dBASE 5 For DOS For Dummies

dBASE Terms You Need to Know

Catalog: A wrapper that goes around all the tables, forms, reports, queries, and other things that work together in a database.

Browse screen: A way of displaying table data in a row-and-column format.

Field: A "slot" in a record that holds an individual data item, such as a first name or an address. Each table is made up of records, and each record is made up of one or more fields.

Field type: The kind of thing a data item is. A data item can be text, a number, a time or date, a memo, and so on.

Form: A way of displaying table data on the PC screen so that it looks like a paper form, with explanatory text and blanks for each data item.

Fun: What you should be having more of with dBASE. If you're not having fun, you're working too hard and missing the point.

Query: A question you ask about your database. You construct a query in the dBASE Query Design screen.

Record: All the data items (fields) about a particular thing, such as a person, a sales transaction, or an inventory item. Each record is made up of fields, and each table is made up of records.

Relation: A link between two or more tables that lets you draw information from the tables just as if they were a single table.

Report: A custom-designed printout of your database data. dBASE lets you create reports in a variety of formats, complete with graphics and calculations if you want.

Table: The basic building block of a dBASE database. A table is made up of one or more records. Each record has information about an individual thing, such as a person or a sales transaction.

Basic Survival Skills

Start dBASE	In your dBASE disk directory, type **dbase** at the DOS prompt. Or, if you're in Windows, double-click on the dBASE icon in the Windows Program Manager.
Start the Control Center	From the opening screen, called the Developer's Desktop, press F2.
Open a catalog	In the Control Center, open the Catalog menu and select *Use a different catalog*.
Create a table	In the Data panel, double-click on *Create*. Then, in the Table Design screen, give the name, field type, and width of each field. To save the structure, select *Save changes and exit* from the Exit menu.
Open a table, form, etc.	Double-click on its name in the Control Center panels.
Add some data to a table	Open the table, then, in the dialog box, select *Modify structure/order*. In the Table Design screen, open the Append menu and select *Enter records from keyboard*.
Quit dBASE	From the Control Center, open the Exit menu and select *Exit to DOS*.
Get an acting job in New York	Work at Zabar's Deli to meet producers; drive a cab; go back to school and finish B.A. in history; wait tables; get M.A. in history; drive a cab; get Ph.D. in history; work at Zabar's; get acting job as a talking potato in off-Broadway show; move back to Cleveland; drive a cab.

...For Dummies: #1 Computer Book Series for Beginners

dBase 5 For DOS For Dummies

Cheat Sheet

Planning Your Database

The basic principles of database design:

1. A catalog is a wrapper that goes around tables, forms, reports, and so on, to keep them together. Always create and open a catalog before you do anything else.

2. Each table should contain only one kind of data. For example, you should not mix customer and sales data in the same table.

3. When you need to combine data from different tables, the data must have a common field, such as an account number. The common field should be indexed.

4. Each piece of data should appear only *once* in the database. For example, you shouldn't have one copy of a sales record in a Sales table and another copy in a Customer table. The duplication wastes disk space and can corrupt your data.

5. Do *not* wear a red-and-white polka dot shirt when designing a database. This will not corrupt your data, but it betrays a complete lack of fashion sense.

Creating Your Database

To create a database, first *plan* the database. Then, start dBASE. Follow these steps:

1. In the Control Center, create the catalog that will hold the parts of the database. To do this, open the Catalog menu, select *Use a different catalog,* and enter the name of your new catalog.

2. With the catalog open, create the tables for your database. To create a table, double-click on the word *Create* in the Data panel. If you need to link the tables in your database, make sure they have a common field (such as account number) and that the field is indexed.

3. Create the other elements of your database, such as forms, reports, and queries, by clicking on the word *Create* in the appropriate Control Center panel for each.

4. Congratulate yourself on a job well done.

Creating a Table

To create a table, first create the catalog it goes into. Then follow these steps:

1. Highlight the word *Create* in the Control Center's Data panel and press Enter.

2. For each "field" in the table (name, address, and so forth), type the field name, pick the field type, specify the width, and say how (or if) it should be indexed.

3. After you create the fields, save the table by opening the Exit menu and selecting *Save changes and exit.*

Copyright © 1994 IDG Books Worldwide. All rights reserved.
Cheat Sheet $2.95 value. Item 188-4.
For more information about IDG Books, call 1-800-762-2974 or 415-312-0650

. . . For Dummies: #1 Computer Book Series for Beginners

References for the Rest of Us

COMPUTER BOOK SERIES FROM IDG

Are you intimidated and confused by computers? Do you find that traditional manuals are overloaded with technical details you'll never use? Do your friends and family always call you to fix simple problems on their PCs? Then the *"... For Dummies"*™ computer book series from IDG is for you.

"... For Dummies" books are written for those frustrated computer users who know they aren't really dumb but find that PC hardware, software, and indeed the unique vocabulary of computing make them feel helpless. *"... For Dummies"* books use a lighthearted approach, a down-to-earth style, and even cartoons and humorous icons to diffuse computer novices' fears and build their confidence. Lighthearted but not lightweight, these books are a perfect survival guide to anyone forced to use a computer.

> *"I like my copy so much I told friends; now they bought copies."*
> — Irene C., Orwell, Ohio

> *"Quick, concise, nontechnical, and humorous."*
> — Jay A., Elburn, IL

> *"Thanks, I needed this book. Now I can sleep at night."*
> — Robin F., British Columbia, Canada

Already, hundreds of thousands of satisfied readers agree. They have made *"... For Dummies"* books the #1 introductory level computer book series and have written asking for more. So if you're looking for the most fun and easy way to learn about computers look to *"... For Dummies"* books to give you a helping hand.

IDG BOOKS

dBASE FOR DOS FOR DUMMIES™

dBASE FOR DOS FOR DUMMIES™

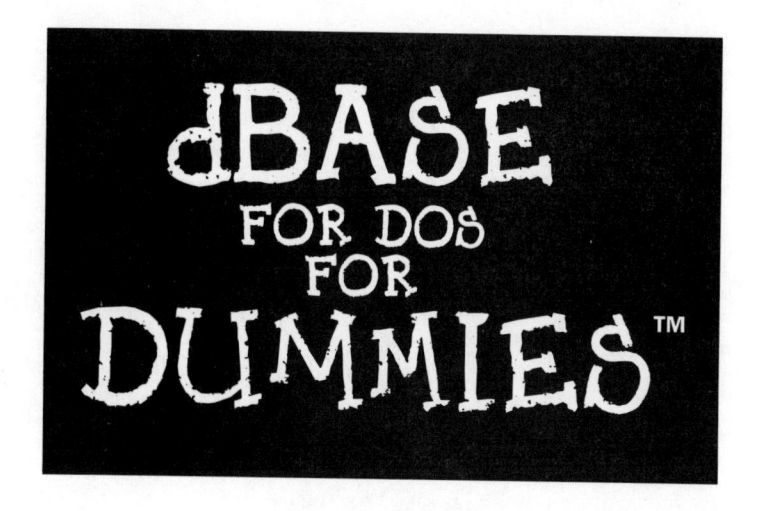

by Scott Palmer
& Michael Stabler

Foreword by Dennis Miller
Product Manager, dBASE 5.0 for DOS

IDG BOOKS

IDG Books Worldwide, Inc.
An International Data Group Company

San Mateo, California ♦ Indianapolis, Indiana ♦ Boston, Massachusetts

dBASE For DOS For Dummies

Published by
IDG Books Worldwide, Inc.
An International Data Group Company
155 Bovet Road, Suite 310
San Mateo, CA 94402

Text *and art* copyright ©1994 by IDG Books Worldwide. All rights reserved. No part of this book may be reproduced or transmitted in any form, by any means (electronic, photocopying, recording, or otherwise) without the prior written permission of the publisher.

Library of Congress Catalog Card No.: 94-76886

ISBN: 1-56884-188-4

Printed in the United States of America

10 9 8 7 6 5 4 3 2 1

Distributed in the United States by IDG Books Worldwide, Inc.

Distributed in Canada by Macmillan of Canada, a Division of Canada Publishing Corporation; by Computer and Technical Books in Miami, Florida, for South America and the Caribbean; by Longman Singapore in Singapore, Malaysia, Thailand, and Korea; by Toppan Co. Ltd. in Japan; by Asia Computerworld in Hong Kong; by Woodslane Pty. Ltd. in Australia and New Zealand; and by Transword Publishers Ltd. in the U.K. and Europe.

For general information on IDG Books in the U.S., including information on discounts and premiums, contact IDG Books at 800-762-2974 or 415-312-0650.

For information on where to purchase IDG Books outside the U.S., contact Christina Turner at 415-312-0633.

For information on translations, contact Marc Jeffrey Mikulich, Foreign Rights Manager, at IDG Books Worldwide; FAX NUMBER 212-286-2747.

For sales inquiries and special prices for bulk quantities, write to the address above or call IDG Books Worldwide at 415-312-0650.

For information on using IDG Books in the classroom, or for ordering examination copies, contact Jim Kelly at 800-434-0650.

Limit of Liability/Disclaimer of Warranty: The author and publisher have used their best efforts in preparing this book. IDG Books Worldwide, Inc., International Data Group, Inc., and the author make no representation or warranties with respect to the accuracy or completeness of the contents of this book and specifically disclaim any implied warranties or merchantability or fitness for any particular purpose and shall in no event be liable for any loss of profit or any other commercial damage, including but not limited to special, incidental, consequential, or other damages.

Trademarks: dBASE is a registered trademark of Borland International. MS-DOS is a registered trademark of Microsoft Corporation. All brand names and product names used in this book are trademarks, registered trademarks, or trade names of their respective holders. IDG Books Worldwide is not associated with any product or vendor mentioned in this book.

is a registered trademark of
IDG Books Worldwide, Inc.

About the Authors

Scott Palmer
Scott Palmer has over ten years of experience in database design, programming, and user training with dBASE (II, III, and IV), Paradox (DOS and Windows), and Access. He is the author of IDG's *Access 2 For Dummies,* and writes a weekly newspaper column for PC users. In his free time, he programs in C++ and writes popular music.

Michael Stabler
Michael Stabler has been involved with the computer industry for over seven years. He's done everything from technical support for private firms to software development for the federal government. He's programmed in several languages and worked extensively with dBASE. He lives in Pittsburgh, PA with his cat Rasputin.

ABOUT IDG BOOKS WORLDWIDE

Welcome to the world of IDG Books Worldwide.

IDG Books Worldwide, Inc., is a subsidiary of International Data Group, the world's largest publisher of business and computer-related information and the leading global provider of information services on information technology. IDG was founded more than 25 years ago and now employs more than 5,700 people worldwide. IDG publishes more than 200 computer publications in 63 countries (see listing below). Forty million people read one or more IDG publications each month.

Launched in 1990, IDG Books is today the fastest-growing publisher of computer and business books in the United States. We are proud to have received 3 awards from the Computer Press Association in recognition of editorial excellence, and our best-selling ...*For Dummies* series has more than 7 million copies in print with translations in more than 20 languages. IDG Books, through a recent joint venture with IDG's Hi-Tech Beijing, became the first U.S. publisher to publish a computer book in the People's Republic of China. In record time, IDG Books has become the first choice for millions of readers around the world who want to learn how to better manage their businesses.

Our mission is simple: Every IDG book is designed to bring extra value and skill-building instructions to the reader. Our books are written by experts who understand and care about our readers. The knowledge base of our editorial staff comes from years of experience in publishing, education, and journalism — experience which we use to produce books for the '90s. In short, we care about books, so we attract the best people. We devote special attention to details such as audience, interior design, use of icons, and illustrations. And because we use an efficient process of authoring, editing, and desktop publishing our books electronically, we can spend more time ensuring superior content and spend less time on the technicalities of making books.

You can count on our commitment to deliver high-quality books at competitive prices on topics customers want to read about. At IDG, we value quality, and we have been delivering quality for more than 25 years. You'll find no better book on a subject than an IDG book.

John J. Kilcullen

John Kilcullen
President and CEO
IDG Books Worldwide, Inc.

VIII WINNER Eighth Annual Computer Press Awards 1992

IX WINNER Ninth Annual Computer Press Awards 1993

IDG Books Worldwide, Inc., is a subsidiary of International Data Group. The officers are Patrick J. McGovern, Founder and Board Chairman; Walter Boyd, President. International Data Group's publications include: **ARGENTINA'S** Computerworld Argentina, Infoworld Argentina; **AUSTRALIA'S** Computerworld Australia, Australian PC World, Australian Macworld, Network World, Mobile Business Australia, Reseller, IDG Sources; **AUSTRIA'S** Computerwelt Oesterreich, PC Test; **BRAZIL'S** Computerworld, Gamepro, Game Power, Mundo IBM, Mundo Unix, PC World, Super Game; **BELGIUM'S** Data News (CW) **BULGARIA'S** Computerworld Bulgaria, Ediworld, PC & Mac World Bulgaria, Network World Bulgaria; **CANADA'S** CIO Canada, Computerworld Canada, Graduate Computerworld, InfoCanada, Network World Canada; **CHILE'S** Computerworld Chile, Informatica; **COLOMBIA'S** Computerworld Colombia, PC World; **CZECH REPUBLIC'S** Computerworld, Elektronika, PC World; **DENMARK'S** Communications World, Computerworld Danmark, Macintosh Produktkatalog, Macworld Danmark, PC World Danmark, PC World Produktguide, Tech World, Windows World; **ECUADOR'S** PC World Ecuador; **EGYPT'S** Computerworld (CW) Middle East, PC World Middle East; **FINLAND'S** MikroPC, Tietoviikko, Tietoverkko; **FRANCE'S** Distributique, GOLDEN MAC, InfoPC, Languages & Systems, Le Guide du Monde Informatique, Le Monde Informatique, Telecoms & Reseaux; **GERMANY'S** Computerwoche, Computerwoche Focus, Computerwoche Extra, Computerwoche Karriere, Information Management, Macwelt, Netzwelt, PC Welt, PC Woche, Publish, Unit; **GREECE'S** Infoworld, PC Games; **HUNGARY'S** Computerworld SZT, PC World; **HONG KONG'S** Computerworld Hong Kong, PC World Hong Kong; **INDIA'S** Computers & Communications; **IRELAND'S** ComputerScope; **ISRAEL'S** Computerworld Israel, PC World Israel; **ITALY'S** Computerworld Italia, Lotus Magazine, Macworld Italia, Networking Italia, PC Shopping, PC World Italia; **JAPAN'S** Computerworld Today, Information Systems World, Macworld Japan, Nikkei Personal Computing, SunWorld Japan, Windows World; **KENYA'S** East African Computer News; **KOREA'S** Computerworld Korea, Macworld Korea, PC World Korea; **MEXICO'S** Compu Edicion, Compu Manufactura, Computacion/Punto de Venta, Computerworld Mexico, MacWorld, Mundo Unix, PC World, Windows; **THE NETHERLANDS'** Computer! Totaal, Computable (CW), LAN Magazine, MacWorld, Totaal "Windows"; **NEW ZEALAND'S** Computer Listings, Computerworld New Zealand, New Zealand PC World, Network World; **NIGERIA'S** PC World Africa; **NORWAY'S** Computerworld Norge, C/World, Lotusworld Norge, Macworld Norge, Networld, PC World Ekspress, PC World Norge, PC World's Produktguide, Publish& Multimedia World, Student Data, Unix World, Windowsworld; IDG Direct Response; **PAKISTAN'S** PC World Pakistan; **PANAMA'S** PC World Panama; **PERU'S** Computerworld Peru, PC World; **PEOPLE'S REPUBLIC OF CHINA'S** China Computerworld, China Infoworld, Electronics Today/Multimedia World, Electronics International, Electronic Product World, China Network World, PC and Communications Magazine, PC World China, Software World Magazine, Telecom Product World; IDG HIGH TECH BEIJING'S New Product World; IDG SHENZHEN'S Computer News Digest; **PHILIPPINES'** Computerworld Philippines, PC Digest (PCW); **POLAND'S** Computerworld Poland, PC World/Komputer; **PORTUGAL'S** Cerebro/PC World, Correio Informatico/Computerworld, Informatica & Comunicacoes Catalogo, MacIn, Nacional de Produtos; **ROMANIA'S** Computerworld, PC World; **RUSSIA'S** Computerworld-Moscow, Mir - PC, Sety; **SINGAPORE'S** Computerworld Southeast Asia, PC World Singapore; **SLOVENIA'S** Monitor Magazine; **SOUTH AFRICA'S** Computer Mail (CIO),Computing S.A.,Network World S.A., Software World; **SPAIN'S** Advanced Systems, Amiga World, Computerworld Espana, Communicaciones World, Macworld Espana, NeXTWORLD, Super Juegos Magazine (GamePro), PC World Espana, Publish; **SWEDEN'S** Attack, ComputerSweden, Corporate Computing, Natverk & Kommunikation, Macworld, Mikrodatorn, PC World, Publishing & Design (CAP), Datalngenjoren, Maxi Data,Windows World; **SWITZERLAND'S** Computerworld Schweiz, Macworld Schweiz, PC Tip; **TAIWAN'S** Computerworld Taiwan, PC World Taiwan; **THAILAND'S** Thai Computerworld; **TURKEY'S** Computerworld Monitor, Macworld Turkiye, PC World Turkiye; **UKRAINE'S** Computerworld; **UNITED KINGDOM'S** Computing /Computerworld, Connexion/Network World, Lotus Magazine, Macworld, Open Computing/Sunworld; **UNITED STATES'** Advanced Systems, AmigaWorld, Cable in the Classroom, CD Review, CIO, Computerworld, Digital Video, DOS Resource Guide, Electronic Entertainment Magazine, Federal Computer Week, Federal Integrator, GamePro, IDG Books, Infoworld, Infoworld Direct, Laser Event, Macworld, Multimedia World, NetworkWorld, PC Letter, PC World, PlayRight, Power PC World, Publish, SWATPro, Video Event; **VENEZUELA'S** Computerworld Venezuela, PC World; **VIETNAM'S** PC World Vietnam

Dedication

From Scott Palmer: For My, inspiration.

From Michael Stabler: To Serena, for the cessation of the cough of a sainted angel, and the beginning. The beginning of that crystal drop of golden-sweet dew on a cool autumn morning, that was spoken of before.

Acknowledgments

Though our names are on the cover, we were not alone in creating *dBASE For DOS For Dummies*. Several other people helped make it the best book for beginning users of dBASE for DOS.

Most involved on a day-to-day basis was Kathy Cox, our editor at IDG Books, who guided the project at every step with encouragement, constructive criticisms, and an endless supply of good ideas. The book's technical editor, Larry Barr, was also a joy to work with and made many helpful suggestions, as did Shawn MacLaren, whose copyediting help was invaluable.

The book originated with Janna Custer and Megg Bonar in the acquisitions department at IDG, whom we thank for giving us the opportunity to work with them. David Solomon, publisher at IDG, and John Kilcullen, IDG's president, also helped to launch the project, and we owe them both our sincere thanks.

Our agent, Connie Clausen of Connie Clausen Associates in New York, handled the business end of the project and continues to give us good advice on just about everything. Our loved ones put up with us all the way and continue to give us good advice (some of which we even take!) on just about everything.

(The publisher would like to give special thanks to Patrick J. McGovern, without whom this book would not have been possible.)

Credits

Publisher
David Solomon

Managing Editor
Mary Bednarek

Acquisitions Editor
Janna Custer

Production Director
Beth Jenkins

Senior Editors
Tracy Barr
Sandra Blackthorn
Diane Graves Steele

Production Coordinator
Cindy L. Phipps

Associate Acquisitions Editor
Megg Bonar

Project Editor
Kathleen M. Cox

Editors
Shawn MacLaren
Pam Mourouzis
Barbara Potter

Editorial Assistant
Laura Schaible

Technical Reviewer
Larry Barr

Production Staff
Valery Bourke
Kent Gish
Angela Hunckler
Drew R. Moore
Steve Peake
Patricia R. Reynolds

Proofreader
Jennifer Kaufeld

Indexer
Sherry Massey

Book Design
University Graphics

Cover Design
Kavish + Kavish

Contents at a Glance

Foreword .... *xxiii*

Introduction *1*

Part I: All the DataBasics You Have to Know *7*
Chapter 1: What the Heck *Is* dBASE, Anyway? 9
Chapter 2: Figuring Out the dBASE Screen 21
Chapter 3: Setting Up a Database: Rule #1 Is Think Ahead! 31
Chapter 4: Cataloging and Creating Tables 43
Chapter 5: Putting Data in Your Database 57
Chapter 6: Here's Looking at Your Data 71

Part II: Playing with Your Data *79*
Chapter 7: Redesigning Your Table 81
Chapter 8: Adding and Using Memo Fields 89
Chapter 9: Creating and Using On-Screen Forms 97
Chapter 10: Finding Stuff *Fast* in Your Database 111
Chapter 11: Using Queries to Find Lots More Stuff 119
Chapter 12: Mastering Logical Operators and Replacing Data 135
Chapter 13: Hot Stuff! Customizing Your Forms 147

Part III: Organizing and Printing Your Data *159*
Chapter 14: Sorting, Indexing, and Other Apodictic Truths 161
Chapter 15: Organizing Stuff with dBASE's DOS Utilities 175
Chapter 16: Creating Simple Reports 187
Chapter 17: Form Letters for Fun and Profit 201
Chapter 18: Designing and Printing Mailing Labels 209

Part IV: Really Advanced Stuff to Impress Your Friends *221*
Chapter 19: Divvying Up Your Database, Then Putting It Back Together 223
Chapter 20: Hot Stuff! Creating Sophisticated Reports 231

Chapter 21: Insanely Great Field Tricks in Forms and Reports 249
Chapter 22: dBASE Utilities and Power Tricks 263
Chapter 23: Exchanging Data with Other Programs 271

Part V: The Part of Tens 275
Chapter 24: Ten Awful Database Words (& Penalties for Using Them) 277
Chapter 25: Ten dBASE Problems and How to Survive Them 281
Chapter 26: Ten Fun Facts About dBASE 289

Part VI: Appendixes 291
Appendix A: Database Data for the Example Table 293
Appendix B: Installing dBASE 297
Appendix C: Stepping Up to the Developer's Desktop 299

Index 303

Reader Response Card .... Back of Book

Cartoons at a Glance
By Rich Tennant

page 221

page 275

page 291

page xxiv

page 7

page 95

page 79

page 199

page 261

page 159

Table of Contents

Foreword .... *xxiii*

Introduction *1*
    About This Book 1
    How to Use This Book 2
    What You're Like (According to Your Mother) 2
    How This Book Is Organized 2
        Part I: All the Databasics You Have To Know 3
        Part II: Playing with Your Data 3
        Part III: Organizing and Printing Your Data 3
        Part IV: Really Advanced Stuff to Impress Your Friends 3
        Part V: The Part of Tens 4
        Part VI: Appendixes 4
    Icons Used in This Book 4
    Where to Go from Here 5

Part I: All the DataBasics You Have to Know *7*

Chapter 1: What the Heck Is dBASE, Anyway? 9
    What Is dBASE? 9
        Ready, set . . . computerize! 11
        Work smarter not harder with dBASE 12
        Smile when you data entry, pardner! 13
    Getting the Data You Need — Easily! 13
        Print reports about your data 14
        Annoy people with form letters and mailing labels 14
        Exchange data with other programs 14
    Starting dBASE 15
        The dBASE 5 Developer's Desktop opening screen:
            Not for regular people 17
        Opening a menu 18
        Getting Help (not including psychiatric help) 19
        It's the dBASE Control Center you really want 19
        Quitting dBASE 20

Chapter 2: Figuring Out the dBASE Screen 21
    The dBASE Developer's Desktop: For Programming Geeks Only 21
    The Control Center 23
        Using the Control Center panels 24
        Making the Control Center start automatically 25

Using the Menus	26
Using shortcut keys	27
Using submenus	27
What the different menus do	27
Getting Help When You Need It	29

Chapter 3: Setting Up a Database: Rule #1 Is Think Ahead! 31

Organizing Your Database	32
Using catalogs to keep database stuff together	32
Thinking about your data	33
Using Tables to Hold Your Data	33
Fields and records and bears — Oh, my!	34
All data has a type	35
Using Queries to Find Your Data	35
Using Forms to Enter Your Data	36
Using Reports to Print Your Data	37
Planning Your Database	37
Creating a Database Catalog	38
Hands on: Creating a Sample Catalog	40

Chapter 4: Cataloging and Creating Tables 43

Planting Fields to Structure Your Table	44
Naming your dBASE fields	46
Typecasting your field data	46
Cataloging Your Table	47
Removing stuff from a catalog	49
Creating a Table	50
Hands on: Creating the Bookcust Table	52

Chapter 5: Putting Data in Your Database 57

Getting Ready: You Look Fine	57
Adding Data to a Table: The Main Event	58
Entering data in Form mode	59
Entering data in Browse mode	61
Looking at your records	62
Moving around in your table	62
Checking Out the Status Bar	63
Editing Data and Fixing Mistakes	64
Basic steps for editing stuff	64
Deleting a record	64
Undeleting a record	65
ZAP! Using the dBASE equivalent of a nuclear bomb	66
Hands on: Pumping Up the Bookcust Table	66
Hands on: Correcting Customer Records	69

Chapter 6: Here's Looking at Your Data 71

Creating Your Own Special Browse Screen 72
    Changing column widths 73
    Locking columns in the Browse screen 74
    Keeping the action in one column only 75
Moving Around in the Browse Screen 76
Power Moving in the Browse Screen 76
    Skipping around in the Browse screen 77
    Moving directly where you want to go 77

Part II: Playing with Your Data 79

Chapter 7: Redesigning Your Table 81

What Changes Can You Make? 82
Changing a Field's Definition 82
Adding a Field 83
    Adding a field to the end of a table 83
    Inserting a field in the middle of the table 84
Deleting Fields 84
Hands on: Adding and Deleting Fields 85

Chapter 8: Adding and Using Memo Fields 89

Adding a Memo Field 90
Entering a Memo 91
Viewing and Editing a Memo 92
Hands on: Entering Memos 93

Chapter 9: Creating and Using On-Screen Forms 97

Why Use Forms? 98
Creating a Form 98
    Basic steps 99
    Secret shortcuts 101
Moving Fields on a Form 102
Viewing Data and Moving Around in a Table 102
Putting Formats into Fields 103
Entering and Changing Data with a Form 104
Hands on: Creating and Changing a Form 105
Hands on: Formatting and Filling the PHONE Field 109

Chapter 10: Finding Stuff *Fast* in Your Database 111

Finding Stuff the Easy Way 112
    Searching a database 113
    Match Capitalization 113

Wild cards 114
To Index or Not to Index? 115
Hands on: Finding a Customer Record 115
Hands on: Looking for Parts of Words 117

Chapter 11: Using Queries to Find Lots More Stuff 119

Keys to Perfect Queries 120
    Understanding the Query Design screen 121
    Moving around in the Query Design screen 122
Creating a Query in dBASE 123
    Selecting fields for the query 123
    Telling dBASE what to look for 124
    Running the query 124
    Saving a query answer 125
    Sorting records in a query answer 126
    Changing the order of fields in the answer 128
    Rerunning a query 129
Using Query Operators, and What It All Means 129
Important Points to Remember 131
Hands on: Drudge Work Alert! Setting Up a Sales Table 131

Chapter 12: Mastering Logical Operators and Replacing Data 135

What Is a Logical Operator? 136
Creating Multiple-Condition Queries 136
    Using AND and OR 136
    Combining conditions with AND 137
    Querying the Bookcust Sales table 140
    Looking for a range of values 141
    Combining conditions with OR 142
    Putting OR conditions in different fields 143
Doing Calculations in a Query 143
Replacing Data in a Table 144

Chapter 13: Hot Stuff! Customizing Your Forms 147

Moving Fields and Text 148
Changing and Adding Text 149
Drawing Boxes and Lines on the Screen 150
    Adding a box 150
    Adding a line 151
Changing a Form's Colors 151
Adding Calculated Fields 153
Adding Automatic Error-Checking for Your Data Entry 154
Using Templates 155

Table of Contents   xix

Part III: Organizing and Printing Your Data 159

Chapter 14: Sorting, Indexing, and Other Apodictic Truths 161

Doing Simple Sorts 162
    The basic steps for sorting records 163
    Sorting on more than one field 165
    Sorting character fields that contain numbers 167
Indexing: Usually Better than Sorting 168
    Stuff you need to know before you index 170
    Making sure that the right fields are indexed 171
    Displaying your records in indexed order 171
    Indexing on multiple fields 172

Chapter 15: Organizing Stuff with dBASE's DOS Utilities 175

The Basics of dBASE's DOS Utilities 176
    dBASE's preprogrammed DOS commands 176
    The DOS shell 176
    Catalogs vs. utilities 176
How to Use the Utilities 177
    The DOS utilities screen 177
    How to mark a file and why you'd want to 178
    Deleting a File 178
    Deleting marked files 179
    Moving and copying a file 181
    Renaming a file 182
On the Menus: Other Important File Utilities 182
    The DOS menu 182
    The Files menu 183
    The Sort menu 183
    The Mark menu 184
    The Operations menu 184
    The Exit menu 185
A Guide to dBASE File Extensions 185

Chapter 16: Creating Simple Reports with dBASE 187

Different Kinds of Reports 188
Creating a Simple Report 188
    What are bands and what are they good for? 191
    What are all those Xs and 9s on my screen? 193
Changing the Look of Your Report 193
    Undeleting and deleting columns 193
    Changing column names 194
    Changing column widths 195
Saving and Printing Your Report 197

  Saving a report layout 197
  Opening a saved report 197
  Printing a report 198

Chapter 17: Form Letters for Fun and Profit 201

  Form Letter Basics 202
   A form letter is nothing more than a glorified report 203
   Creating a form letter with a Mailmerge layout 203
   Form letter tricks, such as changing margins and tab stops 206
   Adding a calculated field to a form letter 207
  Using Type Styles and Other Printing Tricks 208

Chapter 18: Designing and Printing Mailing Labels 209

  dBASE Label Basics 209
   More sizes fit all 210
   Strike out the bands 210
  How to Design, Save, and Print Labels 211
   Indexing your database 211
   Creating your labels 212
   Creating custom label sizes 215
   Adding special style to your text 216
   Saving mailing label designs 216
   Printing mailing labels 217
  Changing a Label Design You've Already Created 217
   To remove a field from the label 217
   To add a field to the label 218
   To move a field 218
   To add or remove text 218
   To switch to a different label size 218

Part IV: Really Advanced Stuff to Impress Your Friends 221

Chapter 19: Divvying Up Your Database and Putting It Back Together 223

  The Basic Idea: Divide and Conquer 224
   Dividing your data into different tables 224
   Linking tables with a query 225
   Different types of relations between tables 225
   To be related, tables must share a field 226
  The Practical Part: Here's How You Do It 227
   Checking the "many" table 227
   Setting up the relation 228
   Deleting a relation 230

Table of Contents

Chapter 20: Hot Stuff! Creating Sophisticated Reports 231
- The Basic Ideas 232
- The Basic Steps 233
- Creating a Grouped Report 234
  - Indexing the grouping field 234
  - Setting up a basic report 236
  - Adding group sections 238
  - Prettying up report section breaks 240
  - Parts of the grouped report design 242
  - Saving the report 243
- Doing Calculations in a Report 243
  - Changing the height of a report band 243
  - Inserting a summary field 243
- Basing a Report on a Query 245
- Creating a Multitable Report 246

Chapter 21: Insanely Great Field Tricks in Forms and Reports 249
- Using the Modify Field Submenu 250
- Tricks with Templates 251
- Using Edit Options 253
- Tricks with Character Fields 254
- Tricks with Number Fields 256
- Displaying Memo Fields in a Form Window 257

Chapter 22: dBASE Utilities and Power Tricks 263
- Changing the Default Directory 263
- Creating Macros 265
- Changing Macros 266
- Customizing dBASE's Settings 267

Chapter 23: Exchanging Data with Other Programs 271
- Filename Extensions 271
- Importing Data from Other Programs 272
- Exporting Data to Other Programs 273

Part V: The Part of Tens 275

Chapter 24: Ten Awful Database Terms (and Suggested Penalties for Using Them) 277
- Application 278
- Field 278
- Easy 278
- Fourth-Generation Language (4GL) 278

dBASE For DOS For Dummies

```
                Key .................................................................................................. 279
                Normalize ...................................................................................... 279
                Post ............................................................................................... 279
                Powerful ........................................................................................ 280
                Relational ..................................................................................... 280
                SQL ................................................................................................ 280

        Chapter 25: Ten dBASE Problems and How to Survive Them ................... 281
                Problem #1: Getting a Disk Error ............................................... 282
                Problem #2: The Control Center Won't Start ............................ 283
                Problem #3: A Drive Not Ready ................................................. 284
                Problem #4: Files Don't Open ..................................................... 284
                Problem #5: dBASE Runs Really Slow Under Windows ............ 285
                Problem #6: Queries Quickly Quietly Quit ................................ 285
                Problem #7: Is Your Disk "Too Full" for a Memo? .................... 286
                Problem #8: You Lost Memo Fields and Indexes ...................... 287
                Problem #9: You Can't Delete a Blank Report Line .................. 287
                Problem #10: You Don't Know Where to Get dBASE Help ....... 288

        Chapter 26: Ten Fun Facts About dBASE ................................................... 289
```

Part VI: Appendixes 291

```
        Appendix A: Database Data for This Book ................................................ 293
                The "Customer Records" Table ................................................. 293
                The "Sales" Table ........................................................................ 295

        Appendix B: Installing dBASE ..................................................................... 297
                What You Need to Install and Run dBASE ................................. 297
                Installing dBASE on Your PC ...................................................... 298

        Appendix C: Stepping Up to the Developer's Desktop ............................. 299
                What's on the Developer's Desktop ........................................... 300
                        Introducing the Command window .................................. 300
                        The dBASE compiler and linker ........................................ 300
                        Creating event-driven forms ............................................. 301
                        The Object Inspector ......................................................... 302
                        The Project Manager ......................................................... 302
```

Index 303

Reader Response Card .... Back of Book

Foreword

It's no exaggeration to say that in the personal computer world, "In the beginning, there was dBASE." For most of the 1980s, PC data management was virtually synonymous with dBASE. Worthy competitors came — and quite a few of them went — but dBASE remained the one to beat.

Now, of course, things are different. With over six million users, dBASE is still the most widely known data manager in the world, as well as one of the most powerful. But it's a powerhouse among equals: depending on your needs, dBASE is one among several excellent data managers, including Paradox and dBASE for Windows. Of course, as product manager, I *still* believe that dBASE is the one to beat — and Borland has produced a new version that adds credence to that belief.

If you are holding this book, it's a safe bet that you now have Borland's exciting new dBASE 5.0 for DOS. You're no "dummy." You chose the most powerful DOS data manager in existence and one that millions of people have already used. So now, what are you going to do with it?

And that's where this book can help. In an easy to understand, friendly style, Scott and Mike show you step by step how to use the most important features of dBASE. With lots of pictures, diagrams, and PC screens to show you what's going on, *dBASE For DOS For Dummies* makes using dBASE almost effortless.

As a dBASE enthusiast myself, I enjoyed the humor and the clear, well-organized chapters, which combine the best aspects of a tutorial with an easy dBASE reference so that you can look things up quickly and easily.

With dBASE 5.0 for DOS, and this book, you stand at the threshold of an exciting — and productive — PC adventure.

Dennis Miller
Product Manager
dBASE 5.0 for DOS

dBASE For DOS For Dummies

The 5th Wave — By Rich Tennant

"I STARTED DESIGNING DATABASE SOFTWARE SYSTEMS AFTER SEEING HOW EASY IT WAS TO DESIGN OFFICE FURNITURE."

Introduction

Do you just *love* computers? When you wake up in the morning, is your first thought about how to frimmitz the programming subroutine to the relational zignab so you can print out reports that nobody but *you* will understand?

If so, then you've got the wrong book.

This book is for people who *have a life* outside of sitting at the computer and want to get their work done as easily, enjoyably, and *quickly* as possible. If you need the answer to a specific question, want to learn how to do something, and *don't* want to waste a lot of time with computer mumbo-jumbo, then this is the book for you.

About This Book

You can read this book in two ways. If you want, you can read it from front to back, just like a novel. When you read it this way, you'll find that each chapter gives you new dBASE skills that you can immediately put to use. Unfortunately, it has much less sex and violence than a novel — but it *does* have lots of nice pictures and cartoons.

If you prefer, you can just dip into this book whenever you need help on a particular topic. Though each chapter builds on the ideas that came before it, the chapters are also self-contained. You can pick and choose what you want to read about. Each chapter begins with a summary of what you need to know to get the most out of the chapter. If you want to pursue things in more depth, there are also cross-references to other parts of the book. For example, by going to a particular chapter, in a few minutes you could learn how to:

- Design a database in dBASE.
- Create and print simple reports that are ready in a matter of seconds.
- Find any data you need, no matter how big your database.
- Create and print form letters and mailing labels.
- Frimmitz the programming subroutine to the relational zignab — no, wait, that's *one* thing you *won't* find in this book!

How to Use This Book

Using a database package like dBASE requires both *knowledge* and *skill*. Knowledge, you can get by reading; skill, you can only get by *doing*.

To give you both knowledge and skill, this book gives you both *instruction* and *hands-on steps*. The instructional parts cover basic ideas that you need to understand, as well as the basic moves involved in database tasks. To read these sections, all you need is a brain: some are so easy that you don't even need that! You can read these parts on the subway, while doing your laundry, or (depending on your job) while sitting in a getaway car outside the bank.

The hands-on steps assume that you're sitting at your PC and working with dBASE. These steps show you the specific things you do to set up databases, print reports, and so on. You can use the same steps either with the example database in the book or with your own "real life" database.

If you're already stuck with a problem in dBASE, then you can jump directly to the chapter you need. Just check out the Table of Contents or the Index. At the beginning of each chapter, you'll see a list of things you can learn in that chapter. If you don't need help on a specific problem, then just browse through the book and read whatever interests you. Or check out the cartoons.

What You're Like (According to Your Mother)

This book assumes that you're a *regular person*. That has nothing to do with a daily serving of bran flakes. It means that you're not a computer expert and, frankly, don't want to be *bothered* with a lot of technical hocus-pocus. You want the facts, plus a little encouragement, and maybe a stupid joke now and then. No 25-syllable words. Just useful information and skills.

It also assumes that you have dBASE 5 for DOS on your PC. However, virtually all of the concepts and techniques you'll learn *also* apply to dBASE IV for DOS.

How This Book Is Organized

This book has six main parts. Each part focuses on giving you specific knowledge and skills. Within each part, the chapters are deliberately kept short so that they're easy to finish without a big time commitment on your part. And inside each chapter, the sections are clearly marked so you can pick and choose the parts you want to read.

Here's the big picture of what's in each part:

Part I: All the Databasics You Have To Know

If you just want to *get to it* in as short a time as possible, this is the place to go. This part gives you all the basic knowledge and skills you need to get started with dBASE *right now*. You'll learn how to plan a database, put information in the database, look at the information when you need it, and get help when you're confused.

Part II: Playing with Your Data

Although Part I shows you how to view your data, this part shows you several more powerful ways to view and find your data, even if your database is really huge. You'll learn how to create on-screen forms that catch errors and explain what's in your database, how to do simple searches for information, and how to use logical operators for *really powerful searches*. It's not necessary for you to work out at a gym before doing really powerful searches, but it helps.

Part III: Organizing and Printing Your Data

Your data gets even easier to find if you know how to organize it the way you want. This part shows you how to sort the information in your database so that it's in alphabetical or numerical order — for example, by last name, account number, or date. You also learn how to design and print simple reports about your data.

Part IV: Really Advanced Stuff to Impress Your Friends

This part shows you how to do things that other people only dream about. You learn how to divide up your database so that it's totally and completely (timid souls might even say *frighteningly*) efficient. You learn how to create reports that group your data and do calculations, design and print form letters and mailing labels, and speed up your work by using macros and dBASE utilities.

Part V: The Part of Tens

This last part tells you things that you probably never wanted to know, but should. If you really get in trouble with dBASE, this part offers tips on how to fix whatever's gone wrong. It also explains database words that only a computer nerd could love, and gives you some little-known facts about dBASE and the goofy characters who have been a part of its history.

Part VI: Appendixes

The final part covers database data for this book, how to install dBASE, and, for closet computer nerds, some basics about dBASE 5's new wonder-programming tool, the Developer's Desktop.

Icons Used in This Book

This icon says that something is technical. Not that you absolutely don't *want* to know this stuff — some of it is pretty interesting, in a "nerds go berserk" sort of way — but you don't really *need* to know it to work with dBASE.

This icon marks a useful tip, "inside information," or a shortcut that helps you work with dBASE more easily.

This icon marks something you should remember, not only because you'll find it useful, but because there'll be a quiz next period.

This icon marks specific exercises you can do using the book's example database.

This icon marks things that can get you into trouble if you aren't careful. Even dBASE, easy and friendly as it is, has a few timebombs hidden here and there. If you pay attention to the Warnings, you shouldn't have any trouble.

This icon marks interesting background information. You don't strictly need to know it, but it helps you understand dBASE better.

This icon marks information in other chapters that can help you understand the current chapter.

Where to Go from Here

At this point, you've spent enough time reading the introduction. It's time to get to it! If you have a specific problem to solve, go ahead and jump to that chapter of the book. If not, start in Part I and learn the basics: just enough to be dangerous. Then get ready to have some fun with dBASE!

Part I
All the DataBasics You Have to Know

The 5th Wave　　　　　　　　　　By Rich Tennant

"YEAH, I STARTED THE COMPANY RIGHT AFTER I GRADUATED FROM COLLEGE. HOW'D YOU GUESS?"

In this part ...

In the early years of database management, people were ignorant. So ignorant, in fact, that many so-called "experts" mistakenly bought automobile repair shops on the theory that they'd be able to use the same tools for both transmissions and databases. A tool is a tool, right?

This part shows you how to use the most basic tools for managing information with dBASE. It shows you how to plan a database, set up a table, and put in the data. Then, it shows you how to look at your data and, if you need help, how to get help on-screen in dBASE.

Sadly, this part does *not* show you how to manage an auto repair shop or fix a transmission. Even the embarrassed database experts from the early days don't know stuff like that.

Chapter 1
What the Heck *Is* dBASE, Anyway?

▸▸

In This Chapter
▸ What is dBASE?
▸ How dBASE organizes your data
▸ How dBASE makes it easy to get data you need
▸ Starting dBASE
▸ Reading the dBASE screen
▸ Getting Help
▸ Quitting dBASE

▸▸

*I*n this chapter, you get an overview of dBASE and how it can make your life easier. *Relax* — we're not going to talk about a lot of abstruse technical stuff that only someone with a pocket protector and a Ph.D. can understand. This chapter explains *just what you need to know* to start dBASE and have some idea of what you're doing. We talk about specific skills (creating a database, printing a report, monster truck driving) in later chapters. Here, you're just getting your feet wet.

To get the most out of this chapter, it helps to have

✓ Installed dBASE on your PC
✓ Paid for this book
✓ Put on clean underwear just in case

What Is dBASE?

The answer is simple: it's a *database management system*. If you don't know what *that* is, don't worry. You've used database management systems all your life. You just haven't *called* them that.

Part I: All the DataBasics You Have to Know

Let's begin with what dBASE is supposed to manage: data. Data is a bunch of disconnected, disorganized information — just like the receipts you shove into your desk or the chapters in the latest best-selling trashy novel. And if you've ever tried to find a receipt in the desk drawer — or the "good parts" of a trashy novel — you know that data by itself often doesn't do you much good. After all, how does buying that life-saving operation for your mother help you if you can't find the receipt at tax time? (Hey, we all love our mothers, but let's be serious: a deduction is a deduction.)

To make data useful, you need a way to manage it. In other words, you need to organize all the scattered receipts (that is, your data) so that you can find what you need when you need it. Any collection of data is a *database*; a *database management system*, or *database manager*, is what organizes the data for you.

For your receipts, your database management system may be a set of file folders labeled *Car expenses*, *House payments*, *Medical expenses*, and so on. Instead of shoving all your receipts into a drawer, you can put each receipt into an appropriate folder. When you need to find a receipt, you no longer have to muddle through a drawer full of wadded paper. You just go to the right file folder, look inside, and presto! There's the receipt you want. Figure 1-1 illustrates this approach to database management.

You see, databases aren't really so mysterious.

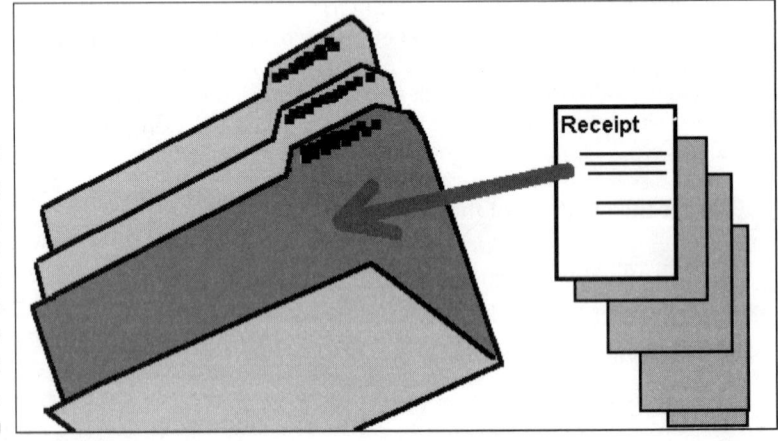

Figure 1-1: Organizing receipts with a simple database management system.

> ### Where did dBASE come from?
>
> dBASE 5 is the newest version of dBASE, one of the most popular PC database management systems in history. Based on work done during the late 1970s by Wayne Ratliff at Jet Propulsion Laboratory in Palo Alto, California, dBASE was the dominant PC database manager of the 1980s. There were versions of dBASE for most small computers, including PCs, and many big computers.
>
> Originally, you did everything in dBASE by typing commands at the infamous *dBASE dot prompt.* Many users came to hate and fear this creature, which just sat there, waiting for someone to type a command — users were left feeling *totally on their own.*
>
> Eventually, Ashton-Tate (which sold dBASE before the company was acquired by Borland International) added some simple drop-down menus to dBASE III. With dBASE IV, Ashton-Tate added an early version of the control center. But these menus didn't really help much, causing some users to give up data management entirely and join the Roller Derby. With dBASE IV, Ashton-Tate added an early version of the Control Center.
>
> Since Borland acquired dBASE, it has made the venerable data manager more powerful and easier to use. dBASE 5's Control Center, for example, lets you use a mouse for most tasks and replaces the dreaded "dot prompt" with a Command window where — if you really get the urge — you can type dBASE commands.

Ready, set . . . computerize!

Some databases are computerized, some aren't. If you bought this book, of course, it's a safe bet that you're interested in computerized database management. With computerized databases, all the data is at your fingertips, so you don't need to get out of your chair (groan!) and make that trek to the filing cabinet (huff, puff!). (Do you ever think of getting more exercise?) And computerized databases offer other advantages as well:

- A computerized database is *fast.* Even if you only have a few hundred file folders, it can take a lot of time to find the file you want. With dBASE, you can go right to the data you need in a matter of seconds.

- A computerized database is *flexible.* If you need to present your data in a variety of ways, dBASE does most of the work for you. Need a row-and-column report? Done. Need a summary of sales totals, grouped by region? Done. Need mailing labels? Done.

- A computerized database is *powerful.* Even a jumbo, heavy-duty file folder can't hold a million employee or sales records. But dBASE can hold as many records as you need — one, a hundred, a million — all on your PC's hard disk.

- A computerized database is *deductible.* Yes, if you use it in your business, dBASE is fully tax deductible; you can use it to offset all those profits you made from offshore oil drilling.

12   Part I: All the DataBasics You Have to Know

That's the scoop! dBASE gives you a fast, flexible, powerful, deductible, and easy way to make sense out of any data you throw at it.

(Technical Stuff icon) Sooner or later, you'll hear someone refer to dBASE as a *relational* database management system. Don't worry about the word *relational*. People get into lots of arguments about what that term really means. For practical purposes, it means that you can divide your computerized data into different "file folders" for efficiency, but also you can easily combine the data from different file folders when you need to retrieve data from your database. Beyond that, it's just a bunch of pointy-headed computer scientists jabbering at each other.

Work smarter not harder with dBASE

A drawback of computerized databases is that they've been hard to work with — until now. With dBASE, you don't need to remember a lot of commands. You don't need to be a database expert. You don't even need to be good-looking, though you are, of course. All you need to do is open menus, click on buttons, and follow the instructions that appear on-screen.

When you create the basic building block of a database — in dBASE, it's called a *table* — the first thing you need to decide is what data should go into it. A customer table, for example, may have each customer's account number, first and last names, address, city, state, ZIP code, and telephone number. Each of these items goes into a separate column in the table, as shown in Figure 1-2. dBASE guides you as you create each column.

```
 Records   Organize   Fields   Go To   Exit
┌─────────┬──────────┬─────────┬───────┬────────────┬──────────────────────┐
│ CUST_ID │ FNAME    │ LNAME   │ MRMS  │ SALUTATION │ ADDRESS              │
├─────────┼──────────┼─────────┼───────┼────────────┼──────────────────────┤
│ 00001   │ James    │ West    │ Prof. │ Jimbo      │ Mythic University    │
│ 00002   │ Harriett │ Stowe   │ Ms.   │ Ms. Stowe  │ 14 Parakeet Lane     │
│ 00003   │ Jules    │ Twombly │ Mr.   │ Jules      │ The ABC Hotel        │
│ 00004   │ Arnold   │ Harris  │ Mr.   │ Arnie      │ 101 Fifth Avenue     │
│ 00005   │ Teri     │ Lane    │ Ms.   │ Ms. Lane   │ 5678 15th Street, #5-│
└─────────┴──────────┴─────────┴───────┴────────────┴──────────────────────┘
 Browse   C:\dbase5\BOOKCUST          Rec 1/5           File  ExclLock  Num
```

Figure 1-2: A row-and-column table of customer data.

NOTE: In older versions of dBASE, a table was called a *database file*. The only reason that the term was changed was to make dBASE terminology easier to understand. There is no difference between a database file and a table, except you also can eat dinner on a table.

Smile when you data entry, pardner!

Data entry is when you sit down at the PC's keyboard and start putting information into a database. When you do so, dBASE helps save you from unnecessary typing and also prevents some common kinds of mistakes.

If you're worried about accidentally inputting the *wrong* data — say, a salary of $100,000 for your most junior clerical employee — you can tell dBASE to refuse any data that looks suspicious. And if someone else is entering the data for you, dBASE can help prevent mix-ups by displaying on-screen an explanation of what each data item is supposed to be.

Getting the Data You Need — Easily!

Of course, putting your data into a database is only the beginning. You also have to get the data *out* of the database when you need it.

dBASE lets you look at your data in two ways: you can view multiple records in a row-and-column screen, as in Figure 1-2, or one record at a time, as in Figure 1-3.

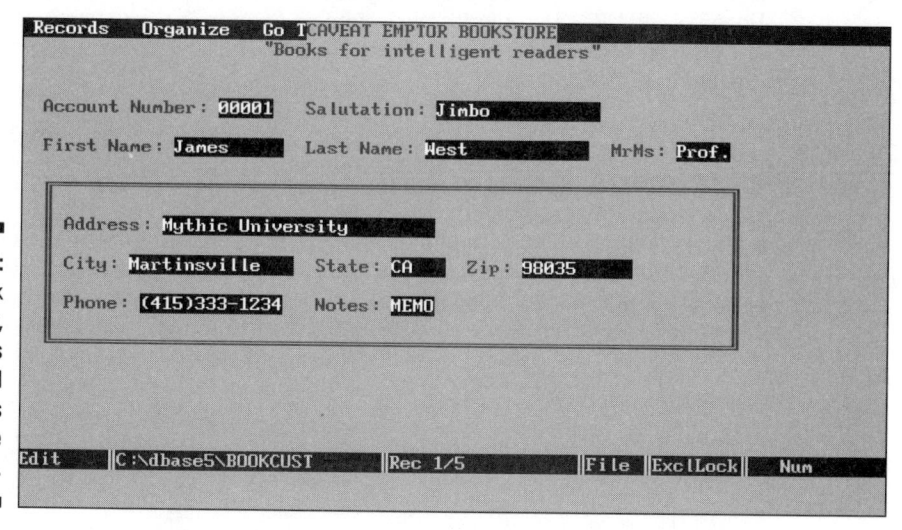

Figure 1-3: If you ask nicely, dBASE lets you see all the details of a single record.

Print reports about your data

dBASE does more than just display your data on-screen. You can print out reports in any format you choose: row and column, one record on a page, summaries only, totals and calculations — you name it. If you're ambitious, you can lay out the report yourself. If you're in a hurry, you can let the dBASE Quick Layout do most of the work for you. Figure 1-4 shows a sample of dBASE's snazzy report capabilities.

Figure 1-4: A snazzy dBASE report (boring dBASE reports sold separately).

Caveat Emptor's Most Beloved Customers

Customer's First Name	Customer's Last Name	City	State
James	West	Martinsville	CA
Harriett	Stowe	New York	NY
Jules	Twombly	Las Vegas	NV
Arnold	Harris	Boise	ID
Teri	Lane	Santa Barbara	CA

Annoy people with form letters and mailing labels

In addition to using your data in reports, you also can use it to create form letters (*"Dear Mr. McMahon: You may already be a winner!"*) and mailing labels. However, dBASE cannot write the letters and stamp the envelopes. But there's always next year.... Figure 1-5 shows a form letter and some mailing labels created in dBASE.

Exchange data with other programs

If you work in an office where different people use different programs, dBASE makes it easy to exchange data with your coworkers. Whether they're using Lotus 1-2-3, Access, Paradox, FoxPro, or even a simple word processor, dBASE can import data from and export data to their programs, as shown in Figure 1-6.

Chapter 1: What the Heck *Is* dBASE, Anyway? 15

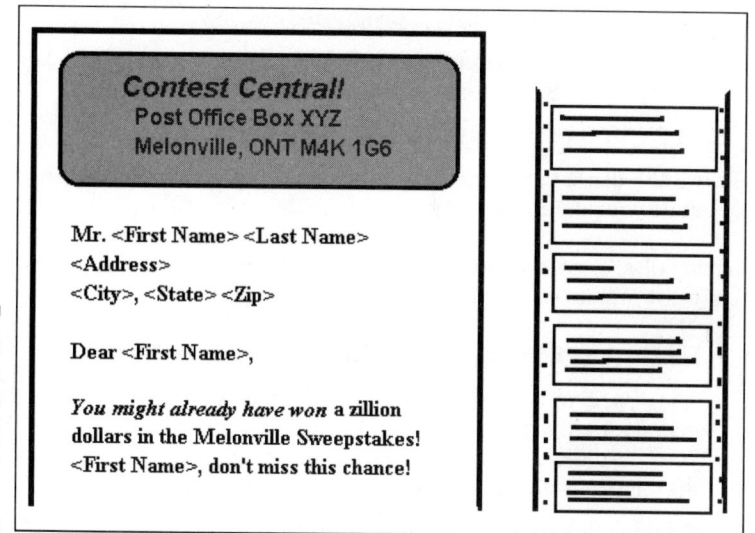

Figure 1-5: dBASE lets you create form letters and mailing labels.

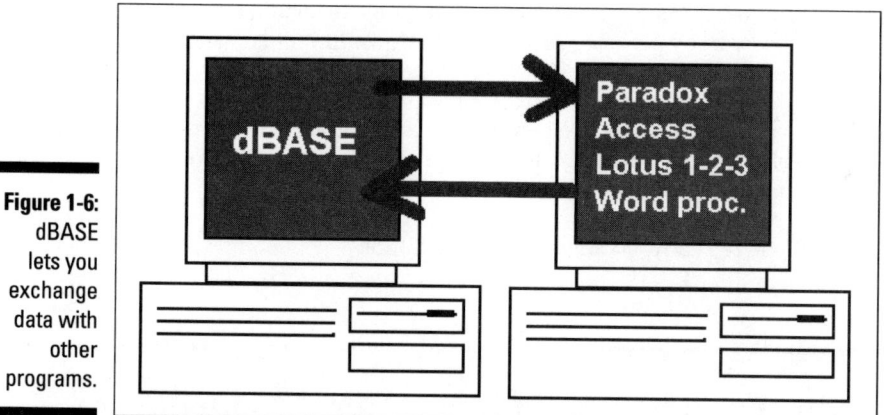

Contest Central!
Post Office Box XYZ
Melonville, ONT M4K 1G6

Mr. <First Name> <Last Name>
<Address>
<City>, <State> <Zip>

Dear <First Name>,

You might already have won a zillion dollars in the Melonville Sweepstakes! <First Name>, don't miss this chance!

Figure 1-6: dBASE lets you exchange data with other programs.

dBASE ↔ Paradox, Access, Lotus 1-2-3, Word proc.

Starting dBASE

Starting dBASE is easy — *if* the program is installed on your PC. If it's not installed, follow the instructions in Appendix B to put dBASE on your hard disk. Don't just copy the dBASE disks to your hard disk because the program won't work if you do.

You can start dBASE from DOS or Microsoft Windows. To start dBASE from DOS, follow these steps:

1. **Switch to the main dBASE program directory.**

   To do so, type **cd\dbase** at the DOS prompt. (If the hard disk is your C drive, the DOS prompt is probably C>.) Then press Enter.

2. **At the DOS prompt, type dbase and press Enter.**

   dBASE displays an opening screen and then sits there, waiting for you to start your database work.

Starting dBASE from Windows is just as easy, but you have to use the mouse. To start dBASE from Windows, follow these steps:

1. **Locate the dBASE program icon in the Program Manager.**

   The dBASE program icon is probably in a group called dBASE. The dBASE installation program creates this group automatically if it sees Windows on your hard disk. Open the group window by double-clicking on its icon. The dBASE program icon is inside the window.

2. **Double-click on the dBASE program icon.**

   dBASE starts up in its own window. Because dBASE is a DOS program, the window takes up the whole screen. You can switch back to Windows, however, by pressing Alt-Tab (hold down the Alt key and press Tab) or Ctrl-Esc.

In the next few sections, we take you on a brief tour of the program. It will probably be more meaningful if you perform the steps that we describe — then you can see what actually happens on-screen.

When you're ready, go ahead and start dBASE.

A mouse can be easier to use than the keyboard.

A mouse is sometimes easier to use than the keyboard. This book assumes that you're using a mouse or at least some kind of pointing device, such as a trackball. You can do most things in dBASE by using either the keyboard or mouse, and we often give instructions for both. dBASE 5, though, is designed to work with a mouse. When you don't have to type a command — and you usually don't — it's normally quicker and easier to use the mouse.

Our advice is simple: If you don't have a mouse, get one. If you have one, use it. And if you find yourself getting sentimental about Mighty Mouse, just keep saying to yourself: *It's only a cartoon. It's only a cartoon.*

The dBASE 5 Developer's Desktop opening screen: Not for regular people

The biggest new feature in dBASE 5 is the Developer's Desktop. The Developer's Desktop is meant for heavy-duty programming geeks, so you'll seldom use it. However, just in case, you should at least know how to get into the Developer's Desktop and get out of it. When you first start dBASE, you'll see the Control Center. To get to the Developer's Desktop, just open the Exit menu and select Exit to Command window, The Developer's Desktop will appear, as shown in Figure 1-7.

Across the top line of the screen is the Menu Bar. You can open any of the menus by clicking on its name in the Menu Bar or by holding down the Alt key and pressing the key for the bold letter in the menu name (known as a *hot key*).

Figure 1-7: The dBASE 5 Developer's Desktop. At the top is the Menu Bar. To the right is the dBASE Command window. At the bottom is the Status Bar.

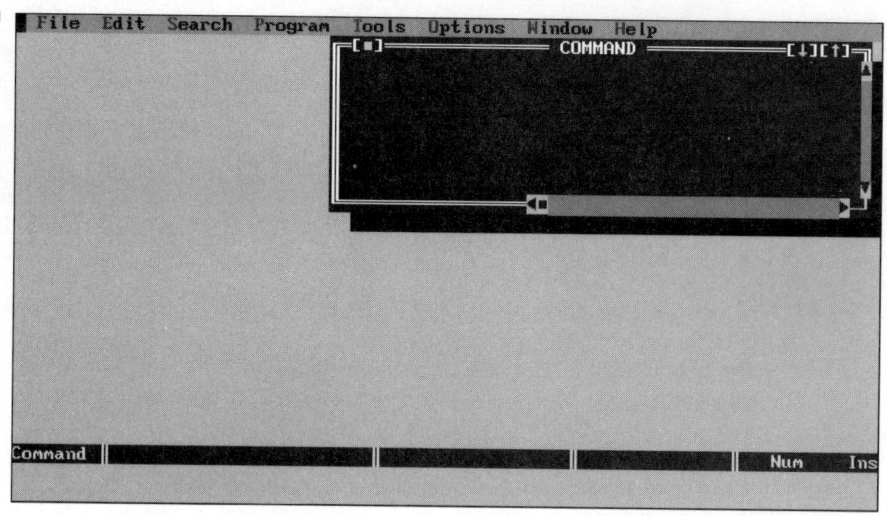

At the right side of the screen is the dBASE Command window. You can type in dBASE commands in this window. You won't have to use it too much unless you want to do something really fancy.

At the bottom of the screen is the Status Bar, which displays helpful information — for example, what different menu choices mean, what your next step should be, and so on.

Opening a menu

Though you won't do a lot with the Developer's Desktop, you *will* use a lot of menus. That's a basic skill you need everywhere, not just in the Developer's Desktop. To open a menu, simply click on the word File in the Menu Bar (or press Alt-F). The File menu appears (see Figure 1-8).

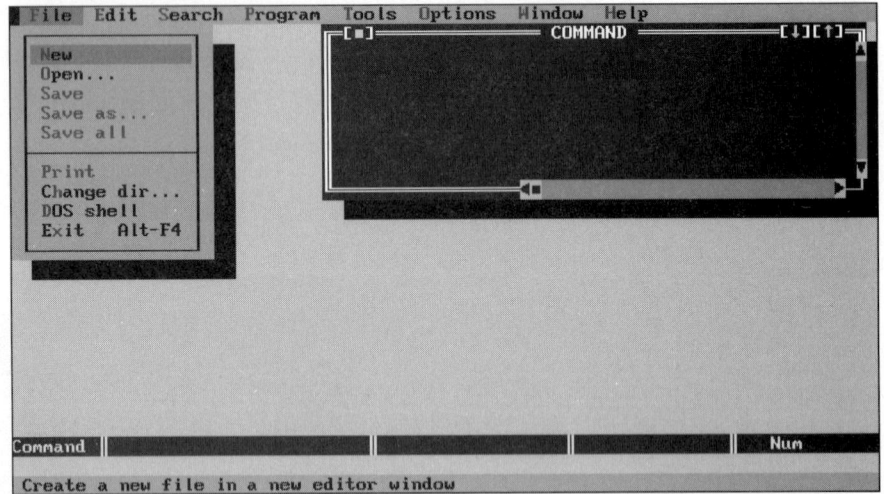

Figure 1-8: The File menu.

To look at the other menus, press the right-arrow key. The other menus contain all kinds of stuff only programmers can use; in fact, these menus may not look too useful for you. But other menus in dBASE *are* useful, and they work the same way.

Keep pressing the right-arrow key until you're back at the File menu. You can close the menu by clicking again on File in the Menu Bar. You also can close a menu by pressing Esc twice (once to close the menu, once to close the Menu Bar).

> **TIP**
> If you see a bold letter in a menu in the Menu Bar, you can open that menu by pressing Alt and the hot key simultaneously. If you see a bold letter in a menu, you can make that menu choice by pressing the hot key — as long as the menu is displayed on-screen. If you don't see any bold letters, the hot key for a menu or menu choice is almost always the Alt key plus the first letter of the menu choice.

Getting Help (not including psychiatric help)

dBASE is simple to use, but any time you have a problem, you can get help easily:

- If a **Help** menu is visible in the Menu Bar, open it (either click on the word *Help* or press Alt-H). From the **Help** menu, select Help Index. A Help window appears.

- If a **Help** menu is not visible in the Menu Bar, press the F1 function key. A Help window appears.

Chapter 2 explains in more detail how to use the Help system.

It's the dBASE Control Center you really want

The reason you don't have to use the Developer's Desktop is that you can do most everything you need from the dBASE Control Center (see Figure 1-9), which is easier, but isn't on the screen at the moment. To see the Control Center from the Developer's Desktop, do one of three things.

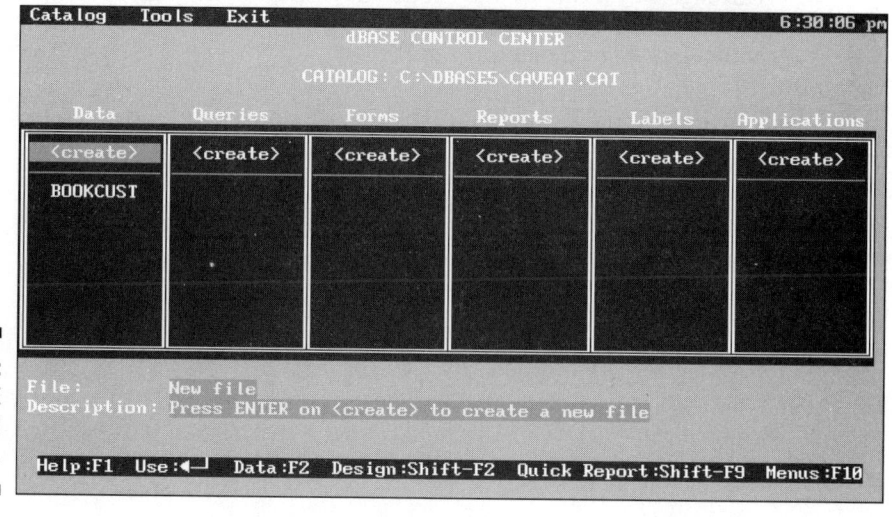

Figure 1-9: The dBASE Control Center.

- Press F2.
- In the Command window, type **assist** and press Enter.
- Click on the word Window in the Menu Bar. In the menu, choose Control Center.

Any time you're in the Developer's Desktop, you can get to the Control Center using one of these three methods. And if the Control Center doesn't appear automatically whenever you start dBASE, Chapter 2 shows you a way to set that up.

Quitting dBASE

Quitting dBASE is as easy as starting up:

- If you're in the Control Center, open the Exit menu and select Quit to DOS.
- If you're in the Developer's Desktop, click in the Command window and type **quit**. Then press Enter.

That's it for this chapter! We've described the basic ideas of a database management system, as well as the main parts of dBASE.

Congratulate yourself and take a break. Have a cappuccino. Learn a foreign language. Buy a cat. Sell the cat and buy a dog. When you're rested, go on to Chapter 2, where you'll learn to find your way around the dBASE screens without getting cat hair on your PC.

Chapter 2
Figuring Out the dBASE Screen

In This Chapter
- The dBASE opening screen
- The Control Center
- Using the Control Center panels
- Using the menus
- Getting help when you need it

*F*ew things are as scary as looking at a blank PC screen and having no idea what to do. Getting mugged in a dark alley comes close; meeting your prospective in-laws for the first time comes even closer.

In this chapter, you learn about the different parts of the dBASE screen and how to use each of them. That way, the only thing to be scared of when you use dBASE will be whether or not you remembered to put out the parakeet and feed the cat, or put out the cat and feed the parakeet, or feed the parakeet to the cat.

To get the most out of this chapter, you need to have

- Installed dBASE
- Had a little practice using the mouse
- Learned about the basic parts of a dBASE database (see Chapter 1)
- Arranged for a sighted person to look at the screen for you (a Seeing Eye dog will do, as long as the dog is very, *very* smart)

The dBASE Developer's Desktop: For Programming Geeks Only

When you first start dBASE 5, you may see the Developer's Desktop, shown in Figure 2-1. Most of the time, this screen isn't very useful unless you're a programming geek with a pocket protector and an I.Q. of 200. You usually just zoom past this screen to the Control Center, where you do *most* of the things you want to do in dBASE.

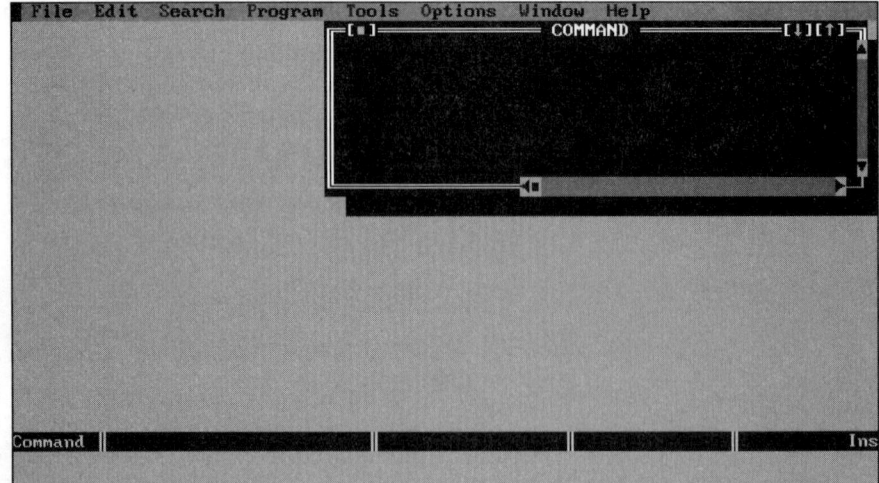

Figure 2-1: The dBASE 5 Developer's Desktop.

If your screens don't *exactly* match those shown in this chapter, don't panic: nothing is wrong. You might have a slightly newer version of dBASE, or the program may just look different on your PC. Any differences are likely to be minor, so the descriptions and instructions should still apply (in other words, don't use this book for kindling).

At the top of the screen sits the Menu Bar, which has different menus depending on the screen you're in at the time. When you're in the Developer's Desktop, the menus let you do only programming-type things, such as loading routines, compiling programs, and staying up until 5:00 a.m. working on the computer. Don't worry about these menus.

At the bottom of the screen is the Status Bar, which tells you something about what dBASE is doing at the moment; it often lists important key commands. Again, you won't need this feature much in the Developer's Desktop. So, just like you do with a really awful TV sitcom, take a quick glance and move on.

However, there is *one* part of the Developer's Desktop that you *will* use from time to time: the Command window in the upper right part of the screen. This is where you can type dBASE commands. In fact, you can do anything in dBASE by typing commands in the Command window.

But if you don't want to spend your life typing, you need to get to the Control Center. There are three ways to do it:

 ✔ Press F2 on your keyboard.

 ✔ In the Command window, type **assist** and press Enter.

 ✔ Click on the word **W**indow in the Menu Bar. In the menu, click on the Co**n**trol Center menu choice.

Chapter 2: Figuring Out the dBASE Screen   **23**

> **NOTE:** Any time you're in the Developer's Desktop, you can go to the Control Center by using one of these three methods.

The Control Center

The dBASE Control Center, shown in Figure 2-2, is divided into several main parts:

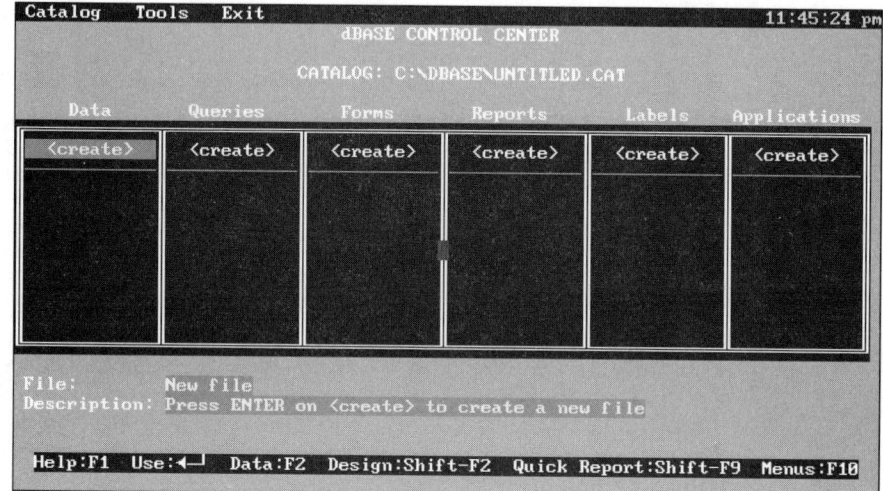

Figure 2-2: The Control Center.

- ✔ **The Menu Bar:** The Menu Bar is the top line on your screen. The Control Center's menus let you change the current catalog, use dBASE tools and utilities, go back to the Developer's Desktop, or exit dBASE. These menus don't have any database management options, such as creating a table, because you do all that through the Control Center panels.

- ✔ **The Status Bar:** The Status Bar is the bottom line on your screen. When you're in the Control Center, the Status Bar lists information about using the Control Center, including important key commands.

> **NOTE:** Whenever you open a menu, the Status Bar disappears, and two lines of text appear in its place. The first line explains how to get around in the open menu. The second line explains what happens if you pick the highlighted menu choice.

- ✔ **The current catalog:** Underneath the Menu Bar is a line that shows the catalog that's currently open. (Catalogs are explained in Chapter 3.) When you first start dBASE, this line will probably say
  `C:\DBASE\UNTITLED.CAT`. You can change the current catalog by using

the Catalog menu (see the "The Catalog menu" section, later in this chapter.

- ✔ **The panels:** The panels are the six big columns in the center of the screen. Each panel is labeled (see the top of each column), detailing the kind of file it handles. Almost everything you do in dBASE, you start in these panels — for example, you start here when you want to create or open a database table, report, form, and so on. (For more information about panels, see the following section.)

- ✔ **The current file:** If a file is highlighted in the panels, the two lines underneath the panels display the file's name and description (which you enter when you create the file). If no file is highlighted (in other words, if create is highlighted), these lines say New File and Press Enter to create a new file.

- ✔ **The current time:** dBASE displays the current time in the top right corner of your screen to keep you from accidentally staying up all night. This feature has saved many a relationship from the rocks (the dreaded "computer divorce").

Using the Control Center panels

The Control Center panels allow you to create or open different kinds of dBASE files.

To *create* a file, use the arrow keys on your keyboard to move to the appropriate column. For example, if you want to create a table called "Customer" to hold the names and addresses of bookstore customers, move to the Data panel. To set up a report so that you can print out the customer's names and addresses, move to the Reports panel — and so on. After you reach the desired column, highlight <create> and press Enter. dBASE takes you to another screen, where you can describe the file you want to create.

After you create a catalog (a kind of "wrapper" for your database) and some database files, the files are listed in the lower part of the panels. If you want to look at the data in a table (in other words, *open* a file), highlight the filename in the lower part of the Data panel and press Enter. dBASE asks what you want to do with the table; after you tell all (don't lie, now), you're off to the races!

As soon as you open a file, such as a customer records table, the filename moves to the top of the panel. You'll see how this works in Chapter 4.

Making the Control Center start automatically

Normally, when dBASE 5 starts up, you'll see the Control Center. However, if a programming geek has been fooling around with your copy of dBASE 5, it's possible that the Developer's Desktop will appear instead.

Here's how to fix the problem so that the Control Center appears automatically whenever you start dBASE. Take a deep breath, count to ten, eat a chocolate donut, and follow these steps:

1. **Get back to the Developer's Desktop.**

   If you're in the Control Center, open the Exit menu and select Exit to the Command window. Be sure that you *don't* accidentally select Exit to DOS, because that will kick you all the way out of dBASE.

2. **In the Command window, type modify command config.db and then press Enter.**

   This command opens the CONFIG.DB file so that you can edit it. This file tells dBASE how you want it to work.

   Most of the time, you won't have to fool around with the CONFIG.DB file, but adding some text to it is the easiest way to make the Control Center appear automatically.

   When you open the file, an editing window appears on-screen, as shown in Figure 2-3. This window is a simple text editor that works just like a word

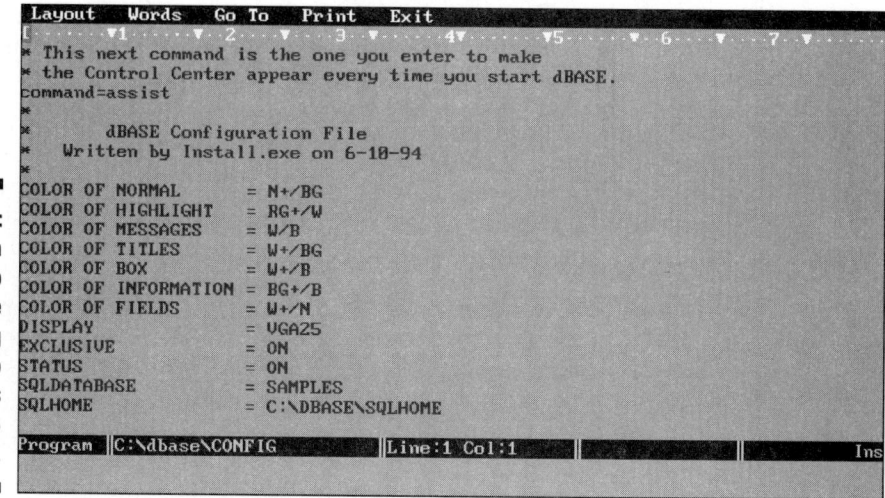

Figure 2-3: Opening a window to type something into dBASE's CONFIG.DB file.

processor, such as WordPerfect or Microsoft Word. You can move around in the window by using the arrow keys on your keyboard.

3. **Use the arrow keys to move to the first blank line at the bottom of the file.**

4. **Type command = assist and press Enter.**

   This line tells dBASE to start the Control Center automatically. If you want, you can add an explanation, called a *comment*, above the command line to remind you (or anyone else who looks at the CONFIG.DB file) what that "command = assist" thing is all about. But make absolutely sure that you begin the comment with an asterisk and a space, as shown in Figure 2-3.

   dBASE ignores any line that begins with an asterisk and a space.

5. **Press Ctrl-End.**

   This action saves the new version of the file to the hard disk.

6. **Press F2 (or type assist in the Command window) to return to the Control Center.**

   The next time you start dBASE, the Control Center will appear automatically.

Using the Menus

Using the dBASE menus is pretty standard stuff if you have spent five minutes around a PC. But you're never too old to learn a few tricks, and it never hurts to rehash the fundamentals.

There are two main ways to open and close menus and select menu choices: with the mouse or with the keyboard. Many people use the mouse, but if you're a keyboard whiz, that may be faster for you:

- ✔ **To open a menu with the mouse,** click on its name in the Menu Bar. For example, to open the Catalog menu, click on the word *Catalog* in the Menu Bar. To close the menu, make a menu choice or click the mouse in a blank area of the screen.

- ✔ **To make a menu choice with the mouse,** click on the choice you want.

- ✔ **To open a menu with the keyboard,** hold down the Alt key and press the hot key, usually the first letter in the menu name. For example, to open the Catalog menu, press Alt-C. To close the menu, press the Escape key once.

- ✔ **To make a menu choice with the keyboard,** either press the choice's hot key or use the arrow keys to highlight the choice and then press Enter.

Chapter 2: Figuring Out the dBASE Screen 27

TIP Any time a menu is open, you can look at the bottom of the dBASE screen to see an explanation of the currently highlighted menu choice. Just above the explanation are instructions for getting around in the menu.

Once the menu is open, you can select a menu choice in three ways:

- Click on the menu choice.
- Press the key for the first letter in the menu choice. For example, in the Tools menu, you can select *Macros* by pressing the M key.
- Use the arrow keys to highlight the menu choice you want. Then, press Enter.

TIP No matter what you're doing, you can usually "back out of it" by pressing Esc. dBASE displays a little box asking whether you really want to quit doing what you're doing. Answer "yes" if you're sure and "no" if you've changed your mind.

Using shortcut keys

After you work with dBASE for a while, you will notice that you sometimes can bypass menus and just press a key combination to do something. These key combinations, called *shortcut keys,* are usually shown on the Status Bar. For example, while looking at data in a Browse screen, you can instantly switch to viewing the data in an on-screen form by pressing F2.

Using submenus

Some menu choices lead you to submenus. You can expect a submenu whenever you see a triangle next to a menu choice (for example, Macros in the Tools menu). Figure 2-4 shows the submenu that appears when you select Macros.

You open a submenu simply by selecting the menu choice. You close a submenu by clicking on the menu choice again with the mouse or by pressing Escape.

What the different menus do

Most of the things that the menus do are concerned with creating and modifying stuff in dBASE. If you're reading this book from front to back, you may not yet understand some of the choices on the menus. But here's an overview:

Part I: All the DataBasics You Have to Know

Figure 2-4: When you see a triangle to the right of a menu choice, it means that selecting that menu choice will open a submenu.

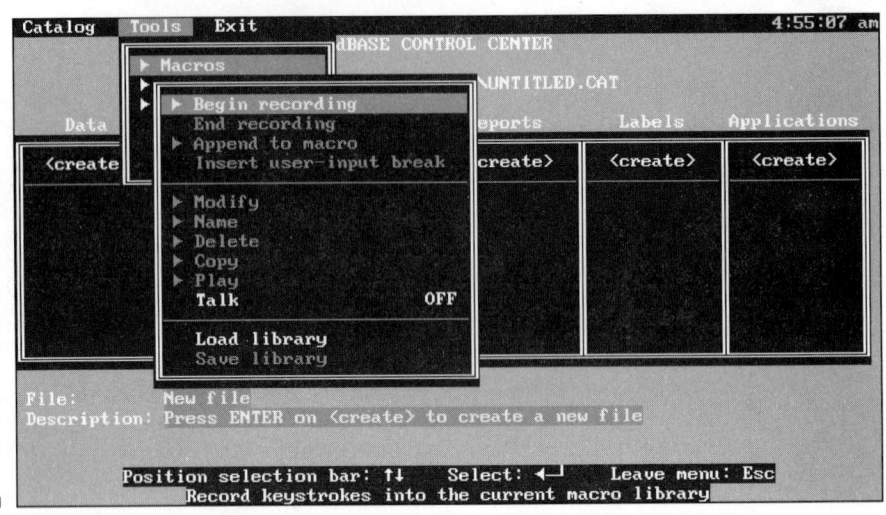

The Catalog menu

The Catalog menu lets you create and manipulate *catalogs*, which keep together all the different files (tables, reports, and so on) that go with a particular database. The important menu choices are:

- **Use a different catalog:** Lets you switch to a different catalog or create and use a new catalog.

- **Modify catalog name:** Lets you change a catalog's name. A catalog name can have up to eight letters, digits, and underscores, but it can't include spaces or punctuation marks. For more information about catalog names, see Chapter 3.

- **Edit description of catalog:** Lets you change a catalog's description, which you create when you first create a catalog. Or you can write a description for the catalog if you didn't do so when you first created the catalog.

- **Add file to catalog:** For a catalog to keep track of all the different files that go with a particular database, the appropriate catalog must be open whenever you create a new file for a database. If you forget to open the catalog before creating a file, however, you still can add it to the catalog via this menu choice.

You don't need to worry about the other choices in the Catalog menu.

The Tools menu

The Tools menu choices work as follows:

- **Macros:** A macro is a series of actions that you can record and play back. This menu choice opens a submenu that lets you record and play back your keystrokes. If you find that you press the same keys over and over — such as opening the same catalog, opening the same table, displaying its data in a Browse screen, and so on — a macro can help save time that's better spent at the local bowling alley.
- **Import:** Lets you import data from other programs — such as Paradox, FoxPro, and Lotus 1-2-3 — into dBASE.
- **Export:** Lets you rearrange data from dBASE (change its *file format*) so that it can be used by other programs, such as Paradox, FoxPro, and Lotus 1-2-3.
- **DOS utilities:** Provides file management capabilities and other features for working with the files on your PC's hard disk.
- **Protect data:** Lets you password-protect your database so that snoopers can't look at it. Of course, if the snoopers are those 14-year-old genius types, you can always try banishing them to their room or taking away their MTV.
- **Settings:** Lets you set various things about how dBASE works. Don't worry about this choice at the moment. It's covered in Chapter 22.

The Exit menu

This menu gives you only two choices:

- **Exit to the Command window:** Gets you out of the Control Center and back to the Developer's Desktop.
- **Quit to DOS:** Shuts down dBASE and returns you to MS-DOS or (if you're running dBASE under Windows) the Windows Program Manager.

Getting Help When You Need It

No, this section isn't about getting psychiatric help. You don't need that kind of help — at least, you don't need it to work with dBASE.

At some point, though, you may need to do something in dBASE but not have a clue how to do it. There are a couple of solutions. First, you could look it up in this book. But what if you loaned the book to a friend or, worse, to a deadly enemy who's *never* going to give it back? What will you do *then?*

Part I: All the DataBasics You Have to Know

Lucky for you, dBASE provides an on-screen explanation of almost anything you'll ever need to do: just press F1 and a Help window appears, as shown in Figure 2-5.

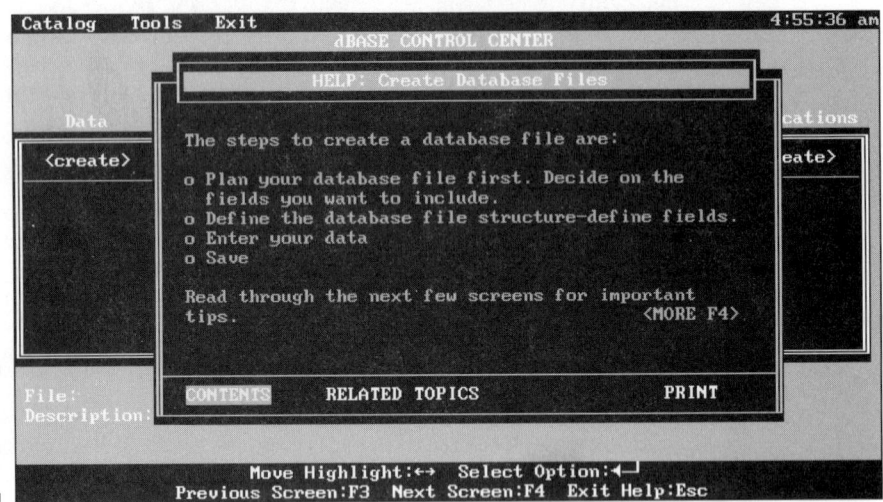

Figure 2-5:
A Help window.

```
Catalog    Tools    Exit                                           4:55:36 am
                           dBASE CONTROL CENTER
                        ┌─────────────────────────────────────┐
                        │      HELP: Create Database Files    │
             Data       │                                     │    cations
           ┌────────────┤ The steps to create a database file are:│  ate>
           │ <create>   │                                     │
           │            │ o Plan your database file first. Decide on the
           │            │   fields you want to include.
           │            │ o Define the database file structure-define fields.
           │            │ o Enter your data
           │            │ o Save
           │            │
           │            │ Read through the next few screens for important
           │            │ tips.                             <MORE F4>
           │            │
           │ File:      │ CONTENTS    RELATED TOPICS              PRINT
           │ Description:
                        Move Highlight:↔  Select Option:↵
                        Previous Screen:F3  Next Screen:F4  Exit Help:Esc
```

When you're in the Help window, you can go to other Help windows by selecting one of the choices displayed across the bottom of the window. Choosing Contents takes you to a list of all dBASE Help topics; choosing Related topics displays other Help windows that are related to the topic of the current Help window.

NOTE

If your printer is hooked up, turned on, and ready to print, you can print the contents of the current Help window.

Chapter 3
Setting Up a Database: Rule #1 Is Think Ahead!

In This Chapter
- What's in a dBASE database?
- What are data types?
- How to plan your database
- Creating a dBASE catalog

Many things in life don't require you to think ahead. Surprise parties, for example. Turning 30 (sigh). Bad movies. Turning 40 (gulp). Unexpected visits by your in-laws. Turning 50 (gasp). Steady, now: keep breathing and these things happen automatically.

But when setting up a database, thinking ahead is a must. If you don't, you'll end up with a jumbled mess of data that won't serve anyone except the computer consultant you hire to bail you out at $100 an hour. Plus tips.

This chapter shows you how to think ahead and plan your database — from analyzing your needs to setting up the dBASE database. We also describe the basic components of a database and what you can do with each.

To get the most out of this chapter, you need to have

- Learned what a database manager can do for you (see Chapter 1)
- Figured out which data you want to manage
- Installed dBASE for DOS on your PC
- Resolved any psychological conflict that made you giggle uncontrollably when you sat down at the computer

Organizing Your Database

Like most PC database managers, dBASE creates a separate disk file for each different thing in the database. For example, if you want a table of customer data, that's one file; if you want to sort the data by each customer's last name, that's another file; and if you want to link the customer data to sales records, that's yet another file. And so on.

The problem is that unless your database is really simple, it gets hard to remember which files go with which database. If you have the files from three different databases all mixed together in the same disk directory, it can be a Nightmare on PC Street, just without the scary bad guy.

Using catalogs to keep database stuff together

dBASE gives you an easier way to manage your database: Before you create anything else in your database, you create a *catalog* and give it a name (how about *Fred*). A catalog is a kind of wrapper that holds all of a database's elements together. With a click of the mouse, you can see a list of all a catalog's tables, reports, and so on (see Figure 3-1).

After you create Fred, everything else you create goes into it — until you change to a different catalog or quit dBASE. Moreover, when you look on-screen, the *only* database files you see are those in Fred.

In essence, the catalog *is* the database. Even if it's called Fred. So a catalog in dBASE is a big thing that keeps all your little things together. You don't absolutely have to create a catalog before you create the other parts of your database. However, unless you create a catalog, dBASE has no way to keep track of what stuff goes with which database.

You can create as many different catalogs as you like.

The information on your PC's hard disk is divided into *disk files*, which are like file folders in a filing cabinet. Every disk file has a name that consists of up to eight letters or digits, followed by a period and an *extension* of up to three letters or digits. Every disk file is kept in a disk *directory*, which is like a drawer in a filing cabinet. Each directory also has a name. If you don't understand what disk files and directories are, check out IDG's *DOS For Dummies*, which explains all that stuff.

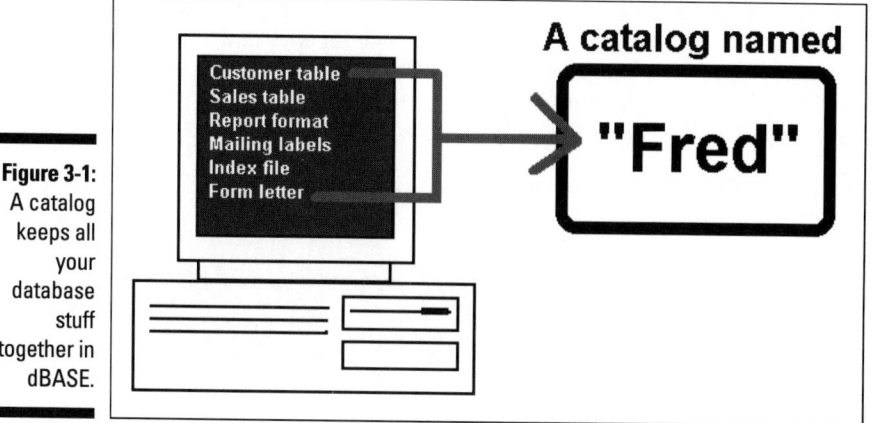

Figure 3-1:
A catalog keeps all your database stuff together in dBASE.

In the old days — *waaaay* back in the 1980s — dBASE didn't have catalogs. Instead, users had to create a separate disk directory for each database. Today, dBASE catalogs make your database life much easier. If you'd prefer not to use catalogs (The Sharper Image and J.C. Penney catalogs notwithstanding), you can still use the old-fashioned approach of creating a separate directory for each group of database files.

Thinking about your data

The catalog is only the wrapper. Your data is the real prize. Before you do anything else on the computer, think about the kinds of data you need to manage. Then you can decide how to divide the data between the different database tools that dBASE provides — tables, forms, reports, and so on. You use each tool to design a particular part of your database.

To make these decisions, of course, you need to know what the database tools that go into a dBASE catalog enable you to do.

Using Tables to Hold Your Data

The starting point of a dBASE database is a *table*, which holds all of a single group of records — with each record holding all the information about one thing, such as one customer or one sale. A table may hold, for example, all your customer records, all your inventory records, or all your sales records. A table shouldn't hold more than one group of records. If you try to keep your customer *and* sales records in a single table, plan on spending two or three weekends trying to figure out what's wrong with your database. (In other words, if a table holds more than one group of data, it's time to visit the bank machine and get that $100 an hour for the consultant in the pin-striped suit.)

Any time you need to combine data from separate tables, you can do so easily.

Fields and records and bears — Oh, my!

The easiest way to think of table data is, well, as a table. Figure 3-2 shows a row-and-column table of data in dBASE. There are no bears. I was only kidding about the bears. Honest.

When you see a table displayed as a row-and-column table, you are in *Browse mode* (and the table is called a *browse table*). The flip side of a browse table is a *form*, which I describe in a minute.

The names of the columns appear at the top of the browse table. In database jargon, columns are called *fields*. A field holds a single kind of information, such as name, address, or the number of TV commercials aired during a single evening.

Rows are called *records*. A record holds *all* the pieces of information about one thing. A customer record, for example, may hold a customer's name, address, and phone number, as well as an account number and the date of first pur-

Figure 3-2:
A dBASE row-and-column table (also called a browse table).

chase. A sales record may hold a customer's account number and an item's description, price, and inventory number. If a table held information about *you*, all of the details about you would go in one record.

> **TIP** All records in a table should hold basically the same types and amount of data. If some records need to hold a lot more data than others, you need to redesign your database. And although the contents of the fields differ, they are the same size in each record. That is, if the contents of the First Name field in one record is 15 letters long, the contents of the First Name field in another record can't be 35 letters long.

All data has a type

Different fields in a dBASE table often contain different *data types*. Just as people categorize everything in the world as solids, liquids, gases, or cream pies, database managers classify data as different data types, such as for text, number, and date. (dBASE for Windows also has types for pictures and other things — even financial worksheets or word processing documents!) Data types help dBASE zip through your data, getting the information you need faster and more efficiently. Chapter 4 covers data types, which are also called field types, in more detail. In the meantime, bear with me. (No, that's *not* a bear with me. There are no bears. Just be patient.)

Using Queries to Find Your Data

After you put data into a database, you sometimes need to search for specific pieces of data. Suppose that you're manning the phones one Sunday night (you *do* work Sunday nights, don't you?), and a customer calls to make sure that you sent an order to the right address.

You can handle the situation in three ways. The first, and easiest, is to put customers on hold until they hang up in disgust. If you have ever called a business on Sunday night, you know how popular this method has become.

Second, scan the customer data table row by row until you see the customer record you want. If you have more than a few dozen records in your table, this method also may cause customers to hang up.

The best choice is to use a *query* to find the record you need. A query is a question that you ask dBASE, such as "What records have the ZIP code 90210?" or "How many customers bought books on bungee jumping?" or "Wouldn't you really rather be a toaster?"

Part I: All the DataBasics You Have to Know

When you create a query, you tell dBASE which field you want to examine — say, last name — and what you want to search for — say, the name Wilds. Then you just click on a little screen picture, and dBASE immediately shows you the record you need. (Unfortunately, the caller's name was West, so he hung up, anyway.)

Using Forms to Enter Your Data

When you fill out a paper form, you write the data in blanks on a page. When you fill out a dBASE *form*, you type the data in blanks on-screen, as shown in Figure 3-3.

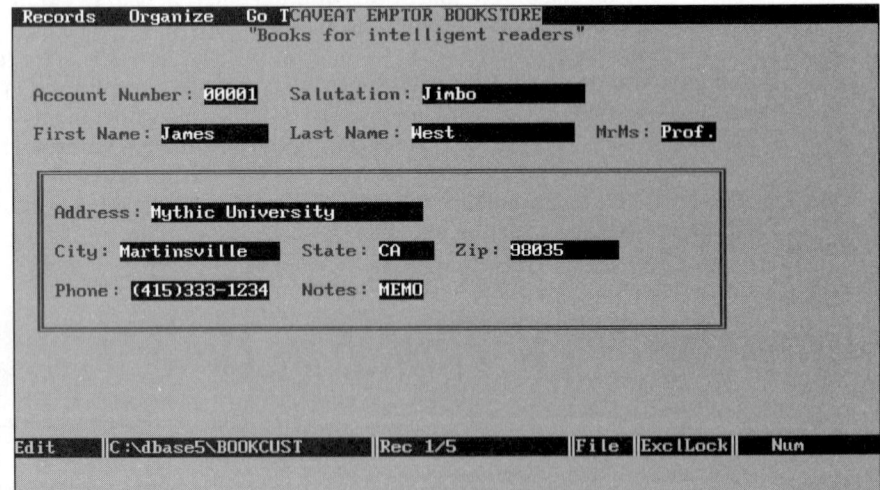

```
Records    Organize    Go TCAVEAT EMPTOR BOOKSTORE
                       "Books for intelligent readers"

   Account Number: 00001    Salutation: Jimbo
   First Name: James        Last Name: West              MrMs: Prof.

       ┌─────────────────────────────────────────────────────┐
       │  Address: Mythic University                         │
       │  City: Martinsville    State: CA    Zip: 98035      │
       │  Phone: (415)333-1234  Notes: MEMO                  │
       └─────────────────────────────────────────────────────┘

Edit      C:\dbase5\BOOKCUST        Rec 1/5        File  ExclLock   Num
```

Figure 3-3: Filling in an on-screen form.

> **TIP**
>
> When you enter data into your own database, it's easy to remember what data goes where. But if other people enter data for you, forms can be a big help. When designing a form, always assume that it will be used by someone who knows nothing about your data and your database. In dBASE, you can include instructions in your form to explain what data goes where; be sure to take advantage of this feature. That way, if a data-entry person doesn't know what kind of data to put into the MrMs blank, help is available on-screen.

Using Reports to Print Your Data

A report is just a printout of your data. It can be plain, or it can get really fancy. In dBASE, you can print reports in a variety of formats.

You can design complete reports, which include all the data in your database; summary reports, which give you totals and calculations; or specialized reports, which contain only one or two fields. You can create row-and-column reports, one-record-at-a-time reports, form letters, or mailing labels. For the complete details, see the chapters on reports.

Planning Your Database

When planning your database, you need to ask yourself two main questions:

- What data do you need to manage?
- What do you need to do with the data?

Suppose that you're the database guru at a fictitious book store called Caveat Emptor, which is Latin for "Let the buyer beware." Your boss is the store owner, a mysterious individual named Honest Janis.

Caveat Emptor has a large number of regular customers, many of whom have accounts at the store. In addition, the store has a vast inventory of used and rare books — including, of course, several copies of *dBASE For DOS For Dummies*. That adds up to two main groups of data:

- Customer names, addresses, and phone numbers
- Sales transactions

In dBASE, each group of data gets its own table. You can combine the data from different tables to create consolidated forms or reports.

Janis decides that he needs to do several things with the data in his database (see Figure 3-4): First, he needs to be able to locate the data for a customer by searching for the customer's account number or last name. Second, he needs to print form letters and mailing labels to keep customers up to date on the store's latest used-book acquisitions. Third, he needs to update the inventory database and print reports. These requirements dictate how he needs to set up the database's tables, forms, and reports.

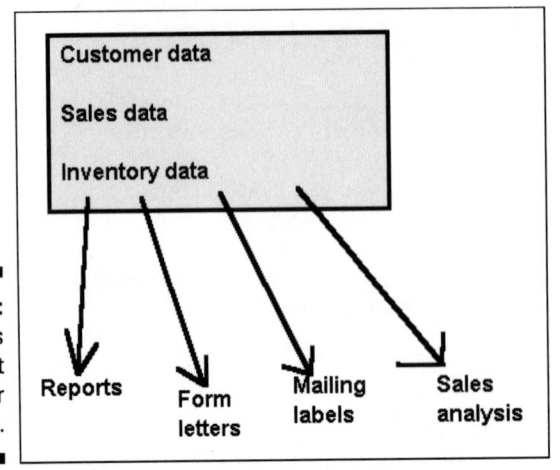

Figure 3-4: Requirements for the Caveat Emptor database.

Customer data
Sales data
Inventory data

→ Reports
→ Form letters
→ Mailing labels
→ Sales analysis

Creating a Database Catalog

Now that you know what data you need to manage and what you want to do with it, you can get to the PC and creating a dBASE catalog — the heart of the database itself. After all that buildup, the actual process of creating a catalog may be anticlimactic. And relax: if you mess up, you just get to start over.

Of course, at a lower salary. In another job. At another company. In another city that's probably awful.

On second thought, try *not* to mess it up.

Quit shaking, this stuff is easier than you think. To create a dBASE catalog:

1. **Start dBASE.**
   - *To start dBASE from DOS:* Switch to the main dBASE directory (probably C:\DBASE). Then type **dbase** at the DOS prompt and press Enter.
   - *To start dBASE from Windows:* Double-click on the dBASE icon in the Program Manager.

2. **If the dBASE Control Center isn't visible, press F2.**

   The Control Center appears on-screen.

3. **Click on Catalog in the Menu Bar (or press Alt-C).**

   This action opens the Catalog menu.

Chapter 3: Setting Up a Database: Rule #1 Is Think Ahead! 39

4. **Select Use a different catalog.**

   You can select the menu choice in any of three ways:

   - Click on it with the mouse.
   - Press U.
   - Use the arrow keys to highlight the menu choice and then press Enter.

   After you select the menu choice, a little box appears at the right side of your screen, as shown in Figure 3-5. In this box, underneath the word *create*, are the names of any catalogs you've already created. If you select *create,* you can create a new catalog. If you select an existing catalog, you open that catalog.

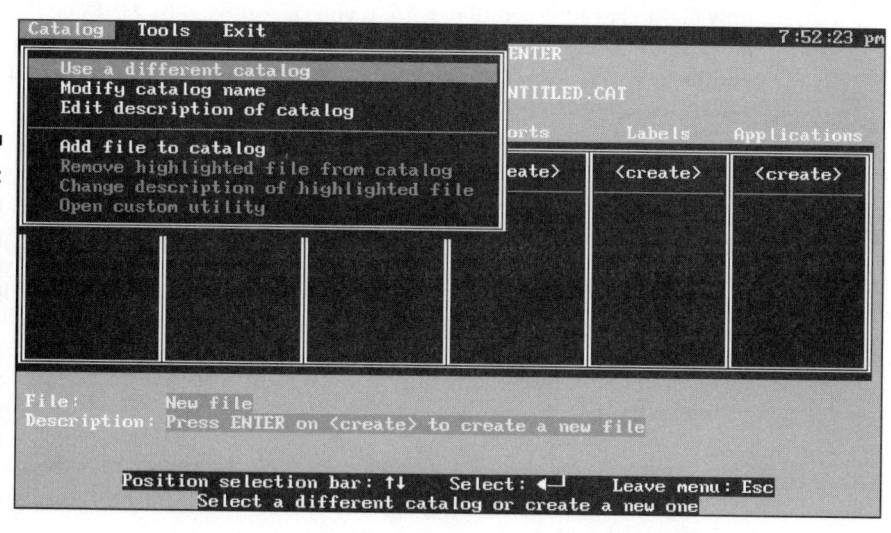

   Figure 3-5: Creating a new catalog or opening an existing catalog. Notice the little box at the right side of the screen.

5. **Select create.**

   dBASE asks you to name the new catalog.

6. **Enter the desired name and press Enter.**

   The catalog name can't be more than eight letters long, and it can only contain letters, numbers, or underscores. dBASE automatically adds the extension .CAT to the name.

7. **Re-open the Catalog menu and select Edit description of catalog.**

   dBASE prompts you to enter a description of the catalog. Type the description, such as **Bookstore customer data,** then press Enter. Presto! You're done!

Part I: All the DataBasics You Have to Know

> **NOTE**
>
> Notice the catalog line in the top-center of the screen. It will look something like:
>
> ```
> C:\DBASE\FILENAME.CAT
> ```
>
> except that FILENAME is replaced by the catalog name you entered. This line provides a quick way to see which catalog you're in. If the filename is UNTITLED, you aren't in any catalog.

> **TECHNICAL STUFF**
>
> The reason that catalog names can't be longer than eight characters (letters, digits, and underscores) has nothing to do with dBASE. It's because MS-DOS, the PC's operating system, keeps track of disk files and limits their names to eight characters, a period, and a three-character extension. dBASE puts the extension .CAT on catalogs and .DBF on the disk file for each table, leaving you only eight characters to play with. If you're confused by MS-DOS, then congratulations! It means you're paying attention. Reading IDG's *DOS For Dummies* is a good way to feel less confused. (Of course, so is hitting yourself on the head with a steel pipe, but reading *DOS For Dummies* isn't injurious.)

Hands on: Creating a Sample Catalog

> **HANDS-ON**
>
> If you like, try creating a catalog for this book's sample database, which chronicles the database management travails of the Caveat Emptor bookstore.
>
> If you aren't already running dBASE, start it up. If the Control Center isn't visible, press F2.
>
> Now create the catalog for the book's example database. Because it's for the Caveat Emptor bookstore, call it CAVEAT. Follow these steps:
>
> 1. **Open the Catalog menu.**
> 2. **Select Use a different catalog.**
> 3. **In the little box that appears at the right side of your screen, select create.**
>
>   dBASE asks you to name the new catalog.
>
> 4. **Type CAVEAT in the blank and then press Enter.**
> 5. **Reopen the Catalog menu and select Edit description of catalog.**
>
>   dBASE prompts you to enter a description of the catalog.
>
> 6. **Type Bookstore Database and press Enter.**

dBASE creates a new catalog named Caveat. Anything you create now will be included in the new catalog. Also in the Sears catalog. But that's another story.

For now, that's it! dBASE automatically saves your catalog to your PC's hard disk, so you can shut down dBASE and take a break.

Whenever you set up a database, remember to analyze the data you need to manage, figure out what you need to do with the data, and use dBASE to create the database. And please, don't feed the bear. Bears are just like cats: Give them a bowl of milk (or a side of beef) and you'll *never* get rid of them.

Chapter 4
Cataloging and Creating Tables

In This Chapter
- Planning the structure of a table
- Understanding fields
- Understanding field types
- Working with catalogs
- Creating a table
- Saving a table

To get the most out of this chapter, you need to understand

- Basic dBASE and database concepts (see Chapter 1)
- What catalogs are and how to create them (see Chapter 3)
- Your subconscious motivations and their traumatic origins (Did you hate your muzzer? Ve alvays look to ze muzzer. Und your dog, Shpot? Did he hate hiz muzzer, too? Hmmm?)

In this chapter, we give you some basic ideas to help you create and use catalogs and tables. If you want to follow along by practicing on the book's example database, you need to have created the Caveat catalog (refer to the hands-on section, "Creating a sample catalog," in Chapter 3).

Chapter 3 showed you how to create a dBASE catalog, which is a wrapper that holds all your different data management tools together. After you create a catalog, you can create your *table,* which is the basic building block of your database. Each table holds data about a particular kind of thing. In this chapter, you learn how to create a table.

The book's example table is called Bookcust, and it will hold all the customer data collected by Janis, the imaginary bookstore owner introduced in Chapter 3.

When you design a table, you should be guided by one consideration: What do you need to accomplish with your database? Because dBASE is so simple to use, you can focus on *what* you're doing rather than *how* you're doing it.

Planting Fields to Structure Your Table

When database people talk about the *structure* of a table, they're simply discussing a table's fields. When creating a table, you need to figure out

- Which fields you need
- What types your fields should be
- How big your fields should be
- If you are truly out standing in your field

These decisions, of course, are determined by what you need to do with the table.

A field is a category of information about the people or things in your database. A field's contents in any record is one piece of information for that category, such as a name, street address, part number, or list price.

Suppose that you're designing a table for the Caveat Emptor bookstore (refer to the hands-on section, "Creating the Bookcust Table," later in this chapter). Also suppose that you want to do the following:

- Keep track of customer names and addresses
- Print reports of customer data
- Print form letters and mailing labels

To keep track of customer names and addresses, you may establish the following fields:

Name

Address

City, State, ZIP

If you were keeping track of your customer information on paper, this three field setup would be fine. (Actually, if you were writing this information on paper, you wouldn't even think about fields. You'd worry only about whether people can read your handwriting!) But dBASE has a lot of power that you can't use if you limit yourself to these three fields.

Suppose that you decide later that you want to put customer records in order by ZIP code or print the first and last names in a different order than they appear in the Name field. You'd be out of luck! With a computer database, you can do these things and more, as long as you separate the different kinds of information into different fields. If you create only three fields, however, you'll be out of luck. You should have "made like glue" and stuck to paper.

To take full advantage of dBASE, you should put separate parts of the name and address data in separate fields, such as the following:

Account Number

First Name

Last Name

Address

City

State

ZIP

That's a lot better. This setup even contains an Account Number field in case two customers have the same first and last names. (This field also will be helpful in Chapter 11 if you create the sample Sales table and want to combine its data with the data from the Bookcust table.)

With this table setup, you can easily take care of your top two goals: keeping track of customer names and addresses and printing reports. But what about the third goal — printing form letters and mailing labels?

Most form letters include a courtesy title (for example, Mr. or Ms.) before the person's name in the address. In addition, you also need a field that indicates which name to use in the salutation ("Dear so-and-so,"). In the case of the Bookcust table, many of the Caveat Emptor customers are friends of the owner. And Honest Janis would never address his pal Jim West as Mr. West, not even in a form letter.

After adding the MrMs and Salutation fields to the mix, the final field list is

Account Number

First Name

Last Name

MrMs

Salutation

Address

City

State

ZIP

There's nothing technical about this stuff. If you have common sense and can think ahead, you can be a database expert with dBASE. If you don't have these qualities, you can be a very successful politician.

Naming your dBASE fields

In working out the table design, you used descriptive names for the fields (Account Number, First Name, and so on). When you create a table in dBASE, however, you can't use just any old names for fields. In dBASE,

- A field name can't be more than ten characters long.
- Only letters, digits (0 to 9), and underscores (_) are allowed.
- A field name must begin with a letter.
- Case doesn't matter (FNAME is the same as fname is the same as fNAME).

Thus, you can use CUST_ID as a field name, but you can't use CUST-ID because it has a hyphen (rule 2). You can't use Account Number because it has a space (rule 2) and it's too long (rule 1). And you can't use 2LiveCrew because it doesn't begin with a letter (rule 3) and lacks talent (rule 5). Oops, there is no rule 5; forget that last part.

Because of these rules, you usually have to modify any descriptive field names. For example, you can change *Account Number* to *CUST_ID*, *First Name* to *FNAME*, and so on.

Typecasting your field data

Each field in a dBASE table has a *field type*, which you have to specify when you set up the table. Why go to all the trouble? The reason is simple: The data type tells dBASE how to treat the field's data.

For example, when you select numeric as the field type, dBASE knows that it can do mathematical operations with the data in that field — something it can't do if you select character (text) as the field type. If you select Android as the field type, dBASE knows that you've gone a little goofy and think you're a character on *Star Trek*. In dBASE, you can specify any of the following field types (notice that Android is *not* on the list):

- **Character:** Use this field type for plain text. Also use it for numbers when you don't need to perform any calculations with them. For example, you can add up all the telephone numbers or ZIP codes in a database, but what's the point?

- **Numeric:** Specify this field type when you need to perform mathematical operations on the data and the field consists of whole numbers (1, 5, 181, and so on) only. Use a numeric field to keep track of how many orders a customer places, for example.

- **Memo:** Use memo fields for free-form text. Most dBASE fields hold a specific amount of information, but a memo field can hold up to 32,000 characters — about eight typed, single-spaced pages of text. Use a memo field, for example, to keep miscellaneous notes about each customer, such as family birthdays, book preferences, a log of telephone calls, and so on. (In fact, you can add a memo field to the sample Bookcust table in Chapter 8.)

- **Logical:** Use logical fields to keep track of yes/no situations, such as "Is this customer's payment overdue?"

- **Date:** If you don't know what this field is for, you should seek immediate medical help. Oh, all right — a date/time field is for holding dates and times, such as the date of a customer's last order.

- **Float:** Use this field type for numbers with decimal points, such as dollar amounts.

One drawback of computerized database management — even with King dBASE — is that fields are limited to a specific size. You can't have one record with a 10-character First Name field and another record with a 1,000-character First Name field. (You can *change* the size of a field, but then all of the fields are limited to the *new* size.) The exception is a memo field, which is stored in a special way that lets it hold a varying amount of data.

Cataloging Your Table

Before you create a table, remember to open a catalog to keep the table together with other files in the same database. (To brush up on catalogs, refer to Chapter 3.)

> **NOTE:** When you start dBASE, it opens the catalog that was open when you last used the program.

To open a catalog, follow these steps:

1. **Open the Catalog menu.**
2. **Select Use a different catalog.**

   At the right side of your screen, a catalog list appears.

3. **Select the catalog you want to use.**

   dBASE opens that catalog for you. You're done!

In theory, some catalog is always open. So if you want to close a catalog, you do so by switching to another catalog (in other words, open a different catalog). If you don't want *any* catalog open (which would be very unusual), in Step 3 select Untitled from the catalog list. Once you open a catalog, it stays open until you open a different one. You don't need to close it.

A newly created table — or any other database thing, such as a report — goes into a catalog if the catalog was open before you created the table. But what can you do if you forget to open the catalog before you create the table? In other words, what if you have something sitting out on your hard disk that *should* be in the catalog but *isn't?*

You can do two things: First, take comfort in the words of Marcus Aurelius, the Roman emperor: "Tomorrow, you may die." (Aurelius was no fun at parties — except when he did the lampshade-on-the-head trick — but he did have a way of putting things into perspective.) Second, you can easily *add* a table or other database file to a catalog even if you didn't open the catalog first! To add stuff to a catalog, follow these steps:

1. **Open the catalog to which you want to add something.**
2. **Move to the Control Center panel that matches the type of file you want to add.**

   For instance, if you want to add a table, make sure that the highlight is in the Data panel; to add a form, the highlight should be in the Forms panel. And so on.

3. **Open the Catalog menu.**
4. **Select Add file to catalog.**

   On the right side of your screen, dBASE lists all the files in the current disk directory that match the Control Center panel selected in Step 2. You can add any of these files to the catalog.

Chapter 4: Cataloging and Creating Tables   49

> If you ever need to switch to a different disk directory, you can find out how to do so in Chapter 22.

5. **In the file list, select the file you want to add (by either clicking on it or using the arrow keys to highlight it) and then press Enter.**

    dBASE adds the file to your catalog.

Removing stuff from a catalog

If you have worked with a computer for more than a few seconds, you probably have discovered how easy it is to delete something. In fact, your computer may sometimes go above and beyond the call of duty and delete an entire directory, or even an entire disk. Because you can delete stuff easily in dBASE, you should always read the on-screen prompts carefully.

Removing a file from a catalog and *deleting* a file from your disk are two very different things in dBASE. *Removing* a file means that you are taking a file out of the catalog. The file still exists on your hard disk, so you can add it to the catalog again whenever you want (see the preceding section). *Deleting* a file means that dBASE erases a file from your hard disk. Then the only way that you can get the file back is to use an undelete utility, such as the DOS undelete command or the more powerful undelete features in such programs as Norton Utilities and PC Tools.

To remove a file from a catalog in dBASE or to delete a file from the hard disk, follow these steps:

1. **Press F2 to get to the Control Center. (If you're already in the Control Center, don't press F2: nothing will happen, so you will have wasted all that finger effort.)**

2. **Make sure that the current catalog is the one you want.**

    dBASE displays the name of the current catalog in the catalog line (in the top-center of the screen). If the file you want to remove is in a different catalog, change to the correct catalog.

3. **Use the arrow keys to highlight the file you want to remove from the catalog.**

4. **Open the Catalog menu.**

5. **Select Remove highlighted file from catalog.**

    dBASE displays a box that asks whether you're sure you want to *remove* the file from the catalog.

Part I: All the DataBasics You Have to Know

6. **Make sure that the box says Remove and not Delete. Then press Y.**

   dBASE next asks whether you want to *delete* the highlighted file. If you want to erase the file from your hard disk, press Y; otherwise, press N.

> **TIP:** Here's a shortcut for removing (or deleting) a file: Highlight the file in the Control Center and press the Delete key on your keyboard. dBASE first asks whether you want to *remove* the file from the catalog; answer "yes." dBASE next asks whether you want to *delete* the highlighted file. If you want to erase the file from your hard disk, answer "yes"; otherwise, answer "no."

Creating a Table

After you know what fields you need in your table, it's time to begin creating your table in dBASE. Later in this chapter, you can follow the hands-on tutorial and create an example table. But first, here are the basic steps for creating any dBASE table:

1. **Decide which fields you need.**
2. **Create or open the catalog in which you want the table included.**
3. **At the top of the Control Center's Data panel, highlight the word Create.**

   The Table Design screen appears (see Figure 4-1).

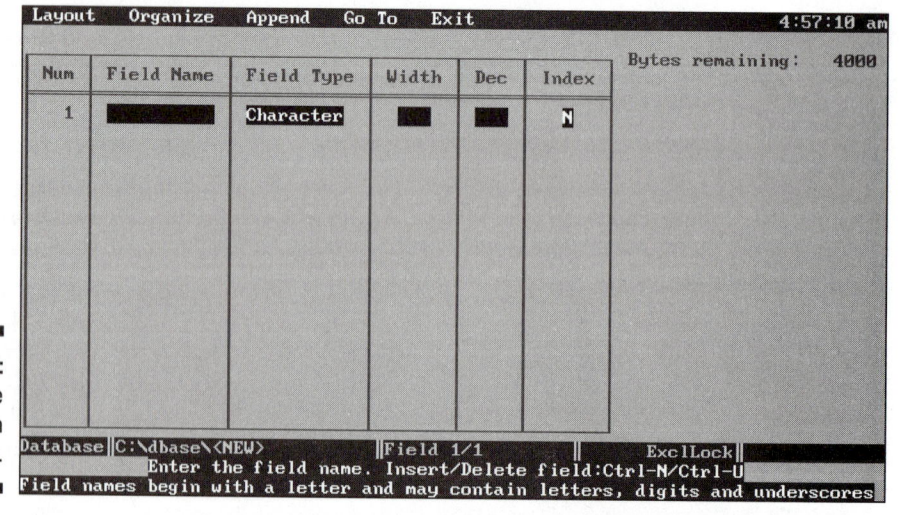

Figure 4-1: The Table Design screen.

Chapter 4: Cataloging and Creating Tables

4. **Enter the name of the first field in the first column of the first line. Press Tab.**

   Notice that as soon as you press Tab, the second column comes to life, and the word *Character* appears.

5. **Choose a field type. Press the spacebar to cycle through the field types. When finished, press Tab.**

   If you accidentally select the incorrect type, press Shift-Tab and the cursor returns to the type column. Press the spacebar to change to the correct type.

6. **Set the width. Press Tab.**

   The width is the maximum width for that field in all records.

7. **Press Y if you want this field indexed. Otherwise, press N.**

   In the last column of the Table Design screen, you tell dBASE whether you want the field indexed. You don't need to know much about this column now; indexes are explained in Chapter 14.

   (If you're one of those type-A overachievers who can't relax for a single second: an index helps dBASE keep your records in order and find stuff faster. If you're often going to be searching for data in a particular field, index the field. In an index, *ascending* means from A to Z; *descending* means from Z to A.)

   For years, what dBASE now calls a *table* was called a *database file*. Sometimes, dBASE experts and even Borland's dBASE manuals slip up and use the old terminology.

8. **Repeat Steps 4 through 7 for every field you need.**

   At the end of Step 7, the cursor moves automatically to the first column of the next row.

9. **Name and save the table design.**

   To save the table design, open the Layout menu and select Save this database file structure. dBASE asks you to name the new table, as shown in Figure 4-2. Type the name (maximum eight letters, with no spaces or punctuation marks) and press Enter.

   Just like a catalog, a table is a file on your PC's hard disk. Therefore, a table name must comply with the same MS-DOS restrictions as a catalog name: it can consist of letters, digits, underscores, and a few special characters — but no commas, periods, or spaces. And a table name can comprise a maximum of eight letters (case does not matter).

Part I: All the DataBasics You Have to Know

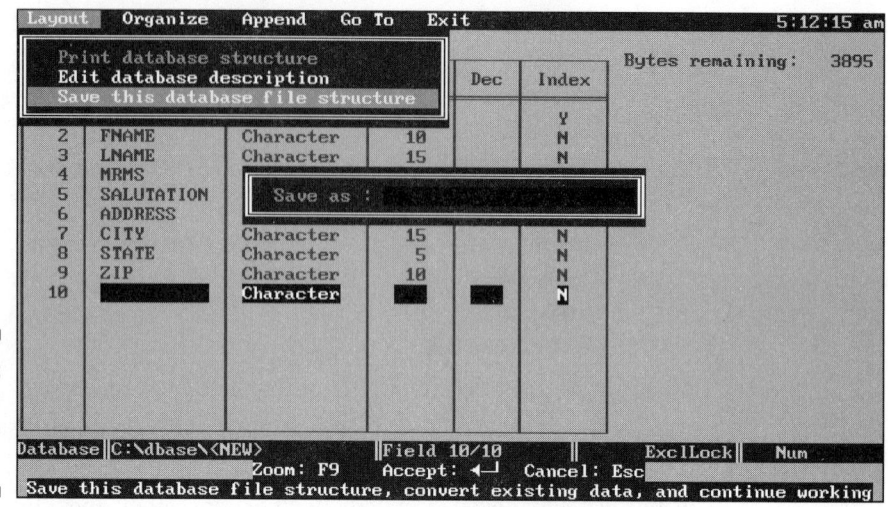

Figure 4-2: Naming and saving the table design.

    10. **Exit the Table Design screen.**

       Since you've already saved the table design, open the Exit menu and select Abandon changes and exit. dBASE automatically returns you to the Control Center. The new table is listed in the Data panel.

> **TIP:** Here are two shortcuts for saving the table design (if you want to bypass the Layout menu):
>
> - Press Ctrl-End. After dBASE prompts you for the table name, type the name you want and press Enter. Presto! The table design is named and saved.
> - Open the Exit menu and select Save changes and exit. In one step, you can save the table design and exit the Table Design screen, returning to the Control Center.

> **TIP:** If you decide that you *don't* want to save the table design, just press Esc. dBASE asks whether you're sure you want to *abandon* the design — which means don't save it — and return to the Control Center. If you're sure, just answer "yes."

Hands on: Creating the Bookcust Table

HANDS-ON: In this section, you actually create a dBASE table to hold customer records for the Caveat Emptor bookstore:

1. **Start dBASE.**
2. **Open the Caveat catalog from the Control Center.**
3. **At the top of the Data panel, highlight Create and then press Enter.**

   The Table Design screen opens.

4. **Type CUST_ID in the first column of the first line to enter the first field's name. Press Tab**

   dBASE creates a field named CUST_ID.

   As soon as you press Tab, the second column comes to life. The word *Character* appears in the column. Scary, isn't it?

5. **Select Character and press Tab.**

   If you accidentally select the incorrect field type, press Shift-Tab and the cursor returns to the type column. You can press the spacebar to cycle through the various field types.

   If you have an inquiring mind, you probably wonder why CUST_ID is a character field when it's going to hold account numbers. (Of course, you also may wonder whether there really is a statue of Elvis on Mars.) CUST_ID is a character field because you won't need to mathematically manipulate account numbers.

   dBASE moves the cursor to the Width column.

6. **Press 5 and then press Tab.**

   dBASE moves the cursor to the Index column.

7. **Press Y.**

   Because you will want to search this field a great deal, you should index this field.

   Notice that dBASE automatically moves the cursor to the next line (see Figure 4-3).

8. **Repeat Steps 4 through 7 to add other fields.**

   Believe it or not, this table won't do you much good with only the CUST_ID field. Most people want to be called by a name rather than a number, and sending all your bills each month "Care of general delivery" is a quick way to go bankrupt.

   So add a second field to the sample table. For example, to define the First Name field: type **fname** and press Tab; accept the suggested field type — character — and press Tab; type **10** and press Tab; and press N for "No, I don't want to index this field."

Part I: All the DataBasics You Have to Know

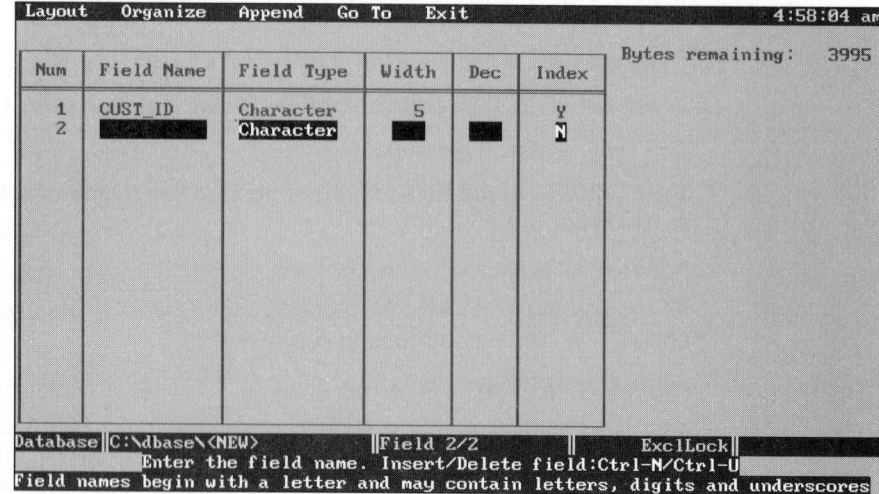

Figure 4-3: The Table Design screen after adding one field.

Define the rest of the fields in your sample table as follows:

Name	Type	Width	Index
LNAME	Character	15	No
MRMS	Character	5	No
SALUTATION	Character	15	No
ADDRESS	Character	25	No
CITY	Character	15	No
STATE	Character	5	No
ZIP	Character	10	No

> **REMEMBER:** You should use the numeric field type only when you plan to perform mathematical operations on the data in the field. That's why the ZIP field, like the CUST_ID field, is a character field type. Another advantage to making the ZIP field a character field type is that you can then include in your database customers who live in countries that use letters in their postal codes.

9. **Save the table design by opening the Layout menu and selecting Save this database file structure.**

   dBASE displays a little box asking you to name the table.

10. **Type BOOKCUST in the blank and press Enter.**

    dBASE saves your table design.

Chapter 4: Cataloging and Creating Tables

11. **Close the Table Design screen by opening the Exit menu and selecting Abandon changes and exit.**

    dBASE automatically takes you back to the Control Center.

    See, you did it! The Bookcust table is now listed in the Data panel.

Wow, you've defined a database table in dBASE! If you want to take a break, shut down dBASE and pull out the old Koosh ball. Unless, of course, you're like me and have a morbid fear of the things.

Chapter 5
Putting Data in Your Database

In This Chapter
▶ Different ways to put stuff in your database
▶ Discovering the Status Bar
▶ Adding records to a table
▶ Deleting records from a table
▶ Editing records and fixing mistakes

*I*f you're reading this book from cover to cover, you have already seen how to plan a database, design a table, and set up the table's fields. You're ready to put some customer data into your table; this is not a difficult task — in fact, compared to entering data in old-style database managers, it's incredibly easy. Nonetheless, there are a few tricks you should learn on the way.

In this chapter, you will see how to enter data into a table. Read the chapter to get the basic ideas and then follow the steps with your own table. If you don't have your own database, you can use the example Caveat Emptor database.

Before you can put data in a table, you need to know

✓ Your way around dBASE (see Chapter 3)
✓ How to create a table and put it in a catalog (see Chapter 4)

To follow along with the book's example database, you need to have created the Caveat catalog (see Chapter 3) and the Bookcust table (see Chapter 4).

Getting Ready: You Look Fine

If you quit dBASE after reading Chapter 4, start it up again. Straighten your tie. Comb your hair. If needed, start the Control Center by pressing F2. If the

Control Center doesn't name the catalog you need as the current catalog, open the Catalog menu and follow these steps:

1. **Select Use a different catalog.**

   On the right side of your screen, dBASE lists the available catalogs.

2. **Select the desired catalog.**

   dBASE opens the catalog and returns you to the Control Center.

If the table you want isn't listed in the Catalog window, you probably forgot to open the catalog before creating the table. No problem! Just move the highlight to the Data panel, open the Catalog menu, and select Add file to catalog. When dBASE displays a list of available tables, highlight the desired table and press Enter to add it to the catalog.

For more detailed instructions on adding an item to a catalog, see Chapter 4.

Adding Data to a Table: The Main Event

After you open a catalog and display a table in the Data panel, you can enter some records. To do so, first open a table; dBASE displays a dialog box that asks what you want to do (see Figure 5-1).

Any time you want to open or select something, you can do so in two ways:

- Double-click on the thing you want to open or select.
- Use the arrow keys to highlight the thing you want to open or select and then press Enter.

To open a table, for example, you can either double-click on its name in the Data panel of the Control Center or highlight its name and press Enter. The bottom line: When you see the words *double-click*, you can usually substitute *highlight and press Enter*, and vice versa.

You can accuse dBASE's designers of a lot of things: Becoming addicted to Twinkies. Collecting 71 unpaid parking tickets. Being computer geeks with no social skills (of course, they'd take that as a compliment). But you have to admit that they *do* have a sense of humor. How else can you explain the fiendish cleverness embedded in the dialog box shown in Figure 5-1? In a million years, would you guess that you can add data to a table by selecting Modify structure/order? I think not.

Chapter 5: Putting Data in Your Database **59**

Figure 5-1: After you open a table, dBASE asks what you want to do next. To enter data, highlight Modify structure/order and press Enter.

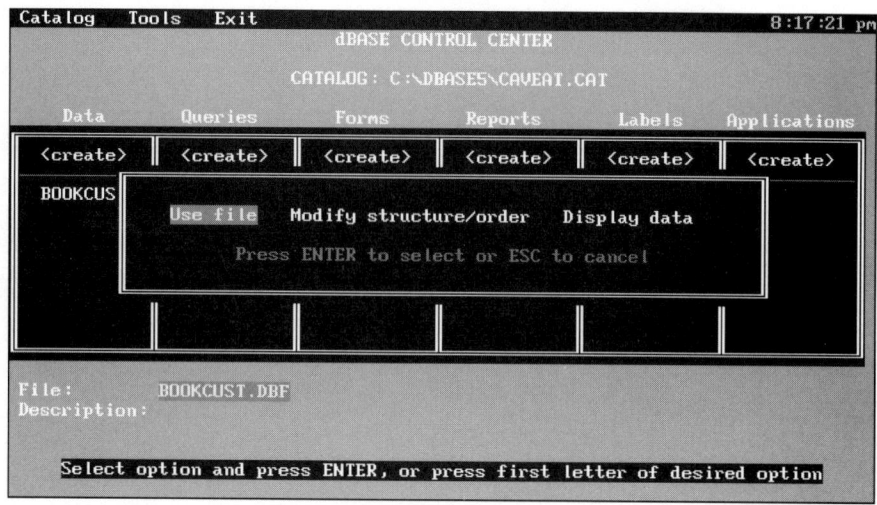

Entering data in Form mode

To add data to a table in Form mode, follow these steps:

1. **Select Modify structure/order.**

    dBASE takes you to the Table Design screen, where you designed the table and set up its fields.

2. **Open the Append menu and select Enter records from keyboard.**

    dBASE displays a blank form in which you can enter new data (see Figure 5-2).

    You can switch between Form mode (as shown in Figure 5-2) and Browse mode (a row-and-column format) by pressing F2. In this case, F2 works as a *toggle,* like a light switch. If you're in Form mode, pressing F2 switches you to Browse mode. Press F2 again and you're back to Form mode.

3. **Enter data into each field.**

    After you type the data for a field, press Enter; dBASE moves you down to the next field. When you fill up a whole field, however, dBASE beeps at you and automatically moves the cursor down to the next field.

    When you press Enter after entering data in the last field, dBASE saves the record and then displays a blank record, ready for you to enter more data. If you want to enter another record, just type the appropriate data in the fields.

Part I: All the DataBasics You Have to Know

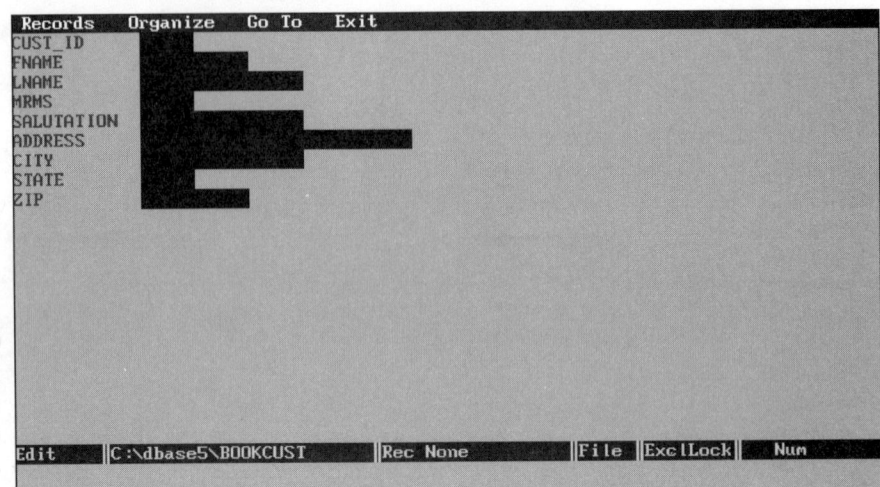

Figure 5-2: A blank form in Form mode.

> **TIP**
>
> When entering numbers that have varying numbers of digits in a character field, be sure to enter zeroes first to fill out the line. If you simply enter numbers without paying attention to the number of digits, dBASE could wind up sorting 100 before 20 (and 20 before 3) because 1 — the first "letter" in 100 — comes before 2 (and 2 comes before 3) and so on. In this case, enter the numbers as 003, 020, and 100. (Refer to Chapter 14 for more information about this and other weird stuff.)

> **TIP**
>
> If you make any mistakes or change your mind about entering some data, you can edit the fields: move to the appropriate fields by using the arrow keys and then use the arrow, Delete, and Backspace keys to delete the old or erroneous data. Then type the new stuff.

  4. **When you're finished entering new records, press Esc.**

     dBASE takes you back to the Table Design screen.

  5. **Open the Exit menu and select Save changes and exit.**

     dBASE returns you to the Control Center. Your new records are now in the table, and you're done!

> **TIP**
>
> If a table already has at least one record and you don't want to go through the Table Design screen, you can add records in another way: In the Control Center, double-click on the table. In the dialog box that appears, select Display data. Then go to the last field of the last record and press Tab. When dBASE asks whether you want to add records, answer "yes."

> **TIP**
>
> If you're a good typist, you also can add records to a table by typing in the Command window

```
use tablename
```

where *tablename* is the name of the table. Press Enter. Then type

```
append
```

and press Enter. When you're finished entering records, press Esc. dBASE returns you to the Command window.

> **Note:** Sometimes, your dBASE manuals and other books talk about *appending* records to a table. This is just fancy technical talk for adding records to a table.

Entering data in Browse mode

Earlier, you saw how to enter records in Form mode — that is, with a blank record displayed on the screen, just like in a paper form. In Browse mode, on the other hand, records are displayed in a row-and-column format. Entering new records in Browse mode works essentially the same as entering new records in Form mode. There's only one limitation: the table must already have at least one record before you can add records in Browse mode.

There are two ways to get into the Browse mode, depending on where you are at the moment:

- If you're in the Control Center, highlight the table name in the Data column and press Enter. When the dialog box appears, select **D**isplay data. A Browse screen (that is, a screen that displays your data in Browse mode) appears.
- If you're in Form mode, just press F2 to switch to Browse mode. When you're in Browse mode, you can switch back to Form mode by pressing F2 again.

To add data to a table in Browse mode, follow these steps:

1. **Type the data you want in the first column and press Tab.**

   dBASE moves you to the next column on the same row.

2. **Type the data for the next column and press Tab.**

   dBASE moves you to the next column on the same row. When you reach the end of the row, dBASE automatically moves you to the first column of the next row.

   > **Tip:** If you want to move to the next row without entering data for all the columns in the current row, just press the down-arrow key. You can use the arrow keys or the mouse to move around in the Browse mode.

3. When you're finished entering data, press Esc.

dBASE automatically saves all the stuff you typed in.

Looking at your records

In Chapter 6, you learn all the tricks you can use to display records. Until then, if you want to look at records — to make sure that they're really there, unlike a politician's conscience — double-click in the Control Center on the table you wish to view. In the dialog box that appears, select Display data.

If, while displaying data, you decide to enter some new records, press Ctrl-PgDn to go to the last record. If you're looking at the table in Browse mode, press the down-arrow key. If you're looking at the table in Form mode, press the down-arrow key until the cursor is in the last field; then press once more. In either case, dBASE asks whether you want to add more records. Answer "yes" and you're off to the races. Drive carefully. If you must drive carelessly, at least wear clean underwear, just in case.

Moving around in your table

Moving around in your table — to the last record, to the first record, and so on — is covered in depth in Chapter 6. However, to get you up to speed quickly with editing your data, here are a few basic moves you can make if your table is displayed in Browse mode. Most of them work exactly the same in Form mode.

Table 5-1	Moving Around in a Table
To Move to This Position	Press This Key
First column in table	Home (in Form mode, this action moves you to the beginning of the current field)
Last column in table	End (in Form mode, this action moves you to the end of the current field)
Next column to the right (next field)	Tab or Enter
Next column to the left (preceding field)	Shift-Tab
Up a row (preceding record)	Up arrow
Down a row (next record)	Down arrow
Up 17 rows	PgUp
Down 17 rows	PgDn
First record in the table	Ctrl-PgUp
Last record in the table	Ctrl-PgDn

If you own a mouse, you can go to any part of the Browse screen by clicking on it. You'll be surprised how quickly moving around in Browse mode becomes second nature.

Checking Out the Status Bar

When you're entering records, the Status Bar (located at the bottom of the screen) gives you information about the table you're in and the record you're on, as shown in Figure 5-3.

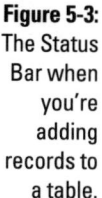

Figure 5-3:
The Status Bar when you're adding records to a table.

`Edit    ||C:\dbase5\BOOKCUST    ||Rec None    ||File ||ExclLock||    Num`

At the far left end of the Status Bar, dBASE tells you whether you're in a Form (Edit) screen or a Browse screen. The other items on the Status Bar are (l-r)

- The name and disk directory of the current table.

- The number of the current record and the total number of records in the table. For example, if you're entering a new record to a table that already has 10 records, this part of the Status Bar would say `Rec EOF/11` (end of file, 11 total records). If you're using the Form screen simply to *view* the fifth of ten records already in the table, this part of the Status Bar would say `Rec 5/10`.

- The source of the data that's displayed on-screen. When you're entering records, this part of the Status Bar says `File`, indicating that the data comes from a table file.

- If you're running dBASE on a network or under Windows, the next part of the Status Bar holds information about how the network is treating your table. Don't worry about this part.

- The status of your keyboard's Num Lock and Caps Lock keys. If Num Lock is turned on, `Num` appears at the far right end of the Status Bar; if Caps Lock is turned on, `Caps` appears.

64 Part I: All the DataBasics You Have to Know

> **TIP:** In case you're not familiar with the Num Lock and Caps Lock keys, here's what they do: Most PC keyboards have a numeric keypad, which you can use to enter numbers. But these keys also serve as arrow keys. If Num Lock is turned on, these keys are number keys; if it's turned off, they're arrow keys. The Caps Lock key makes all letters uppercase. If Caps Lock is turned on, you can make lowercase letters by holding down Shift as you type.

Editing Data and Fixing Mistakes

What happens if you make a couple of mistakes when you enter the data? Oh, I know that you enter everything just as you are supposed to, but the big boss is going to get mad at somebody about any errors in the file, and I'm going to blame you. (I can't afford to lose this job; I have two cats and five credit cards to support. You understand.)

Basic steps for editing stuff

The basic steps for editing data are simplicity itself. Not hyperbole itself, not alliteration itself, nor even tergiversation itself, but simplicity. Here are the steps:

1. **Display your table in Browse or Form mode.**
2. **Move to the record you want to edit.**
3. **Move to the field you want to change.**
4. **Delete the old stuff and type in new stuff.**
5. **Be sure to save your table with the new data.**

> **TIP:** Normally, when you type something in a field, dBASE is in *overstrike mode* — that is, if the cursor is to the left of some text that already exists in a field, any new text you type simply replaces (overstrikes) what was there. The opposite of overstrike mode is *insert mode* — that is, any new text you type simply pushes old text to the right. You activate insert mode by pressing the Insert key on your keyboard. You can toggle back to overstrike mode by pressing the Insert key again.

Deleting a record

Deleting a record is as easy as editing it. dBASE requires a two-step process to delete a record, however, so that you'll be less likely to delete a record by accident.

To delete one or more records,

1. **Display a table in Browse mode.**
2. **Move the cursor to the record you want to delete.**
3. **Press Ctrl-U.**

    Notice that Del appears in the Status Bar, indicating that the current record is marked for deletion — or as dBASE experts say, "marked for extermination." (dBASE experts tend to be a hyperaggressive bunch.) If you move the cursor out of the marked record, Del disappears from the Status Bar because the cursor is now on a record that *hasn't* been marked for deletion.

4. **If you want to delete any other records, repeat Steps 2 and 3.**
5. **Double-check to make sure that you haven't marked any records by mistake.**

    Common-sense alert: This is your last chance to change your mind about deleting any of the records.

6. **If you don't want to delete a marked record, move the cursor to that record and press Ctrl-U.**

    Ctrl-U is a toggle: pressing it once marks a record for deletion, pressing it again *unmarks* the record.

7. **Open the Organize menu and select Erase marked records.**

    dBASE asks whether you're sure. If you are, press Y and dBASE deletes all the marked records. This process of deleting marked records used to be called "packing the database," and you still see it called that every once in a while. No one knows why it was called that, but fortunately no one really cares, anyway.

Undeleting a record

You cannot get a record back after you select Erase marked records from the Organize menu. At any time before you take the final, fateful step, however, you can change your mind and unmark the records. That's why we stress double-checking which records you have marked.

Even after you delete a record, however, you can retrieve a copy of it *if* you backed up the file on your hard disk. If you're not sure how to make backup copies, check out IDG's *DOS For Dummies,* written by the venerable Dan Gookin, an inspiration to us all.

ZAP! Using the dBASE equivalent of a nuclear bomb

Deleting records one at a time is an OK solution for most situations. But once in a while, you may want to delete *all* the records from a table and start fresh. Let me introduce ZAP, a dBASE command that deletes *all* the records in a table, leaving only the empty table structure.

Use ZAP with great caution. In particular, don't take it internally. If it gets in your eyes, flush them immediately with large quantities of cold water; if water isn't handy, beer will do fine (domestic and imported brands work equally well).

To delete all the records in a table by using ZAP,

1. **From the Control Center, open the Exit menu.**
2. **Select Exit to Command window.**
3. **In the Command window, type use filename and press Enter.**

   Filename is the name of the file you want to zap. When you enter the command **use filename**, dBASE opens the file.

4. **Type zap and press Enter.**

   dBASE asks whether you're really, truly sure that you want to zap the file. Ask yourself a few questions: *In my heart, am I sure about this? Or are my emotions just playing with my head? And who made all those 900-number calls on my phone?*

5. **If you're really, truly sure, press Y.**

   dBASE deletes all the records in the table.

Hands on: Pumping Up the Bookcust Table

The best way to learn how to enter data is to do it. Open dBASE if you need to. In the Control Center, make sure that the Caveat catalog is open. The Bookcust table should be displayed in the Data panel, as shown in Figure 5-4.

First, either double-click on the Bookcust table or highlight it and press Enter. dBASE displays the dialog box you saw earlier in Figure 5-1. Then, follow these steps:

Chapter 5: Putting Data in Your Database   67

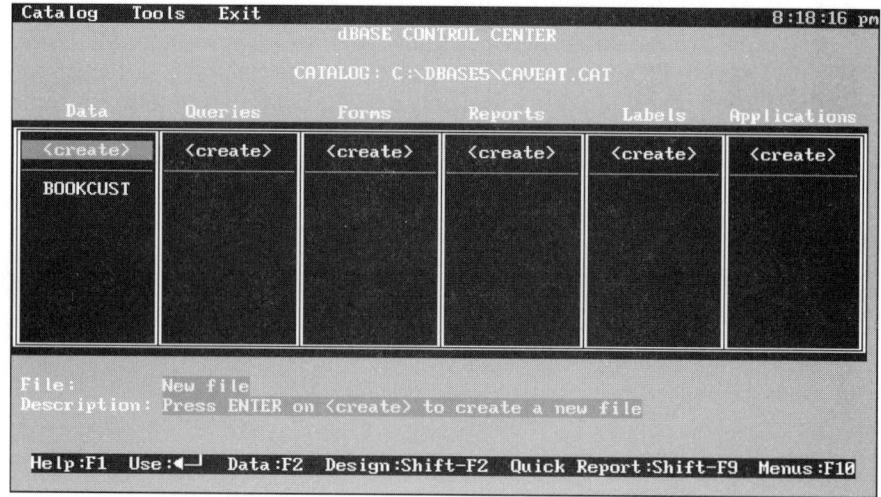

```
Catalog   Tools   Exit                                          8:18:16 pm
                         dBASE CONTROL CENTER
                     CATALOG: C:\DBASE5\CAVEAT.CAT
     Data         Queries       Forms       Reports     Labels     Applications
   <create>      <create>     <create>     <create>    <create>      <create>
   BOOKCUST




 File:         New file
 Description:  Press ENTER on <create> to create a new file
 Help:F1  Use:↵  Data:F2   Design:Shift-F2   Quick Report:Shift-F9  Menus:F10
```

Figure 5-4:
Preparing to enter data into the Bookcust table.

1. **In the dialog box, select Modify structure/order.**
2. **Open the Append menu and select Enter records from keyboard.**

   dBASE displays a blank form in which you can enter new data. Right now, the cursor is in the CUST_ID blank.

3. **Type 00001 (indicating that this is the first customer record) for the customer ID.**

   Notice that as soon as you finish typing, dBASE beeps and moves you to the next column (that is, the next field). When you entered the fifth digit, you filled up the CUST_ID field (remember that you gave the field a width of 5).

   dBASE needs the leading zeroes to put the customer account numbers in the correct order.

7. **In the FNAME field, type James and press Tab.**

   dBASE automatically moves you to the next field, LNAME.

Go ahead and enter the rest of the data for this record. Remember to press Tab to move to the next field. (By the way, if you make any mistakes typing, don't worry about them right now.) To enter the last name, type **West**. For MrMs, type **Prof**. For Salutation, type **Jimbo**.

When you press the Tab key after typing the salutation, the cursor automatically moves to the next field, ADDRESS. To complete the sample record, enter the following data: for Address, type **Mythic University**; for City, type **Martinsville**; for State, **CA**; and for ZIP, **98035**. After you enter the ZIP code and press Tab, dBASE automatically displays a blank form so that you can enter another record.

Part I: All the DataBasics You Have to Know

> **REMEMBER:** Every time you finish entering a record — that is, when you complete a row in the Browse screen and move down to the next row — dBASE saves the record to your PC's hard disk. That way, even if the electricity goes off and your computer shuts down, you only lose the data from the current record.

The Bookcust table has 15 records, which are listed in Appendix A. You can enter as many or as few as you want. For now, though, just enter the following four.

> **NOTE:** This customer data contain a couple of deliberate mistakes. You learn how to correct them later in this chapter.

CUST_ID: 00002
FNAME: Harriett
LNAME: Smith
MRMS: Ms.
SALUTATION: Ms. Stowe
ADDRESS: 14 Parakeet Lane
CITY: New York
STATE: NY
ZIP: 10087

CUST_ID: 00003
FNAME: Jules
LNAME: Twombly
MRMS: Mr.
SALUTATION: Jules
ADDRESS: The AB Hotel
CITY: Las Vegas
STATE: NV
ZIP: 34567

CUST_ID: 00004
FNAME: Arnold

Chapter 5: Putting Data in Your Database

LNAME: Harris
MRMS: Mr.
SALUTATION: Arnie
ADDRESS: 101 Fifth Avenue
CITY: Boise
STATE: ID
ZIP: 23413

CUST_ID: 00005
FNAME: Teri
LNAME: Lane
MRMS: Ms.
SALUTATION: Ms. Lane
ADDRESS: 5678 15th St., #5-A
CITY: Santa Barbara
STATE: CA
ZIP: 93101

After you enter the last field of the last record, press Tab; dBASE saves the record and displays a blank record on your screen. Open the Exit menu and select Exit.

Hands on: Correcting Customer Records

Display the newly revised Bookcust table in a Browse screen. In the second record of the sample table, Harriett's last name should be *Stowe,* not *Smith.* To correct the record, follow these steps:

1. **Press Ctrl-PgUp and then press Home.**

   This action moves you to the top left corner of the Browse screen. The cursor should be in the CUST_ID column of the first record.

2. **Press the down-arrow key.**

   This takes you to the Harriett Stowe record.

3. Press Tab twice.

The cursor moves to the LNAME cell. (Cell is the name for the intersection of a row and a column.)

4. Press the Delete key five times.

This action deletes the name *Smith*.

5. Type Stowe and then press the down-arrow key.

As soon as you move out of the record, dBASE saves the change.

Now follow the same process to correct Jules Twombly's record. It turns out that he doesn't live at the AB Hotel in Las Vegas — it's a nice enough hotel, but it's frequented by gangsters, computer book writers, and Wayne Newton impersonators. Instead, Jules lives at the ABC Hotel, a $2,500-a-night place on the Las Vegas Strip.

To edit Jules's address, follow these steps:

1. Move to the appropriate record and then press Tab three times.

The cursor moves to the ADDRESS cell in the Jules Twombly record.

2. Press the right-arrow key six times.

The cursor moves just to the right of AB.

3. Type C and press the down-arrow key once.

The cursor moves down to the next row, and dBASE saves the change.

Now that you have learned all about entering and editing your data, it's time to take a break. Go for a walk. Go hang-gliding. Eat a chocolate cake.

Chapter 6

Here's Looking at Your Data

In This Chapter

▶ Creating your own special Browse screen
▶ Changing column widths
▶ Locking columns in the Browse screen
▶ Limiting your powers of editing to one column
▶ Moving around in the Browse screen
▶ Power moving in the Browse screen

*F*ace reality. dBASE would be pretty impractical without the capability to retrieve data. Sure, it's fun to sit around and create tables. But eventually, you or (worse) your boss may want some usefulness from your computer. With today's gee-whizzy computer, usefulness is an easy thing to delay. You can (though of course *you* wouldn't) send your company's spreadsheet to the background while you play solitaire in the foreground. ("Just one more game, and then I'll get to those figures.") Should an emergency ever arise, you can call up the spreadsheet and look busy. But, alas, we know that even this switch is only temporary.

In this chapter, we will help prepare you for the Day After, when you'll need to retrieve your data. You'll learn all about the Browse mode — dBASE's window to your data — and how to make the Browse screen more attractive and legible.

Before you can change how your records are displayed in the Browse mode, it helps if you can

✔ Create a table (see Chapter 4) and put some data in it (see Chapter 5).
✔ Display and edit your data in the Browse mode (see Chapter 5).
✔ Turn off solitaire.

If you have gone off like a wild man and you're using the Browse screen with your own real-life database, that's great! Just substitute your own database for the sample that gets browsed. You rebel.

Creating Your Own Special Browse Screen

If you want to make your Browse screen easier to read and more attractive to other Browse screens — in essence, if you want to even out its flaws — you can change column width, limit your ability to edit columns, or even limit what you see to a few, crucial columns.

Before you do so, though, take comfort in the knowledge that nothing you do to change the look of the Browse screen can hurt your table or its data. So have fun, go a little crazy. But if you happen to hear a shrill, whining sound from the computer, run away real fast.

To get some idea of how to change your Browse layout, look at the Browse screen from the Caveat database shown in Figure 6-1. If you've been following along with the sample database, you can use the Control Center to load the Caveat database into the Browse screen. If you're not sure how, refer to Chapter 4.

You can improve this Browse layout in a number of ways. For starters,

- Several columns (CUST_ID, FNAME, LNAME, SALUTATION, and so on) are wider than they need to be. You can shrink them and make more of the other fields visible.
- You can lock the three most important columns (CUST_ID, FNAME, and LNAME) to the screen so that they are always visible, no matter where you go.

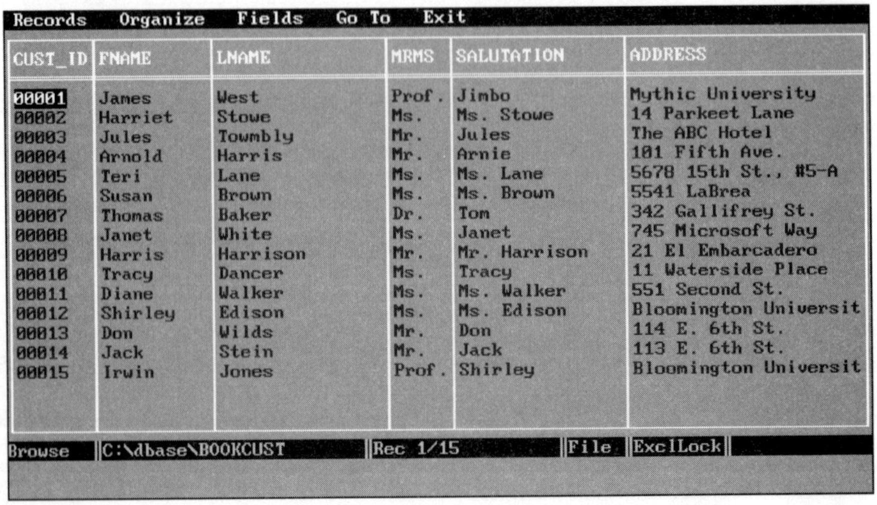

Figure 6-1:
The Bookcust Browse screen.

Changing column widths

You can change a column's width in two ways: with the mouse or with the keyboard.

> **NOTE:** Changing the column width in the Browse screen does not affect the field length in the table. Making a column narrower doesn't reduce the amount of data you can put in a field, and making it wider doesn't increase the amount of data you can enter. The only reason to change column widths is to make the Browse screen a happier place to be.

Using the mouse

To change a column's width by using the mouse, follow these steps:

1. **Display a table in a Browse screen.**
2. **Position the mouse pointer on the column's right vertical border.**

   You can position the pointer anywhere on the vertical line. It's easier to grab the line, however, if you place the pointer near the top row, where the column labels are located.

3. **Press and hold down the left mouse button.**

   This action grabs the column border so that you can drag it horizontally.

4. **With the mouse button depressed, move the mouse to the left or right.**

   Roll the mouse left to narrow the column and right to widen it.

5. **When the column is the desired width, release the mouse button.**

   dBASE drops the column border in its new position, changing the column's width.

For practice, try using this method to narrow the column for the CUST_ID field in the Bookcust table. Then adjust the width of other columns as needed.

Using the keyboard

If you prefer using the keyboard instead of a mouse, then we're with you. However, we also must urge you to get a mouse because the battle is over, and those hateful meeces have won. But until they abolish keyboards altogether, you can resize your columns by following these steps:

1. **Display a table in a Browse screen.**
2. **Use the arrow keys to highlight the column you want to resize.**
3. **Open the Fields menu.**

Part I: All the DataBasics You Have to Know

4. **Select Size of fields.**

5. **Use the arrow keys to change the column width.**

6. **When you have the desired width, press Enter.**

> **TIP:** Because changing column widths doesn't affect the underlying table, you can make the columns narrower than the data in them. Not only is this always great fun around the office, but also you can see more columns on-screen.

Locking columns in the Browse screen

When you have a table with as many fields as the Bookcust table (or more), you may find it helpful to lock some of the columns into place. Doing so allows you to keep important fields on-screen while you scroll through the remaining fields. Normally, you only want to lock one or two fields: more than that, and there won't be any room on the screen for the fields you want to move through.

Locking a field in place

Follow these steps (if you dare) when locking a field: forward with your right foot, to the side with your left foot, back with your right foot, now dip, spin around three times, jump, and land in your desk chair. Oops! Right steps. Wrong dance.

To lock a field in place,

1. **Display a table in a Browse screen.**

2. **Open the Fields menu.**

   Notice that there's a zero next to the first option, Lock fields on left. The number in brackets is the number of fields currently locked.

3. **Select Lock fields on left.**

   dBASE asks you how many fields you want to lock. The first column locked in place is the leftmost column displayed on-screen, *not* the leftmost column in the table.

4. **Type the number of fields you want to lock.**

   You don't need to press Enter. As soon as you press a number key (1 to 9), dBASE beeps and uses that as the number of fields to lock in place.

That's that. Just try to lose the locked fields.

> **TIP:** If you want to lock a column in place and not display any columns to its left, tab to the right until the desired column is the first displayed on-screen. Then select Lock fields on left and press 1.

Unlocking locked fields

To unlock all fields that you've previously locked, follow the same steps as you do to lock the fields except enter 0 as the number of fields to lock.

Keeping the action in one column only

If you have the second-clumsiest fingers in the world (the line starts to my right), you may find it helpful to limit your supreme database abilities. By *freezing* a field, or limiting your cursor movement (and thus your editing power) to that one column, you can guard against accidental changes while you're in Browse mode.

Freezing a field

To freeze a field, follow these steps:

1. **Display a table in a Browse screen.**
2. **Open the Fields menu.**
3. **Select Freeze field.**

    dBASE asks you which field you want to freeze.

4. **Enter the name of the field you want to freeze.**

    dBASE freezes the field. You are now restricted to that field.

Unfreezing a field

To unfreeze a field, follow these steps:

1. **Display a table in a Browse screen.**
2. **Open the Fields menu.**
3. **Select Freeze field.**

    dBASE displays a dialog box, asking which field you want to freeze. The name of the currently frozen field is shown in the blank.

4. **Use the Backspace key to delete the field name.**
5. **Press Enter.**

    dBASE unfreezes the field. You now can move around anywhere in the Browse screen.

Moving Around in the Browse Screen

Moving around in the Browse screen may sound disgusting, but, trust me, dBASE doesn't mind. Besides, you'll be the life of every party if you know your way around a good Browse screen. And it helps prevent hair loss, too.

Experiment a little by moving around in your Browse screen. Experiment a lot by tossing your monitor around with the Browse screen displayed (but do so only if you're an experienced dBASE user). The following table lists the basics of moving around in the Browse mode.

NOTE: If you make changes to your data while you're in the Browse mode, dBASE saves the changes automatically. It's such a good program.

Table 6-1   Moving Around in the Browse Mode

To Move to This Position	Press This Key
First column in table	Home
Last column in table	End
Next column to the right	Tab or Enter
Next column to the left	Shift-Tab
Up a row	Up arrow
Down a row	Down arrow
Up 17 rows	PgUp
Down 17 rows	PgDn
First record in the table	Ctrl-PgUp
Last record in the table	Ctrl-PgDn

If you own a mouse, you can go to any part of the Browse screen by clicking on it. You'll be surprised how quickly moving around in Browse mode becomes second nature.

Power Moving in the Browse Screen

As Table 6-1 indicates, pressing PgUp or PgDn moves you up or down 17 rows (or one screen's worth), respectively. So if you have a database with 10,000 records, you must press PgDn almost 600 times to get to the bottom of the table! Without a workaround, browsing your data would become a planned event. You would have to clear your schedule for a week. You would have to take some nonperishable food to your computer desk. And you would definitely have to go to the bathroom first.

An easy way to relieve this dilemma is to press Ctrl-PgDn, which takes you to the last record in your table. If you want to see record #5,000, however, you still must press PgUp over 290 times.

Luckily, dBASE offers you two ways to get around this problem; we describe these ways in the following sections.

Skipping around in the Browse screen

If you don't know the exact location of the record you want to see, try *skipping*. As you know, every time you press PgUp or PgDn, you skip up or down 17 records. The master databaser, however, can make dBASE skip any number of records by using the Skip command. For example, if you're on record #5, and you tell dBASE to skip ahead 2, it will move to record #7. To skip around freely, follow these steps:

1. **Open the Go To menu.**
2. **Select Skip.**

    A dialog box appears, asking you for the number of records to skip.

3. **Enter the number of records you want dBASE to skip.**

    If you want, you can move backwards in the table by putting a minus sign (–) in front of the number.

A good skipping interval is usually 1/20 of your database. That way, you can move around fairly quickly, but you can still see enough of the records to have an idea of where you are in the database.

dBASE requires you to sing while you skip.

Moving directly where you want to go

If you know the exact number of the record you want to see, you can tell dBASE to move directly to that record. Talk about power browsing!

To move to a specific record, follow these steps:

1. **Open the Go To menu.**

Part I: All the DataBasics You Have to Know

> ### Skipping through the Command window
>
> Wonder why dBASE uses a weird word like *skip* for the menu choice that lets you move up and down in a Browse screen? Well, the *Skip* command is part of dBASE's built-in language, which was first created in the late 1970s, when skipping was more popular than even disco.
>
> If you use the dBASE Command window to move around in the Bookcust table, you enter commands like the following:
>
> ```
> use bookcust
> skip 5
> display record
> skip -3
> display record
> ```
>
> ```
> go top
> skip
> browse
> ```
>
> The first line, use bookcust, opens the Bookcust table. Because you're at record #1 when you first open the table, skip 5 moves you down to record #6. Display record shows you the data in the current record. Skip -3 moves you back three records to record #3. Go top takes you back to record #1. Skip moves you down one record to record #2. Browse displays a Browse screen.
>
> If you can type, entering commands in the Command window is a lot of fun. If you can't type, it's like watching 30 consecutive episodes of *America's Funniest Bank Robbers*.

---

   2. **Select Record Number.**

      A dialog box appears, asking you to enter the number of the record you want to see.

   3. **Type the number of the record you want and press Enter.**

      dBASE jumps to the record that you type (as long as it exists), and you can continue browsing from there.

You have come far in a short time, databaser. You now can call yourself Master of the Browse Mode. Why you would want to, we don't know.

That's all for the Browse screen, so take a rest. Go on, you deserve it. Play some solitaire.

Part II
Playing with Your Data

The 5th Wave   By Rich Tennant

Futurists predict that eventually all people will be required to do some personal computing on a regular basis. But not everyone will own a PC. As more homes and apartments come equipped with washers and dryers, we will see the inevitable conversion of laundromats into...

DataMats

The "Amana PC" will be the leader in the field followed by the "IBM Front-loader," with its controversial spin-cycle architecture.

Maytag will introduce a dot matrix printer that retains its commercial dryer capabilities for shrinking 5¼-inch disks to 3½-inch size.

Please DO NOT OVERLOAD YOUR RAM CACHE

All Datamats will have vending machines that dispense basic software.

Datamats will, however, suffer from the reputation of occasionally losing one document from any matching pair of documents a user arrives with.

In this part ...

Basic skills are important. If you didn't know how to make change, balance a budget, or write your name, you'd have few career options except to run for Congress.

But basic skills, which are covered in Part I, can only take you so far. This part teaches you more advanced stuff you can do with dBASE. You learn how to change a table design, create on-screen forms that explain your database and catch errors, and search for data.

And if you *still* want to run for Congress, well, that option is always open for you.

Chapter 7
Redesigning Your Table

In This Chapter
- ▶ Changing a field's characteristics
- ▶ Adding fields at the end of a table
- ▶ Inserting fields in the middle of a table
- ▶ Deleting fields

Hardly anything is perfect on the first try. Mozart supposedly could knock out a perfect string quartet in an afternoon, but music historians now believe that the story was made up by his publicist. The philosopher Ludwig Wittgenstein thought he'd arrived at a perfect solution for metaphysical problems when he wrote his first book, *Tractatus Logico-Philosophicus*; but when he sobered up the next morning, he wished that he'd written a detective novel instead. Thus, the only perfect things are chocolate-almond ice cream, the Los Angeles Lakers, and the Violent Femmes' "Why Do Birds Sing?" CD.

It's next to impossible to set up the perfect table on your first try. In fact, just when you think that you have set up the Bookcust table perfectly, your boss — who knows you're a database whiz — requests some changes, confident that you can make them quickly and easily. And guess what? With dBASE, you *are* and you *can*.

Before you can redesign a table, you need to

- ✔ Create the table.
- ✔ Understand basic table concepts, such as fields and data types.
- ✔ Eat a good, healthy breakfast. None of that greasy stuff. No eggs and bacon or pancakes with lots of syrup. Just some wholesome American grains, skim milk, and fruit. Then top it off with a piece of dry toast for a totally pleasure-free dining experience.

Part II: Playing with Your Data

In this chapter, we detail the basics of how to redesign a table. You can follow the steps with your own table. To follow along with the book's example database, you need to have created the Bookcust table (see Chapter 4); the data for this table is in Chapter 5.

What Changes Can You Make?

What can you change about your table? In a word, lots of things. (OK, that's three words. So sue me.) You can change a field's definition, add and delete fields, and Marshall Fields. In this chapter, you learn how to do all these things. And it's a good thing, because your boss has suddenly got *lots* of good ideas for you to put in the database design.

If you need to redesign a database, don't beat yourself up about it (unless you *like* doing that sort of thing). In most cases, changes aren't required as a result of anything you did wrong, but because your database users

- Change their minds about what they want
- Think of a feature they want you to add
- Didn't explain what they really needed in the first place

The last is the worst cause of database design changes because it's the most avoidable. When you design a database, make the users be clear about what they want. If they refuse — well, we don't sanction violence, but....

Changing a Field's Definition

A field's definition is the easiest thing to change. You can change the name, type, width, number of decimal places, and indexing — in a word, any-of-a-field's-characteristics. (See? One word. Happy?)

To change a field's definition, follow these steps:

1. In the Control Center, select the table whose field you want to change.

You can select a table in two ways:

- Highlight the table and press Enter.
- Double-click on the table name.

    dBASE displays a dialog box that asks what you want to do.

2. **Select Modify structure/order.**

   The Table Design screen opens with the table you selected.

3. **Use the arrow keys to move to the field you want to change.**

4. **Enter a new name, data type, width, number of decimal places, or index option.**

5. **Open the Exit menu and select Save changes and exit.**

   dBASE asks whether you're sure that you want to save the changes in the table. If you are, answer Yes; dBASE saves the table with the new field definition and returns you to the Control Center.

WARNING! If you change a field type or reduce the field width, you may lose some or all of the data in the field. Before you make *any* changes in a table design, it's a good idea to back up your table either on a disk or in a different directory of your PC's hard disk.

Adding a Field

Adding a new field is one of the most common things you can do. The best way to learn how to add a field (or any other database-creation task) is to actually add a field to a database. With that in mind, we show you in the following sections how to change a database. At the end of this chapter, you show off your new knowledge and change the Caveat database.

NOTE Adding a field to a table design doesn't add any data in the new field. If the table already contains records, you need to go back and add the data into the new field.

Adding a field to the end of a table

The easiest place to add a field is at the end of a table. To add a field, follow these steps:

1. **In the Control Center, select the table you want to add a field to.**

   dBASE asks what you want to do.

2. **Select Modify structure/order.**

   The Table Design screen appears.

3. **Move the cursor to the line below the last field.**

   dBASE opens up a blank line for you to define the new field.

4. **Enter the new field name and press Tab.**

5. **Select a field type.**

   If you are not going to do arithmetic with any data in a field that contains numbers, accept the default field type: character.

6. **Specify the field width and press Tab.**

7. **Open the Exit menu and select Save changes and exit.**

   dBASE asks whether you're sure that you want to save the changes in the table. If you are, answer Yes; dBASE saves the table with the new field definition and returns you to the Control Center.

Inserting a field in the middle of the table

Adding a field at the end of a table is pretty easy. Inserting a new field anywhere else is trickier. Here's the basic technique:

1. **Move to the line *below* where you want to insert the new field.**
2. **Press Ctrl-N.**
3. **Enter the field name and press Tab.**
4. **Choose a field type.**
5. **Open the Exit menu and select Save changes and exit.**

Deleting Fields

Deleting a field is another thing dBASE makes easy. To delete a field, follow these steps:

1. **Move to the field you want to delete.**
2. **Press Ctrl-U.**

   dBASE deletes the selected row.

3. **Open the Exit menu and select Save changes and exit.**

   dBASE saves your modified table design.

Chapter 7: Redesigning Your Table   85

Hands on: Adding and Deleting Fields

Suppose that Honest Janis — the imaginary bookstore owner — wants to add a phone number field to the table. The easiest place to add the field is at the end of the table, underneath the line for the ZIP field.

To add the phone number field, follow these steps:

1. **If you haven't already done so, start up dBASE and make sure that the Caveat catalog is open in the Control Center.**
2. **In the Control Center, select the Bookcust table.**
3. **Select Modify structure/order.**
4. **Move the cursor to the line below the ZIP field.**

    dBASE opens up a blank line for you to define the new field.

5. **Enter PHONE as the field name and press Tab.**
6. **Accept the default data type: Character.**
7. **In the Width column, type 13 and press Tab.**
8. **Open the Exit menu and select Save changes and exit.**

    dBASE asks whether you're sure that you want to save the changes in the table. If you are, answer Yes; dBASE saves the table with the new field definition and returns you to the Control Center.

Don't forget that creating a new field doesn't add any data to the table! As a result, you still have to add the phone numbers for Janis. But wait until you read Chapter 9 before you enter any of the phone numbers; in Chapter 9, we describe how to insert special formatting characters into a field (and do lots of other neat field tricks).

Adding a field at the end of a table is pretty easy. Now try inserting a field in the middle of the table. To insert and define a field that holds the date of customers' first purchase, follow these steps:

1. **In the Table Design screen, move to the line for the PHONE field.**

    The PHONE field is just below where you want the new field to go.

2. **Press Ctrl-N.**

    dBASE opens a blank line above the PHONE field.

3. **Type FIRSTSALE and press Tab.**

Part II: Playing with Your Data

4. **Press the spacebar to cycle through the data types and then select date as the field type.**

   Your screen should look like Figure 7-1.

5. **Open the Exit menu and select Save changes and exit.**

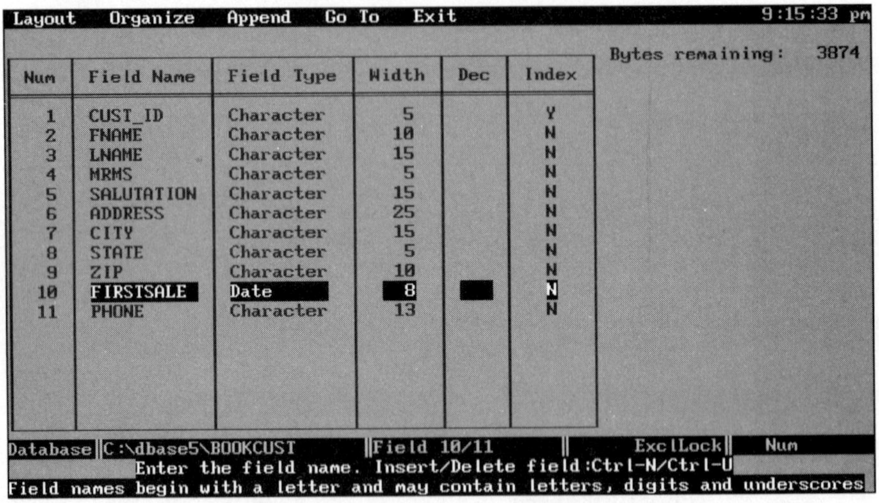

Figure 7-1: The sample table after you insert the PHONE and FIRSTSALE fields.

Suppose that after you move the FIRSTSALE field, Honest Janis decides that the table doesn't need a FIRSTSALE field after all. You now need to delete the field. But you stay calm because Janis promised to buy you a first edition of this book if the database is ready on schedule. (Come to think of it, you already *have* a first edition of this book, so why are you working so hard?)

To delete a field, follow these steps:

1. **Move to the row for the FIRSTSALE field.**
2. **Press Ctrl-U.**

   dBASE deletes the selected row. Your screen should now look something like Figure 7-2.

3. **Open the Exit menu and select Save changes and exit.**

See, you don't have to worry about creating the perfect database on your first attempt because dBASE makes it so easy for you to make revisions. Now that you have redesigned the sample table to Honest Janis's liking, shut down dBASE and enjoy his good mood. Then move to the next chapter, where we describe even more impressive tricks you can do with dBASE.

Chapter 7: Redesigning Your Table

```
Layout   Organize   Append   Go To   Exit                    9:15:51 pm
                                              Bytes remaining:    3882
 Num   Field Name   Field Type   Width   Dec   Index
   1   CUST_ID      Character      5            Y
   2   FNAME        Character     10            N
   3   LNAME        Character     15            N
   4   MRMS         Character      5            N
   5   SALUTATION   Character     15            N
   6   ADDRESS      Character     25            N
   7   CITY         Character     15            N
   8   STATE        Character      5            N
   9   ZIP          Character     10            N
  10   PHONE        Character     13            N

Database C:\dbase5\BOOKCUST      Field 10/10       ExclLock   Num
          Enter the field name. Insert/Delete field:Ctrl-N/Ctrl-U
Field names begin with a letter and may contain letters, digits and underscores
```

Figure 7-2: The Bookcust table design after you delete the FIRSTSALE field.

Chapter 8
Adding and Using Memo Fields

In This Chapter
▶ Adding a memo field
▶ Entering a memo
▶ Viewing and editing a memo

*M*emo is from the Latin word *memoria*, which means either "memory" or "kill the umpire" (depending on the context). In dBASE, a *memo* is what you use to keep detailed notes about the data in your database. In this chapter, we show you so much stuff about memos that you'll become positively giddy. We know because we've seen it happen before: it's not a pretty sight, but medication can help.

To explain memos, we again reference Janis and his bookstore. If you don't believe in imaginary bookstores, simply substitute your own database where we talk about Janis's database. But beware, imaginary bookstores remain imaginary only until you get stuck on their mailing lists.

Before you can create a memo field, you need to have

- ✓ Learned basic database concepts (see Chapters 1 and 2)
- ✓ Created a table (see Chapter 4)
- ✓ Entered data in a table (see Chapter 5)
- ✓ Determined humanity's place and purpose in the universe (optional)

If you're adding a memo field to your own real-life table, follow the steps in this chapter. To do the exercises with the book's example database, you need to have created the Bookcust table (see Chapter 4), put data in it (see Chapter 5), and added the PHONE field (see Chapter 7).

Adding a Memo Field

dBASE memos don't have to be the same size, so you may enter into a memo field absolutely nothing or pages of data (in fact, a memo field can hold as much data as you have room on your hard disk).

REMEMBER

Other types of fields limit data entries to a specific width (which you define) and maximum possible width (which dBASE defines). dBASE limits a character field to a maximum of 254 characters, for example. And if you specify a width of 10 for a character field, no record in the table can have more than 10 characters in that field.

You add a memo field to a table in the same way that you add any other field. To add a memo field, follow these steps:

1. **Open a catalog in the Control Center.**

   If you're using the example, open the Caveat catalog.

REMEMBER

2. **Select the desired table.**

   You can select a table in two ways:
   - Highlight the table and press Enter.
   - Double-click on the table name.

   In the example, select the Bookcust table. As soon as you select a table, a window appears, asking what you want to do with the table.

3. **Select Modify structure/order.**

   The Table Design screen appears.

4. **Press Esc to close the menu that's already open.**

5. **Using the mouse or down-arrow key, move to the first blank line in your table design.**

   In the Bookcust table, this line is just below the PHONE field, as shown in Figure 8-1.

6. **Enter the field name.**

   In the Bookcust table, the field name should be NOTES.

7. **Press Tab to go to the Field Type column. Enter memo as the field type.**

   Press the spacebar to cycle through field types until you get to the memo type.

8. **Open the Exit menu and select Save changes and exit.**

   dBASE displays a dialog box that asks whether you're sure that you want to save the modified structure.

9. **Press Y for yes.**

Chapter 8: Adding and Using Memo Fields

```
 Layout   Organize   Append   Go To   Exit                    7:01:36 am
                                                   Bytes remaining:  3882
 Num  Field Name   Field Type   Width   Dec   Index
  1   CUST_ID      Character      5             Y
  2   FNAME        Character     10             N
  3   LNAME        Character     15             N
  4   MRMS         Character      5             N
  5   SALUTATION   Character     15             N
  6   ADDRESS      Character     25             N
  7   CITY         Character     15             N
  8   STATE        Character      5             N
  9   ZIP          Character     10             N
 10   PHONE        Character     13             N
 11                Character                    N

 Database C:\dbase\BOOKCUST        Field 11/11         ExclLock   Num
              Enter the field name.  Insert/Delete field:Ctrl-N/Ctrl-U
 Field names begin with a letter and may contain letters, digits and underscores
```

Figure 8-1:
Adding the memo field.

Memo fields can hold a great deal of data because dBASE puts their contents into a file that is separate from the table. Rather than cram a lot of unnecessary text into a table, dBASE places a *pointer* in the memo field to remind itself where it put the memo. Memo field files take their tables' name but end with a .DBT extension. (For example, for a table named BOOKCUST, the associated memo file is called BOOKCUST.DBT.) When you open a memo field, dBASE follows the pointer and then retrieves the data from the .DBT file. A .DBT file is created only if a table has memo fields.

Entering a Memo

Clearly, the greatest thing about memo fields, other than their natural beauty, is that you can put anything in them but you don't need to put anything in them. Heck, you can put tons of notes in the memo field of one record and ignore the rest. dBASE doesn't mind.

Here are the basic steps for entering a memo:

1. **Make sure that the correct catalog is open in the Control Center.**
2. **Open the table in the Browse mode.**

    Generally, it's easiest to enter memo text if you have the table displayed in Form mode. If you haven't created a form yet, however, the Browse mode is the way to go.

3. **When dBASE asks what you want to do, select Display data.**

4. **Move to the record to which you want to add a memo.**

   You can do so by using the PgUp or PgDn keys, the arrow keys, or the options on the GoTo menu (see Chapter 6).

5. **Move to the column with the memo field and then press Ctrl-Home.**

   The Memo Editor appears on-screen.

6. **Type the text you want.**

   You can use most standard keyboard techniques, including the arrow, backspace, and delete keys.

7. **Press Ctrl-End.**

   This action saves the memo and returns you to the Browse screen.

   If you change your mind while entering text in the Memo Editor, you can simply press Esc to get out without saving the memo. dBASE will laugh at you, though.

   When you get back to the Browse screen, notice that the word *MEMO* is in all capital letters in the field you just modified. If the field were still empty, it would be *memo*. You can use that little trick to tell whether a memo field is empty.

Viewing and Editing a Memo

You open a memo field for viewing or editing in exactly the same way as you do when you enter memo text.

1. **Move to the memo field of the record you want to view.**

2. **Press Ctrl-Home.**

   The Memo Editor appears.

3. **Edit the memo text.**

   Use the arrow keys to move the cursor as needed. Use Delete to erase text. Type in your new text.

4. **Press Ctrl-End to save the changes.**

   To select text for deletion in the Memo Editor, position the cursor immediately before the text you want to delete. Then hold down the Shift and Ctrl keys and press the right- or left-arrow key as needed. After you select the text you want to delete, press the Delete key.

Chapter 8: Adding and Using Memo Fields *93*

Hands on: Entering Memos

Try entering some memos into the book's example database.

1. **Make sure that the Caveat catalog is open in the Control Center.**
2. **Select the Bookcust table.**
3. **When dBASE asks what you want to do, select Display data.**

   The table should appear in a Browse screen, as shown in Figure 8-2. (If you aren't in Browse mode, press F2 to get there.)

```
Records   Organize   Fields   Go To   Exit
CUST_ID FNAME    LNAME     MRMS  SALUTATION    ADDRESS
00001   James    West      Prof. Jimbo         Mythic University
00002   Harriet  Stowe     Ms.   Ms. Stowe     14 Parkeet Lane
00003   Jules    Twombly   Mr.   Jules         The ABC Hotel
00004   Arnold   Harris    Mr.   Arnie         101 Fifth Ave.
00005   Teri     Lane      Ms.   Ms. Lane      5678 15th St., #5-A
00006   Susan    Brown     Ms.   Ms. Brown     5541 LaBrea
00007   Thomas   Baker     Dr.   Tom           342 Gallifrey St.
00008   Janet    White     Ms.   Janet         745 Microsoft Way
00009   Harris   Harrison  Mr.   Mr. Harrison  21 El Embarcadero
00010   Tracy    Dancer    Ms.   Tracy         11 Waterside Place
00011   Diane    Walker    Ms.   Ms. Walker    551 Second St.
00012   Shirley  Edison    Ms.   Ms. Edison    Bloomington Universit
00013   Don      Wilds     Mr.   Don           114 E. 6th St.
00014   Jack     Stein     Mr.   Jack          113 E. 6th St.
00015   Irwin    Jones     Prof. Shirley       Bloomington Universit
Browse  C:\dbase\BOOKCUST           Rec 1/15        File  ExclLock
```

Figure 8-2: Getting ready to enter data into the NOTES memo field.

4. **In the row for James West, move to the NOTES field and press Ctrl-Home.**

   The Memo Editor appears on-screen.

5. **Type the following: A good customer for many years.**
6. **Press Ctrl-End.**

   dBASE thoughtfully saves the memo and returns you to the Browse screen..

Now try entering a longer memo.

1. **Press PgDn to move to the record for Jules Twombly.**
2. **Highlight the NOTES field and press Ctrl-Home.**
3. **Type the following: Jules is a heck of a guy. Always pays his bills on time, and has great taste in books too. Wife: Becky. Two daughters: Lori and Sarah.**

When you finish typing, the Memo Editor should look like Figure 8-3.

4. Press Ctrl-End to close the Memo Editor and save the text.

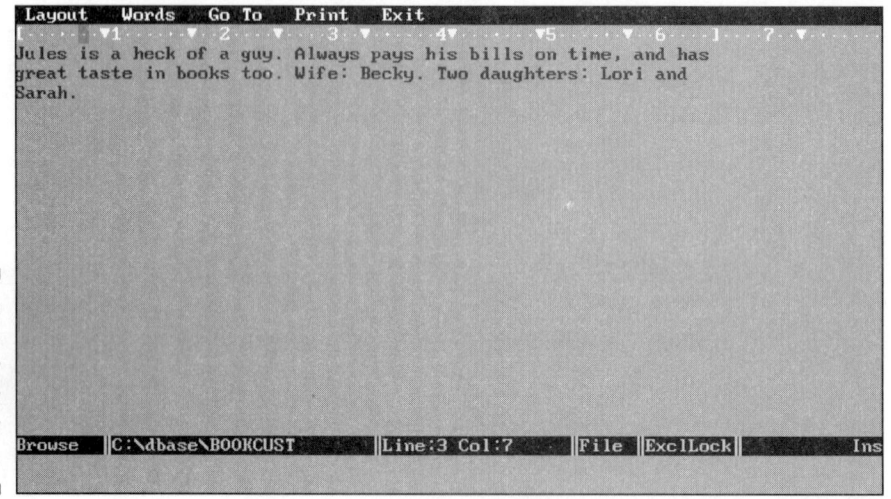

Figure 8-3:
The Memo Editor screen after you enter some text.

Say you decide to change your notes on James West. Here's how to do so:

1. In the record for James West, tab over to the NOTES field.

2. Press Ctrl-Home.

The memo for James West appears in the Memo Editor screen.

Remember that how the table is displayed doesn't matter. These steps work equally well in Browse, Form, or Columnar layout.

3. Use the arrow keys to move the cursor just to the left of the *g* in *good*.

4. Type the following: really.

The memo now reads: A really good customer for many years.

5. Holding down the Ctrl key, press the right-arrow key three times.

This action moves the cursor to the first letter of the word *many*.

6. Press Delete to erase the words *many years*. In its place, type the following: a long, long time.

7. Press Ctrl-End to save the changes.

That's about it for creating, entering, and editing memos. Take a break, you memo writing fool. Too much databasing is bad for the hairline. Go play a nice game of Tetris.

Chapter 8: Adding and Using Memo Fields *95*

Chapter 9
Creating and Using On-Screen Forms

● ●

In This Chapter
▶ What are forms good for? Lots!
▶ Types of forms you can create
▶ Moving stuff around on a form
▶ Formatting fields in a form
▶ Moving around in your table with a form
▶ Entering data with a form

● ●

*F*orms are a part of modern life. There's the graceful form your best friend's daughter exhibits in her ballet recital (deny it at your own risk!); the form that the "earth was without, and void" you hear about in church; the tai chi forms that your spouse is always bugging you to try; and, of course, the dreaded IRS Form 1040.

None of these forms has anything to do with dBASE forms. dBASE forms, in fact, are much more useful (except maybe that one about the earth having form, which keeps us from flying off into space). In dBASE, *forms* give you another way — a very powerful way — to enter and view the stuff in your database.

Before you can create a form, you need to have

  ✔ Created a table. A form is used to enter data into a table or display data from a table; without the table, you have nada. (Well, that's not quite true: you have your health and good looks.)

  ✔ Put data in the table. (OK, you don't have to, but with no data, there's nothing to look at with the form.)

  ✔ Learned basic database concepts, such as *table* and *field*.

Read this chapter to pick up the basics for creating a form. If you want to follow the steps with the book's example database, you need to have created the Bookcust table (see Chapter 4) and put data in it (see Chapter 5). You *should* have created and opened the Caveat catalog (see Chapter 3).

Why Use Forms?

What are forms and what good are they? Saying that "forms are powerful," or that they "get your wash 44 percent brighter," or that they perform other miracles tells you nothing. Those are the words of TV commercials.

We've described how you can use the Browse screen to enter and view all records in a table (that is, a row-and-column format). But the Browse screen is not always the best layout to use:

- You can view many records at a time, but you normally can't view *all* the data in each record because some columns disappear off the right side of the screen. (Yes, you can improve this situation by calling up a simple Form screen — to do so, press F2 when you're in a Browse screen — but there's an even better solution.)

- Apart from the column captions, you can't put text in a Browse screen to explain the meaning of each field. If new employees are entering data, they may get confused. In a simple table, such as the one created for the bookstore customers, this limitation isn't much of a problem. In more complex databases, however, it can be a *serious* problem. For example, suppose that you work in a nuclear power plant and you ask your friend Homer to enter data about the control rods. When he gets to the field named Frimmitz, will he know what it means? A little explanatory text on-screen could prevent a major meltdown.

- Although you can enter records by using a Browse screen, it's easier when the screen looks more like a paper form, with captions, blanks, and explanatory text.

Customized forms let you overcome the Browse screen's disadvantages; you can create forms that display all fields for one record on-screen at the same time, include explanatory text, and look like paper forms. If you're an absolute genius (and you will be by the time you finish reading this book), you can make a form to check data for errors, do calculations, and sport pretty little boxes that make the screen easier to read.

Creating a Form

Like most things in dBASE, creating a form is easy. You can create a form in two ways (one is easy and very flexible, the other is even easier but slightly less flexible):

Chapter 9: Creating and Using On-Screen Forms

✔ You can lay out the form by hand. dBASE gives you a blank form, and you put the fields where you want them, along with labels and explanatory text. This approach takes a few more steps but gives you the most flexibility in determining how your form looks and works. You'll learn some of these techniques in Chapter 13.

✔ You can tell dBASE to do a Quick Layout form — in other words, dBASE does the work *for* you. You then can modify the form to suit your taste. This is the easiest way to create a form, and, for most purposes, it is the best way.

In this chapter, we describe how to create and modify a Quick Layout form. In either case — "Quick" or "by hand" — you can always go back and fine-tune your form design as needed.

Basic steps

Here are the basic moves you make to create a Quick Layout form:

1. **In the Control Center, make sure that the correct catalog is open.**

   This action ensures that the form you create is included in the correct catalog. The current catalog is listed at the top middle of the Control Center screen. If you need to load a different catalog, open the **Catalog** menu and select **Use a different catalog**. dBASE lists the available catalogs at the right side of your screen; highlight the one you want and press Enter.

   Any time you see the phrase "highlight and press Enter," you can do the same thing by double-clicking. In a few cases, you can even do the same by intimidating dBASE: just look very sternly at the screen and say, "Now, this time, I mean it."

2. **Open the table for which you're creating a form.**

   Available tables are listed in the Control Center's Data panel. Highlight the table you want and press Enter. When the dialog box appears, select Use file.

3. **In the Forms panel, highlight <create> and press Enter.**

   The Forms Design screen appears (see Figure 9-1). Notice that the **Layout** menu is already open and the **Quick Layout** option is highlighted.

4. **Press Enter again to choose the Quick Layout menu choice.**

   Instantly, dBASE lays out the fields from your table on the form. To the left of each field is its name in the table. If you want, you can save and use the new form as is; it will work just fine. However, the Quick Layout form doesn't really do what you need a form to do: there's no explanatory text; you may prefer descriptive labels for the fields, such as First Name rather

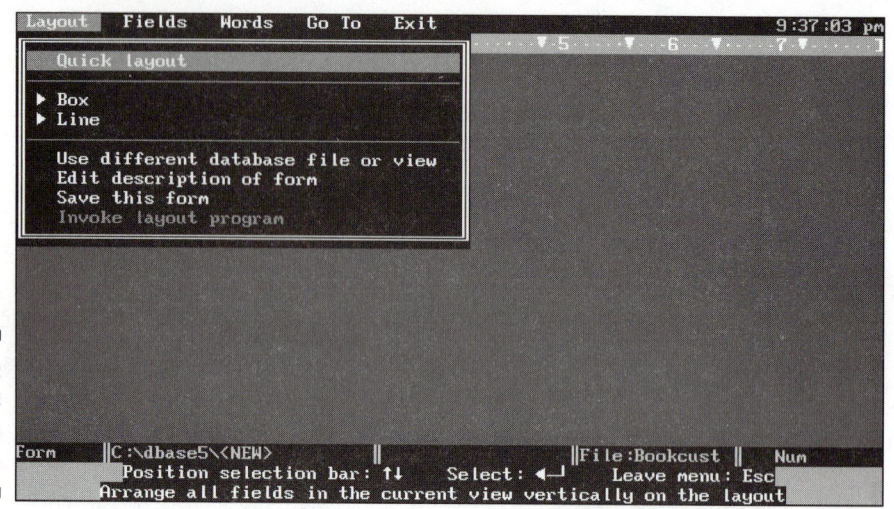

Figure 9-1: The Forms Design screen.

than FNAME; and you may want to arrange the fields so that the form is easier to read. For those reasons and others (including putting special formats in fields, which we describe later in this chapter, and checking for data entry mistakes, which you can read about in Chapter 13), you'll probably want to modify the Quick Layout.

5. If desired, modify the Quick Layout.

You can modify the Quick Layout by moving fields around, entering new text as field labels, typing explanatory text and titles directly on the form, and so on. You can read more about modifying the Quick Layout later in this chapter.

6. Open the Exit menu and select Save changes and exit.

After you enter a name for the form, dBASE saves it to your hard disk. Now you or anyone else can use the form to enter or view data in the table.

> A form doesn't have to include *all* the fields in a table. You can include as many or as few fields as you want. For entering new records, though, it's best to create a form that includes all fields in the table. If a form for our imaginary bookstore's table included only the Last Name, City, and ZIP fields, you would need to switch to the Bookcust Browse screen to enter data into the other six fields; the form would be a waste of time.

Secret shortcuts

- **Add a field to a form:** Press F5.
- **Delete a field:** Position the cursor on the field and then press Delete.
- **Select text or a field:** Position the cursor on the text or field, press F6, and then press Enter.
- **Select multiple text or fields:** Position the cursor at the upper left corner of the area that contains what you want to select. Press F6. Then press the down- and right-arrow keys until the highlight covers everything you want to select. Press Enter.
- **Deselect text or field(s):** Press Esc.
- **Move text or field(s):** After selecting what you want to move, press F7 and then use the arrow keys to move the highlighted text or field(s). When you reach the desired location, press Enter.
- **Turn insert mode on/off:** Press the Insert key to toggle. When insert mode is on, the letters **Ins** appear at the right end of the Status Bar, the third line from the bottom of your screen.

> Insert mode is one of those computerese things that's pretty obvious when you see it. If the cursor is to the left of some text, and insert mode is turned on, anything you type will push the old text off to the right. The old text will still be there on the form, just bumped over by whatever you typed. If insert mode is turned off, the new stuff you type will *replace* the old stuff.

- **Insert a new line:** Turn on insert mode. Position the cursor at the left end of the line *below* where you want to insert the new line. Then press Enter.
- **Delete a line:** Position the cursor on the line you want to delete. Then press Ctrl-Y.
- **Add text to a form:** Position the cursor where you want to add text. Then start typing.
- **Move to the next text or field:** Press Ctrl-F.
- **Move to the preceding text or field:** Press Ctrl-A.
- **Move to the left end of a line:** Press Home.
- **Move to the right end of a line:** Press End.
- **Move right, left, up, or down:** Press the corresponding arrow key.

Moving Fields on a Form

After you have a Quick Layout, you can rearrange the fields and write new field labels, making your form easier to understand. Follow these steps:

1. **Position the cursor at the top left corner of a block you plan to move.**
2. **Press F6.**

    This action tells dBASE that you want to select some stuff.

3. **Press the down- and right-arrow keys until you have highlighted the desired block.**
4. **Press Enter.**

    This tells dBASE that you have selected everything you want.

5. **Press F7.**

    This tells dBASE that you want to move whatever is currently selected.

6. **Press the down- and right-arrow keys to move the block.**

    Move the block to the bottom part of the screen so that it is out of the way.

7. **When you reach the desired location, press Enter.**

    dBASE drops the block.

8. **Press Esc.**

    This deselects the block. The highlight disappears.

> **TIP:** You can use the same technique to highlight and move anything on a form. You can highlight a piece of text, a field, or even an on-screen box, like the one we describe how to create in Chapter 13.

Viewing Data and Moving Around in a Table

In this section, you learn about moving around in a table when you're looking at it with a form. That's different from moving around *under* a table, which you do when you want to pick up loose change or find a contact lens.

But rest easy: moving around your table with a form is very similar to moving around it with a Browse screen.

1. **In the Control Center, highlight the form you want and press Enter.**
2. **When the dialog box appears, select Display data.**

   The form appears on-screen, showing you the first record in the table.

3. **To move around in the table, do the following:**
   - To move to the first record: Press Ctrl-PgUp.
   - To move to the last record: Press Ctrl-PgDn.
   - To move to the next record: Press PgDn.
   - To move to the preceding record: Press PgUp.

   Play around with the key combinations a few times just to get the feel of them. It's easier than you think.

4. **When you finish, press Esc.**

   dBASE returns you to the Control Center.

Putting Formats into Fields

Ready to learn something a little fancy? You can put special formats into fields so that all you have to do is enter a few keystrokes and dBASE automatically formats the field the way you want. You can fix a phone number field so that after you enter the numbers, dBASE adds parentheses around the area code and a hyphen after the prefix.

We call what you put into the field a *template*; others call it a *field format* or an *edit mask*.

1. **In the Control Center, highlight the field you want and press Enter.**

   A dialog box appears.

2. **Select Modify layout.**

   The Forms Design screen appears.

3. **Position the cursor on the field you want to format.**
4. **Open the Fields menu and select Modify field.**

   The Modify field submenu appears, as shown in Figure 9-2. Notice that the **T**emplate menu choice is already highlighted.

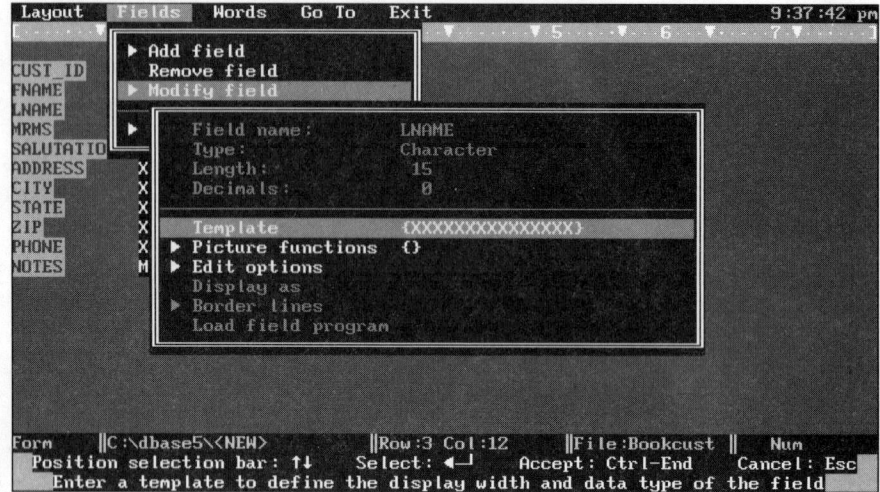

Figure 9-2: The Modify field submenu, with the Template menu choice highlighted.

5. **Press Enter to select the Template menu choice.**

    A mini-Help screen appears, telling you about things you can use in the template.

6. **Type in your new text and press Enter.**

7. **Press Ctrl-End.**

    This action tells dBASE that you're finished modifying the field. dBASE returns you to the Forms Design screen.

8. **Open the Exit menu and selecting Save changes and exit.**

    dBASE saves the modified form layout and returns you to the Control Center.

We describe more tricks with field formatting in Chapter 13.

Entering and Changing Data with a Form

Entering data with a form is just as easy as entering data with a Browse screen. To enter new records by using a form, follow these steps:

1. **In the Control Center, highlight the form and press Enter.**

2. **In the dialog box, select Display data.**

    The form appears, with the first record displayed.

Chapter 9: Creating and Using On-Screen Forms

3. Press Ctrl-PgDn to move to the last record in the table.

4. Press the PgDn key to move beyond the last record in the table.

dBASE asks whether you want to add more records.

5. Press Y to answer "yes."

dBASE displays a blank form. Now you can enter a new record.

6. When you reach the last field, press Enter.

dBASE saves the record and displays another blank form. You can now enter another record.

7. After you enter the last record, press Ctrl-End.

dBASE saves the record and returns you to the Control Center.

Changing data in existing records is even easier: Follow Steps 1 and 2 to display the first record in the table. Then, if needed, move to the record you want to change. Tab down to the field you want to change and type in the new data. When you're finished, press Ctrl-End to save your changes.

Hands on: Creating and Changing a Form

To create a form for the book's example database, first start up dBASE and open the Caveat catalog and then follow these steps:

1. In the Data panel, highlight the Bookcust table and press Enter.

2. In the dialog box, select Use file.

3. In the Forms panel, highlight `<create>` and press Enter.

This action tells dBASE that you want to create a form. The Forms Design screen appears. Notice that the Layout menu is already open and the Quick Layout option is highlighted.

4. Press Enter to select Quick Layout.

dBASE lays out the fields on the form, as shown in Figure 9-3.

After you have a Quick Layout, you can rearrange the fields and write new field labels to make your form easier to understand.

Follow these steps to move the Cust_ID field and the ones under it so that they're out of the way while you're arranging the form.

Part II: Playing with Your Data

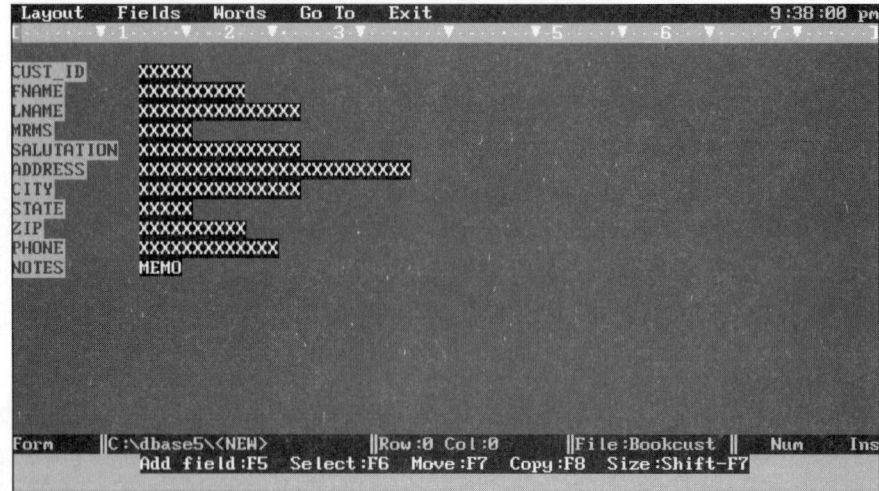

Figure 9-3: A Quick Layout automatically arranges the fields and field names on the form.

1. Position the cursor on the first letter of the CUST_ID field label.
2. Press F6.
3. Press the down- and right-arrow keys until the Cust_ID field label, the Cust_ID field, and all the fields below it are highlighted (see Figure 9-4).

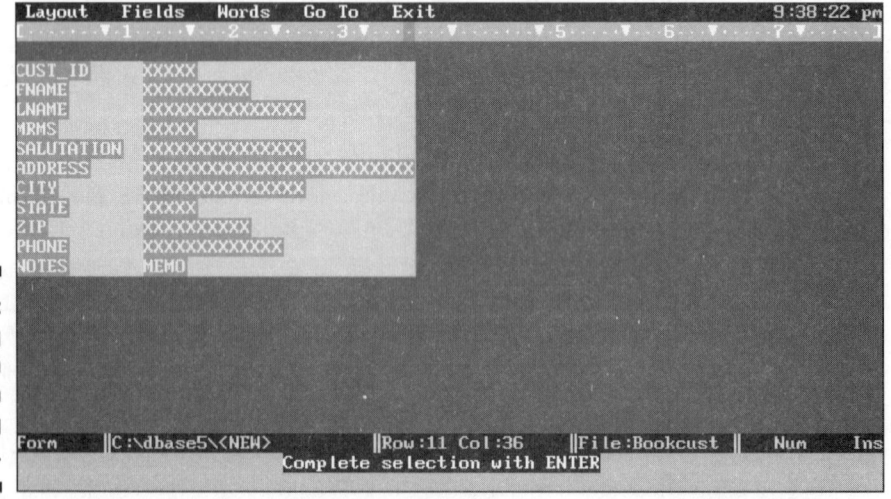

Figure 9-4: Highlighting stuff in preparation for moving it.

4. Press Enter.

   This action tells dBASE that you have selected everything you want.

5. Press F7.

Chapter 9: Creating and Using On-Screen Forms

6. Press the down- and right-arrow keys to move the block.

Move the block down to the bottom part of the screen so that it's out of the way.

7. When it's where you want, press Enter.

This action tells dBASE that you're finished moving stuff.

8. Press Esc.

This deselects the block you moved. The highlight disappears.

Now use the same basic techniques to rearrange all the fields and type new field labels. Follow these steps:

1. Position the cursor at the top left corner of the screen. Type Bookstore Customer Record.

This action gives the data entry form a title.

2. Move the title where you want it to go.

If insert mode is turned on, you can simply press the spacebar until the title is centered on the top line of the screen. Or you can select the title and press F7 to move it.

3. Move the cursor to Row 3, Column 4. Type Acct Num: (as a new, more descriptive field label for the Cust_ID field).

dBASE reports the cursor position in the center of the Status Bar.

4. Position the cursor on the field label CUST_ID.

Make sure that you get the text, not the blank with the Xs in it.

5. Press Delete a few times to delete the original field label.

6. Select the Cust_ID field blank and move it up to Row 3, Column 14 (in other words, move the field up next to its new label). Press Enter to confirm the move.

You don't need to press Esc to remove the highlight because only a single field is selected. As soon as you move the cursor out of the field blank, the highlight disappears.

You can repeat Steps 3 to 6 with the other fields until the form looks the way you want.

With the book's example, use the labels and positions shown in the following table. In each case, the field blank should be just to the right of the field label, separated by a space. The finished screen should look something like Figure 9-5.

Part II: Playing with Your Data

Screen Position	New Field Label
Row 3, Column 27	Salutation:
Row 5, Column 4	First Name:
Row 5, Column 28	Last Name:
Row 5, Column 56	MrMs:
Row 9, Column 4	Address:
Row 11, Column 4	City:
Row 11, Column 29	State:
Row 11, Column 44	Postal Code:
Row 13, Column 4	Phone:
Row 13, Column 29	Notes:

7. **Open the Exit menu and select Save changes and exit.**

   A dialog box appears, asking for the form's name.

8. **Type CUSTFORM and press Enter.**

   dBASE saves the form as a file on your PC's hard disk and then returns you to the Control Center.

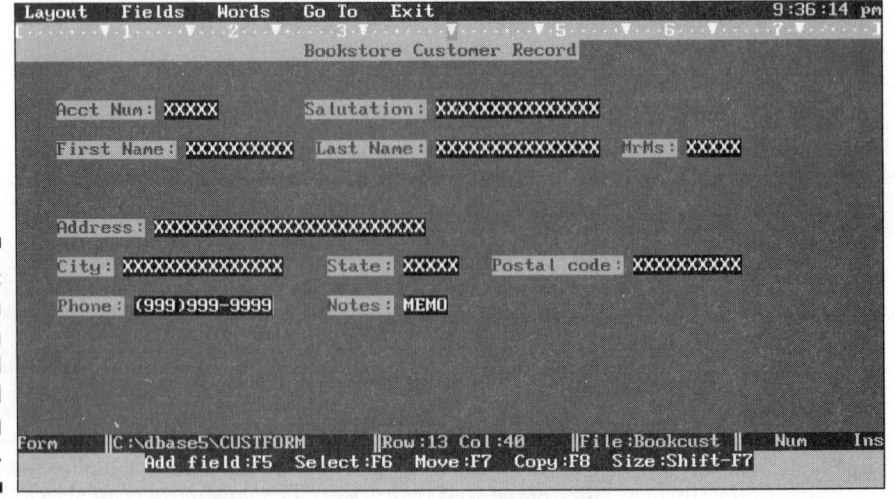

Figure 9-5: The form after adding new field labels and moving fields.

Hands on: Formatting and Filling the PHONE Field

In this section, we describe how to put a template into the PHONE field so that the user only has to enter the digits: dBASE will automatically add parentheses around the area code and a hyphen after the prefix.

In the Control Center, highlight the Custform field and press Enter. When the dialog box appears, select Modify layout. The Forms Design screen appears. Follow these steps:

1. **Position the cursor on the field blank for the PHONE field.**
2. **Open the Fields menu and select Modify field.**
3. **Press Enter to select the Template menu choice.**
4. **Press the Backspace key to erase the Xs in the field blank. Then type (999)999-9999 and press Enter.**
5. **Press Ctrl-End.**

    This returns you to the Forms Design screen. Notice that the PHONE field now contains the template.

6. **Open the Exit menu and select Save changes and exit.**

This template does two things. First, the 9s prevent the user from entering anything but numerals into the field (wherever a field has a 9, dBASE allows only a numeral). Second, it tells dBASE to insert parentheses and a hyphen.

As a final housekeeping detail, open the Bookcust table in the sample database and fill in the PHONE fields for the five existing records. Remember, when you type the phone numbers, don't worry about typing the parentheses and the hyphen: dBASE puts them in the field for you.

James West: 415 555 4678

Harriett Stowe: 212 555 2345

Jules Twombly: 201 555 6213

Arnold Harris: 321 555 9876

Teri Lane: 805 555 1234

1. **In the Control Center, highlight the form and press Enter.**
2. **In the dialog box, select Display data.**

    The form appears, with the first record displayed.

3. Tab to the PHONE field and type only the numbers. Then press Enter.
4. Repeat Step 3 until all PHONE fields are complete.
5. After you enter the last record, press Ctrl-End.

Get up and stretch your legs. Better yet, make those legs walk you to the nearest ice cream store and indulge in some chocolate almond. Consider it a "form" of reward for your hard work.

Chapter 10
Finding Stuff *Fast* in Your Database

In This Chapter
- Searching for a data string
- Using Match Capitalization and wild cards
- Looking for parts of words

*T*he primary purpose of dBASE is to find information quickly. To this end, dBASE comes with a few nifty gadgets that allow you to get the data you want without having to endure long, complicated procedures. In this chapter, we detail each of these gadgets. By the time you finish reading this chapter, you'll be able to find names, addresses, tax shelters, and Waldo! Actually, tax shelters may lie beyond dBASE's reach, but you can try.

Before you can find stuff in a database, you need to have

- Created a table (see Chapter 4).
- Put some data in the table (see Chapter 5) so that you have something to find.
- Gotten over the fear that you'll be electrocuted through the keyboard. You may do some shocking things with your keyboard, but nothing fatal.

If you have escaped Janis's tyrannical grasp and are now following along with your own real-life database, simply substitute your database whenever you see the example database. If the instructions don't work, you can shoot your computer. If you want to follow along with the book's example database, you need to have created the Caveat catalog (see Chapter 3) and the Bookcust table (see Chapter 4) and have entered customer records into the table (see Chapter 5).

dBASE's searching abilities can be broken down into two main categories:

- The nifty gadgets
- Queries (see Chapter 11)

Part II: Playing with Your Data

dBASE's nifty gadgets enable you to quickly find a particular record in your database. Suppose that the Caveat Emptor database has a thousand records; obviously, it would be highly impractical to find a record by moving through the records with the arrow keys. But a dBASE gadget called the *search* lets you look through the entire database and find the record in seconds. For example, you can tell dBASE to search for all the customers who have the last name Lane, or all the customers who live in California, or all the customers with the first name James, and so on. Searching is a perfect method for this kind of simple, one-field information hunt. Pretty nifty, huh?

If, by chance, you need to search for a record by using more than one field, you must use a query (covered in Chapter 11). Queries also can be used to limit the fields that are displayed on-screen, and they can be used to do complicated searches, too. For now, though, don't worry about queries. Just know that they're there. They appreciate the recognition.

Finding Stuff the Easy Way

The fastest, easiest, best, most productive, and natural way to find a record is to look for it. With dBASE, you can find a record by the data in its fields.

For instance, suppose that Teri Lane, one of the Caveat Emptor customers, calls you in a panic. For some inexplicable reason, she can't remember her address. But she knows that you can have the information at your fingertips — in the Caveat Emptor customer database. You don't want to search the entire database, so you tell dBASE to look through the first name field for the word *Teri*. There's only one Teri, so dBASE moves the cursor to her record and you can easily remind Teri what her address is. (She then asks you what planet she's on, but she screams and hangs up before you can come up with a suitably cynical answer.)

This example illustrates how useful it is to search a database for a particular word (or in database jargon, a *string*). It also illustrates why some people screen their calls.

Searching a database for a particular string is such a common thing to do that dBASE comes with a special tool, the *query*, for it. Queries are covered in depth in Chapter 11.

Searching a database

To get in the mood, you can whisper sweet nothings to your computer, but don't let anybody catch you. Not everyone appreciates that computers have feelings, too.

To search your database for a particular string, follow these steps:

1. **In the Browse mode, open the table that you want dBASE to search.**

   If you're not sure how to open the Browse mode, check out Chapter 6.

2. **Move the highlight bar to the field that you want dBASE to search.**

3. **Press F10 to make the menu drop down.**

4. **Use the arrow keys to highlight the Forward search option in the Go To menu and press Enter.**

   A dialog box appears, demanding that you enter a string that dBASE should search for. Don't annoy a dialog box.

   Forward search simply means that you want dBASE to search from the current record *forward* to the end of the table. Backward search means that dBASE should search from the current record *backward* to the beginning of the table.

5. **Type the string you want dBASE to search for and press Enter.**

   If dBASE says that no matching records were found and you're sure that the record exists, try toggling the Match Capitalization option (see the following section) by selecting the Match Capitalization option from the Go To menu (make it say No by highlighting it and pressing Enter). Then try to forward search again.

   If the string is in the database, dBASE moves you to the appropriate record. If more than one record has that string, do another forward search; dBASE moves the cursor to the second record that matches. And so on.

Match Capitalization

The Match Capitalization option, located in the Go To menu, tells dBASE whether the case matters. For example, if you search the Caveat database for customers with the first name James, dBASE will take you to the record of James West. However, if you look through the database for people with the first name JAMES (all capitals), dBASE will tell you that no matching records were found. Why? Because dBASE considers James and JAMES to be two different strings.

Part II: Playing with Your Data

> **NOTE:** dBASE also won't find a matching record if you tell it to search for jaMES or jaMes or JaMeS.

To derail dBASE's meticulous approach, you can switch the Match Capitalization option to No: dBASE then finds your record, regardless of which letters are capitalized.

> **NOTE:** Every time you start to search again, dBASE automatically turns Match Capitalization back on.

Wild cards

If you're in the correct field and you've set Match Capitalization to No, but dBASE still can't find the record you need, you may want to try a *wild card*, which can stand for anything. A wild card can be useful in three situations:

- When you don't know the exact string that you're looking for
- When you want to find more than one record
- When you suspect that misspelled data has been entered into the database

To use a wild card, all you have to do is add an asterisk or a question mark to the string.

When you use the asterisk wild card, dBASE finds everything possible. For example, if you want to search through a typical first name field for all of the customers whose first names began with J, enter **J***: dBASE will find Joe, Jill, Johann, Jeremy, and so on. If you type **Jo***, however, dBASE will find Joe and Johann, but not Jill or Jeremy.

If you want dBASE to be more specific, you can use the question mark wild card. Enter **J???** and dBASE searches for all first names that begin with J and have exactly four letters (J plus one for each question mark). Thus, dBASE will find John, Joan, and Jill, but not Jeremy, Johann, or Jorge.

You can use the asterisk and question mark in the middle of a string; for example, entering **J*n** finds John, Joan, and Johann. And you can even use them together, as in **J?n*e** to find Jennie but not Johnie.

To Index or Not to Index?

Index, schmindex. Don't worry about indexes right now; we cover them in detail in Chapter 14.

On the other hand, you will need to know what to do when that know-it-all dBASEr peers over your shoulder and says (with that really cheesy smile), "You know, you can make that search go faster if you index." Especially because the jerk inevitably will do so right when your boss is walking by. And then you will have to admit that you don't know how to index. Which will postpone that raise until the next century and leave you feeling like the gum on the bottom of the bathroom floor at the stadium. (At least, that's what nine out of ten said when surveyed.)

To emerge from this all-too-common scenario victorious, politely turn to the jerk and say in an even, sure voice that he's wrong. Or at least mostly wrong. And then tell him to clean the spot on his tie.

Indexes *do* make your searches go faster, but dBASE is so blindingly fast that even the know-it-all can't notice much of a difference unless you have a very large database. Unless you have more than a thousand records, you won't search much faster with an index than without one.

An *index* is something that you can do to the fields in your table that puts your data in order. By putting the data in order, any searches will theoretically go faster. However, unless your database is fairly large, the index won't have a noticeable effect.

Hands on: Finding a Customer Record

Try using a forward search in the sample Bookcust table. Suppose that you want to find the records of all customers who live in California. To do so, follow these steps:

1. **Make sure that the Caveat catalog is opened.**

    See Chapters 3 and 4 if you need a review about catalogs.

2. **Open the Bookcust table by highlighting it and pressing F2.**

3. **Press F2 again to switch to Form mode.**

    Now you can see an entire record on-screen at once.

Part II: Playing with Your Data

> **TIP:** dBASE searches *down* from your current position in the table. So if you aren't looking at the first record in the table (the James West record), press Ctrl-PgUp to move to the record #1, the "top" of the table.

4. **Move the highlight bar to the State field (see Figure 10-1).**
5. **Select the Forward search option from the Go To menu.**

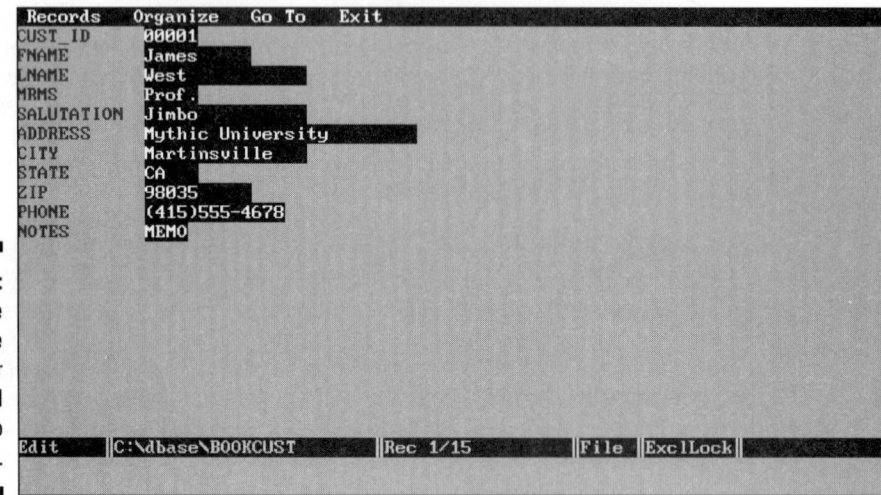

```
Records    Organize   Go To     Exit
CUST_ID    00001
FNAME      James
LNAME      West
MRMS       Prof.
SALUTATION Jimbo
ADDRESS    Mythic University
CITY       Martinsville
STATE      CA
ZIP        98035
PHONE      (415)555-4678
NOTES      MEMO




Edit      C:\dbase\BOOKCUST          Rec 1/15         File  ExclLock
```

Figure 10-1: Make sure that the highlight bar is in the field you want to search.

A dialog box appears, asking for the string you want to look for.

6. **In the dialog box, type CA and press Enter.**

   Doing so tells dBASE what you want to search for. dBASE finds the first record with CA in the STATE field. That's the record for James West, or Jimbo as he's known to friends, family, and parole officer.

7. **Select the Forward search option again from the Go To menu.**

   dBASE produces the dialog box with CA already in it.

8. **Press Enter.**

   dBASE moves to the record for Teri Lane, who lives in Santa Barbara, California.

9. **Select the Forward search option again from the Go To menu and press Enter.**

   dBASE moves to the James West record again because there are no more corresponding entries. dBASE simply cycled back to the beginning and came up with good old Jimbo.

Hands on: Looking for Parts of Words

Suppose that you get a call from one of the Caveat Emptor customers. She's calling you from one of those great car phones. She wants to know how many books she bought last month. Just as she gives you her last name to look up in your database, the phone signal dies out, and you hear only the last part of her name: "owe." You ask her to spell the name, but the phone fades momentarily, and all you get are the last three letters. Both you and she are beginning to get fed up, but what can you do? Nothing, you say? Oh, but there is something. A wild card search.

1. **In the Browse screen, move the highlight bar to the LNAME field.**

   This action tells dBASE which field you want to search.

2. **Toggle the Match Capitalization option from the Go To menu so that it's set at No.**

   This allows dBASE to find the record regardless of case.

3. **Select the Forward search option from the Go To menu, and press Enter.**

   A dialog box appears, asking you to enter the string to search for.

4. **In the dialog box, type *owe*.**

   This tells dBASE what you want to search for. The asterisks are wild cards.

dBASE finds the first record with "owe" in the LNAME field, which is the record for Harriett Stowe, who is virtually unknown but was once mistaken for the famous author of *Uncle Tom's Cabin* and other great works of American literature.

If you do the search again, dBASE will take you right back to Ms. Stowe because she's the only person in the database who matches the search string.

Whew. Searching isn't so bad, is it? OK, so it is. But you're done now, so go out and have some fun hoeing fields (corn fields, not dBASE fields).

Chapter 11
Using Queries to Find Lots More Stuff

In This Chapter
▶ What is a query?
▶ Understanding the Query Design screen
▶ Doing simple queries
▶ Using query operators
▶ Saving a query to use later
▶ Reusing a saved query

You have to put up with lots of weird words every day. For example, there's *microprocessor* (a boss who's always looking over your shoulder); *short meeting* (forget about getting anything done for the rest of the afternoon); *revenue enhancement* (never seems to enhance *your* revenue); and the always-popular *epistemology* (the study of knowing). Well, get ready for another: *query*.

In the last chapter, we described how to use the **F**orward search and **B**ackward search menu choices. Although they enable you to search quickly and easily, there are some problems. First, you can search for only *one thing* at a time. Second, you can't view just the fields that interest you. Third, you can look only for matches of one kind or another. In a sales table, for example, you can look for all records in which the price is *exactly* $10, but not for all records in which the sale price is *less than* or *more than* $10.

In this chapter, we cover how to use queries to find information in your database. Queries require a little more effort than choosing **F**ind Record, but they offer a lot more power. You can handle it; you're *psycho-epistemologically well-integrated* (ready).

To understand the ideas in this chapter, you should know the basic database concepts, such as *table*, *field*, and *field type* (see Chapter 3). To create a query for your own real-life database, read this chapter to get the basics. Then follow

Part II: Playing with Your Data

the steps using your own table rather than the example table. To practice using queries with the book's database, you can use the Sales table that we tell you how to create in this chapter.

Query is just a fancy word for a question you ask dBASE about a table or database. *Running a query* just means asking the question. Without queries, you couldn't find your data as easily. And without words like *query,* database experts couldn't get $100 an hour.

Keys to Perfect Queries

Before you wade into query specifics, it's important to understand the big picture. When you set up a query, you specify three things (see Figure 11-1):

- **The fields you want to see in the answer.** You may not want to see all the fields of the records found by the query. When you run a query, you must tell dBASE which fields you want to see when it displays the *view*, or answer to your query.

- **The fields you want to search.** For example, if you want the records for all customers named Smith who live in ZIP code 90210, you tell dBASE to search the LNAME (last name) and ZIP fields.

- **What you're looking for.** For the preceding example, you tell dBASE to show you all the records in which Smith is in the LNAME field *and* 90210 is in the ZIP field.

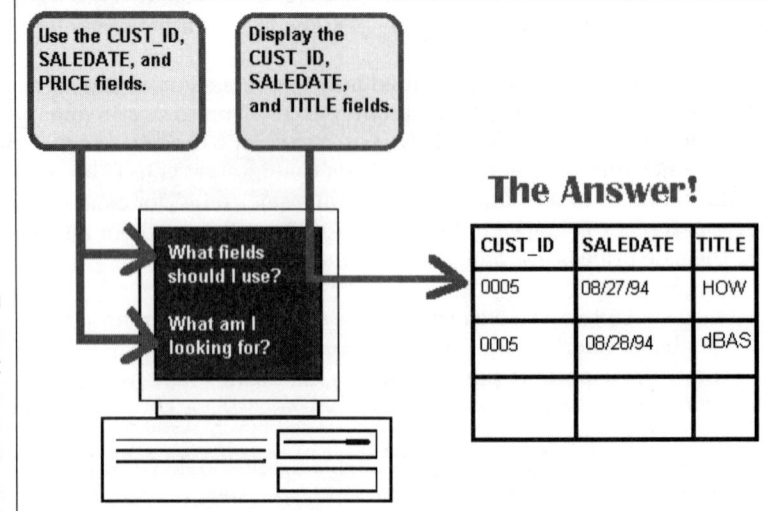

Figure 11-1: What happens when you create and run a query.

Chapter 11: Using Queries to Find Lots More Stuff

You also can specify the order in which you want dBASE to display the records (A to Z or Z to A) and what field to use for putting the records in order.

Because queries often are more complicated than the simple searches you do by choosing **F**orward Search or **B**ackward search, it would be a pain in the neck if you had to redo them every time you needed to get the same information from your database. Luckily, dBASE enables you to *save* queries and reuse them whenever you want.

Understanding the Query Design screen

You construct queries in the Query Design screen. Before you actually learn how to create a query, take a moment to familiarize yourself with this screen. To get to the Query Design screen, open a table. (If you want to follow along with the book's example Bookcust table, which we use to illustrate the steps in this chapter, open it.) Then, in the Control Center's Queries panel, highlight <create> and press Enter. The Query Design screen appears (see Figure 11-2).

> **TIP**
>
> If you're already looking at the table in a Browse or Form screen, you can go directly to the Query Design screen by pressing Shift-F2. If you have really tiny hands and can't quite manage that key combination, you also can open the **E**xit menu and select **T**ransfer to Query Design.

The Query Design screen has three main parts. Each plays a vital role in constructing a query.

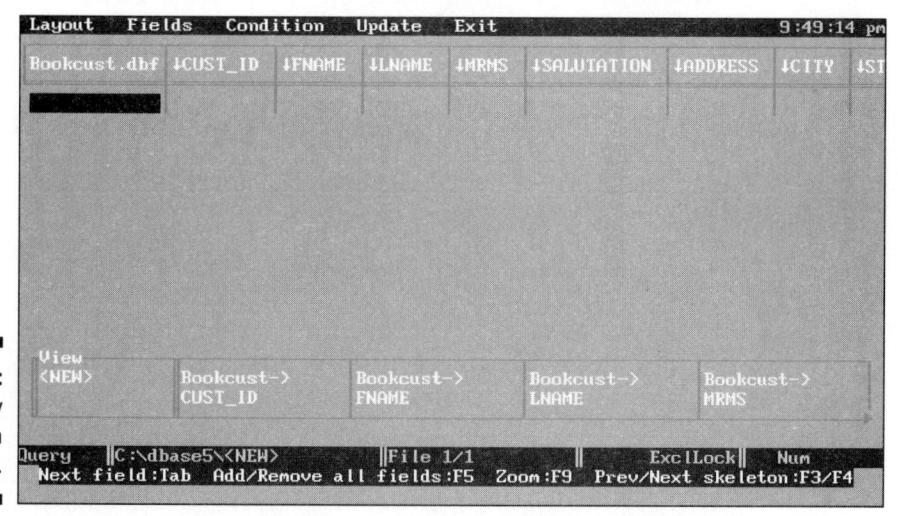

Figure 11-2: The Query Design screen.

- **The table (or file) skeleton:** The row of field names at the top of the screen. Here you select the fields that should be displayed in the answer. When you first arrive in a Query Design screen, a down arrow is to the left of each field name, indicating that each field is selected to appear in the query answer. You can deselect any or all of the fields, and you can reselect them one at a time or all at once (we describe how in a moment). This is also where you tell dBASE what to look for in the query.

- **The view (or the query answer) skeleton:** The row of field names toward the bottom of the screen. Here dBASE shows you which fields are going to be included in the query answer. All of the fields in the table are included initially because they're all checked (the down arrows) in the table skeleton. Next to each field name is the name of the table, a feature that will help you create queries using fields from more than one table.

- **The Status Bar:** As usual, the Status Bar provides you with a great deal of helpful information. At the left end, you see the word Query — in case you forget what you're doing. To the right is the name of the table you're using in the query. Next is the number of the current table: if you're using the example, since you're only using one table, it's File 1 of 1. Next is some technical stuff about networking that you can (and should) ignore. Finally, you see Num if your keyboard's NumLock feature is on and Ins if insert mode is turned on.

The method you use to create queries is called *Query by Example*. Invented in the late 1980s, it makes it easier for database users to create queries. Before that, creating a query required typing some long and complicated commands. With Query by Example, or *QBE*, the work is all visual: on the screen, you just select the fields you want, tell dBASE what to look for, and it's done! Easy as gaining 10 pounds over the holiday season.

Moving around in the Query Design screen

Here are a few simple tricks for moving around in the Query Design screen:

To Move	Press This
To the next field	Tab
To the preceding field	Shift-Tab
To the left end of the skeleton	Home
To the right end of the skeleton	End
Between the table skeleton and the view skeleton	F3 or F4*

* If you have more than two skeletons displayed in the Query Design screen (for example, when creating a query that uses more than one table), F3 takes you to the *next* skeleton and F4 takes you to the *preceding* skeleton. These keystrokes are borrowed from Borland's Paradox database package.

Creating a Query in dBASE

Here are the basic steps for creating a query in dBASE. If you're doing a query with your own real-life table, just follow the steps below. To follow along with the book's example, use the Bookcust table you created in Chapter 4 and filled with data in Chapter 5.

Selecting fields for the query

Selecting fields to display in the query answer is easy. If you want *all* the table's fields to be included in the query answer, you shouldn't need to do anything: when the Query Design screen opens, all the fields in the currently open table should be selected — that is, in the table skeleton, a down arrow is next to each field. If only some or none of the fields are selected, move the cursor to the table skeleton's leftmost column: that's where you see the table's name. Then press F5. All the fields will be selected.

The same trick works in reverse: if the fields are *already* selected, pressing F5 while the cursor is in the leftmost column deselects them. (Guess what: F5 is another toggle.)

To select (or deselect) an individual field, move the cursor to the field's column and press F5. If the field isn't already selected, doing so will select it. If the field is already selected, doing so will deselect it.

You can tell whether a field is selected in two ways:

- A down arrow is next to the field name in the table skeleton.
- The field name is included in the view skeleton.

If the field name isn't in the view skeleton, it's not going to be in the query answer.

You do *not* have to include a field in the query answer in order to search for something in that field. For example, you may tell the query to look for all customers whose account numbers run from 00010 to 00020. However, you don't need to display the account number field in the query answer unless you want it there. You can enter search conditions in a field without selecting that field for inclusion in the answer.

Telling dBASE what to look for

After you select the fields you want to see in the query answer, you can tell dBASE to look only for *specific* records. In a Sales table, for example, you may be looking for only those sales where the dollar amount is over $12, or sales made after a certain date. By entering a condition, you tell dBASE to display only the records that match the condition.

Remember, when creating a query, you tell dBASE which fields to look at and what to look for. You do so by entering a value in the blank under a field name in the table skeleton. There are some special rules for entering values in field blanks, and we describe these rules in the next section. For example, if you are looking for a customer whose first name was Teri, you need to enter =**"Teri"** into the first name (FNAME) field blank: instead of just typing **Teri**, you have to add an equal sign and put the name in quotation marks.

If you're following along with the book's example table, make sure that Bookcust is open and that a table skeleton of its fields is displayed in the Query Design screen. Then follow these steps:

1. **In the table skeleton, move the cursor to the field you want to search.**

   In the book's example table, move the cursor to the LNAME field.

2. **Tell dBASE what to look for.**

   In the example table, try looking for all customers whose last name is Lane. To do so, enter =**"Lane"** in the LNAME field. (Use an equal sign because you're looking for an exact match.)

Running the query

Running the query means telling dBASE to do its search and then display the records on-screen as a query answer. dBASE finds all the records that match your search criteria (if any exist) and displays them in a Browse screen.

1. **Press F2 to run the query and get your answer.**

   After working for a few moments, dBASE shows you a Browse screen that holds all the records that match your query.

2. **If the answer isn't quite what you wanted, fine-tune the query. To go from the query answer back to the Query Design screen, open the Exit menu and select Transfer to query design.**

   dBASE takes you back so that you can fine-tune your query or check it for errors. With simple queries, such as looking for customers with a particular last name, very little can go wrong. But when you run more powerful (and, inevitably, more complicated) queries, as in Chapter 12, you may need to do some fine-tuning once in a while.

3. **When everything's OK, use the query answer.**

   To *use* the query answer means to look at it or save it as a table. If you want to use the query in a report, you can either use the saved query answer or the query itself: dBASE can use either, and the result is the same. For now, just look at it. You can read how to save the query itself in the next section.

4. **When you have the answer you want, open the Exit menu and select Transfer to query design. Back in the Query Design screen, open the Layout menu and select Save this query.**

   dBASE asks you to name the query. If you want, you also can type in a description of what the query does by reopening the Layout menu and selecting Edit description of query.

Query names follow the same rules as table names (or, for that matter, any other DOS disk file). They can have a maximum of eight letters, digits, or underscore characters; no spaces or punctuation marks are allowed.

If you're using the book's example table, save the query as **Lane**. (Don't type the period.)

If you're done designing the query, another way to save the query is to open the **Exit** menu and select **S**ave changes and exit. After you save the query, it's time to head for the beach and hit the waves. Surf's up! Don't forget your sunscreen!

You don't have to enter conditions to run a query. You can enter a no-conditions query

- To see a Browse screen with only the fields you want, instead of all the fields in the table
- To see a Browse screen with the records in order by a particular field
- To see a Browse screen that combines fields from different tables

These are all very common uses of queries; none requires that you enter any conditions.

Saving a query answer

You can do one of two things with a query answer. You can look at it — unless you're in a sunlit room trying to work on one of those old laptop PCs with a lousy screen. But sometimes you want to save it as a table for later use — either in a report (see Chapter 16) or to give someone the query answer in table form. To save a query as a table, follow these steps:

1. **Get to the Query Design screen.**

   If you're still looking at the query answer, open the **Exit** menu and select **Transfer to query design**. If you're in the Control Center, highlight the query and press Enter; in the dialog box, select **Modify** query.

2. **Open the Layout menu and select Write view as a database file.**

   "Database file" is just the old name for a "table." A little box appears, asking for a table name. dBASE suggests that you use the same name for the table as you do for the query. This doesn't cause a problem because all table names end in .DBF while all query names have a .QBE extension.

3. **Type the table name you want and then press Enter.**

   If you're content to use the name dBASE suggests, just press Enter; you don't have to type anything.

Now, simply *file* the query answer and eat a peanut butter sandwich.

Sorting records in a query answer

Unless you tell dBASE otherwise, it displays the query answer records in the same order as they appear in the table itself (something you can change, as we note in Chapter 14). But you can sort the query answer any way you like.

Suppose that you create a query to look for all customers who live in California. In the Bookcust table, this means that the query answer contains the records for James West and Teri Lane — in that order because that's the order in which their records appear in the table.

To *sort* records means to order them. For example, you can sort customer records in alphabetic order by last name or in numerical order by ZIP code. You can sort sales records in order by the date the sale was made, in numerical order by dollar amount, or alphabetic order by book title. Sorting can be done in *ascending* (A to Z, 1 to 10) order or *descending* (Z to A, 10 to 1) order. There are also some fine points about upper- and lowercase letters, but you can generally ignore those. Sorting is explained in more detail in Chapter 14.

But suppose you want to see the records in order by last name? You can make the query sort the records, using any field you like. Just follow these steps:

Chapter 11: Using Queries to Find Lots More Stuff   127

1. **Enter the search condition (if any).**

    You don't *have* to enter a search condition. You can use a query merely to see your records in a particular order. If you're following along with the book's example, move the cursor to the State field and type =**"CA"** in the blank.

2. **Now move the cursor to the field you want to use for sorting the records.**

    If you're using the Bookcust table, move the cursor to the LNAME field.

3. **Open the Fields menu and select Sort on this field.**

    The Sorting submenu appears, as shown in Figure 11-3. **A**scending ASCII (that is, A to Z) is already selected.

ASCII is one of those weird acronyms that computer people seem to love, just as they love triple-strength coffee, jeans, and the Violent Femmes. What ASCII (pronounced "ask-ee") stands for is *American Standard Code for Information Interchange.* Now you know. There will be a quiz next period.

4. **If you want the records in A to Z order, press Enter to select Ascending ASCII.**

    The table skeleton now shows `Asc1` in the LNAME field.

5. **Press F2 to run the query.**

    dBASE orders the records by last name.

You now can save the query itself or save the query answer to a table, just as we described earlier in the chapter.

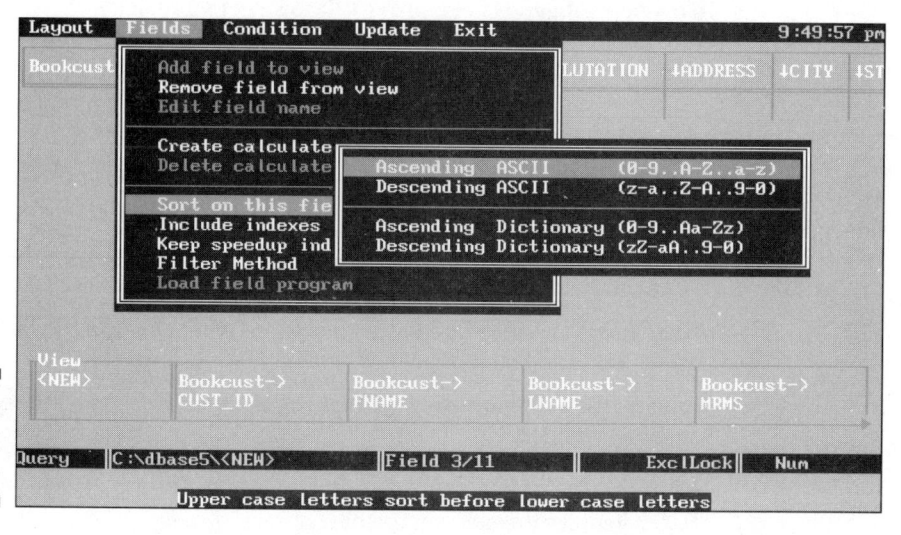

Figure 11-3: The Sorting submenu.

128   Part II: Playing with Your Data

> **TIP**
>
> Normally, a query answer contains *live* data, which means you can edit the data just as if you had displayed it in a regular Browse screen. The only exception: if you sort the records on more than one field (such as last name *and* first name), the data in the query answer is *read-only*, which means you can't change it from the query answer.

Changing the order of fields in the answer

Normally, the fields in the query answer appear in the same order as they appear in the table, even if the query answer doesn't display all the fields.

But suppose that you want the query answer to display fields in a different order — for example, CITY, LNAME, and then FNAME, which would make sense if you were sorting the records by city. Can you change the order of fields in the query answer? Is a chicken Catholic? Does the Pope have lips? Wait a minute, I always get those two mixed up. . . .

It's easy to rearrange the order of fields in the query answer: In the view skeleton, select the field you want to move and then move it. Follow these steps:

1. **Press F3 to switch the cursor from the table skeleton to the view skeleton.**
2. **Tab to the field you want to move.**
3. **Press F6 and then press Enter.**

   Pressing F6 selects the field you want to move. If you want to move more than one contiguous field, press Tab to select more fields to the right (or Shift-Tab to select more fields to the left) before you press Enter.

4. **Press F7.**

   This tells dBASE that you want to move the field.

5. **Move the field.**

   If you want to move the field to the right, press Tab; to move the field to the left, press Shift-Tab.

6. **When the field reaches the desired location, press Enter.**

   dBASE drops the field into its new location. When you run the query, the answer fields appears in the new order.

7. **If you need to do more work designing the query, press F3 to return to the table skeleton.**
8. **When you're ready, run the query.**

   dBASE displays the fields in the new order.

Rerunning a query

The queries we've been talking about are fairly simple. But when you get to be a real dBASE guru, you undoubtedly will want to create bigger databases and more complex queries — and to run the same query more than once. Luckily, because it would be wasteful and time-consuming to set up the same query each time you wanted to run it, dBASE makes it *easy* to rerun a saved query. To rerun a query, highlight it in the Control Center's Queries panel and press Enter. The query answer appears, just as before.

Of course, rerunning a query is useful whether or not the query is complicated. For example, suppose that you design a query to identify all customers living in California. The answer could change from month to month. Each time you rerun the California query, you get an updated list of your California-based customers.

Using Query Operators, and What It All Means

In principle, adding a condition to a query is easy. All you do is enter what you're looking for in the field that may have it. In practice, it's a little more complicated: you have to combine what you're looking for with dBASE *operators* so that dBASE knows exactly how to look for your data. Here are the operators you use:

Operator	What It Means
>	greater than
<	less than
=	equal to
<>	not equal to
>=	greater than or equal to
<=	less than or equal to
$	contains
Like	pattern match

NOTE: Operators that compare two things are sometimes called *relational* operators — they try to see what the relation is between the two things. Are they equal? Is one bigger than the other? When the term *relational* is used to describe an operator, it has nothing to do with *relational databases*, such as those you can create with dBASE.

Part II: Playing with Your Data

Some of the operators are pretty obvious. If you managed to stay awake during seventh grade, you know what the *greater than* operator means, for example. (To search for a number in a field that's greater than 10, enter **>10** in the table skeleton's blank under that field name.) The not-so-obvious operators — not equal to, contains, and pattern match — are as easy to understand. Here are some examples of how the operators work:

What You Type	What dBASE Looks For
="Teri"	Any record with exactly the word *Teri* in the field. Nothing else can be in the field.
$"Teri"	Any record containing *Teri* in the field, no matter what else is in the field.
>10	Any record containing a number greater than 10 in the field.
<>9.95	Any record not containing the number 9.95 in the field.
Like"*ne"	Any record containing text that ends in the letters *ne*. The asterisk is a wild card.

TIP

When looking for text, you must enclose the text in quotation marks and combine it with an operator. For example, $"Teri" searches for all records that contain "Teri" in the search field, no matter what else is also in the field; ="Teri" searches for all records that have *exactly* "Teri" in the field, and nothing else. You also can use the other relational operators with text. Entering >"B", for example, tells dBASE to look for all records where the field begins with a letter after *B*.

REMEMBER

You can use a wild card whenever you're not exactly sure what you're looking for. Wild cards are a way of telling dBASE that it should ignore any letters except the ones you've specified. The asterisk wild card says it should ignore any number of letters; the question mark wild card tells dBASE to ignore only one character. Here are some examples of wild cards in action:

What You Enter	What dBASE Looks For
J*	Any text beginning with the letter *J*. In a customer table, dBASE may find the names John, Jane, Jim, Jonathan, Joseph, Joan, Jurgen, Jorge, and Juanita.
J*n	Any text beginning with *J* and ending with *n*. dBASE may find John, Jonathan, and Jurgen.
J??n	Any text beginning with *J*, having two unknown letters, and ending with *n*. dBASE may find John and Joan.
J???	Any text beginning with *J* and followed by any three letters. dBASE may find John, Jane, and Joan.

Important Points to Remember

There are several important things to remember about setting up a query in the Query Design screen:

- ✔ The fields you search and the fields shown in the answer don't need to be the same. Just because you search for data in a field doesn't mean it has to appear in the query answer.

- ✔ You can search on one or more fields, but you don't *have* to search for data in *any* fields. You can use a query just to see your records in order or to display only certain fields. Searching for data in more than one field is explained in the next chapter.

- ✔ You can have the query answer display one or more fields. You can display all the fields or just the ones you want.

- ✔ You can rearrange the order of fields in the answer. You do so by moving the fields around in the view skeleton.

- ✔ You can sort the answer records on one or more fields.

- ✔ If you sort on more than one field, the query answer data isn't *live* data but *read-only,* which means you can't change the data in a table by changing it in the query answer.

- ✔ Unless the answer is read-only, you can edit the data in the query answer.

Hands on: Drudge Work Alert! Setting Up a Sales Table

To help you see the full power of queries in the following chapters, we suggest that you set up another sample table. (This table records all book sales at Caveat Emptor, the imaginary bookstore owned by the imaginary Honest Janis introduced in Chapter 3.) If you've been playing hooky (hookey? hockey? hooey?) since you finished Chapter 10, start up dBASE again and open the Caveat catalog. Then create the Sales table with the fields listed in Table 11-1. Don't worry: you'll use the table *plenty* later in the book.

We described how to set up a table in Chapter 4, but we'll repeat the basics in case you're a little hazy. For more information, refer back to Chapter 4. Note also that when you see N/A in the table, it means that something is not applicable. For example, for the SALEDATE field, the Width column contains N/A because dBASE automatically sets the field size of a Time/Date field.

Part II: Playing with Your Data

Table 11-1		Fields for the Sales Table		
Name	Type	Width	Decimal	Indexed
CUST_ID	Character	5	N/A	Ascend (Yes)
SALEDATE	Date	N/A	N/A	No
TITLE	Character	50	N/A	No
AUTHOR	Character	25	N/A	No
PRICE	Float	8	2	No

To set up your new table, follow these steps:

1. **In the Control Center's Data panel, highlight `<create>`.**
2. **Enter CUST_ID, the name of the first field, in the first column of the first line. Press Tab.**
3. **Choose a field type: character. Press Tab.**

   If you accidentally select the incorrect type, press Shift-Tab and the cursor returns to the field type column. Press the spacebar to change to the correct type.

4. **Set the width: 5. Press Tab.**
5. **Press Y to index this field. For the other fields, press N.**
6. **Repeat Steps 2 through 5 for every field you need.**

   At the end of Step 5, the cursor moves automatically to the first column of the next row.

7. **Name and save the table design.**

   Save the table under the name Sales. To do so, open the Exit menu and select **S**ave changes and exit.

Now enter the following five records into the Sales table. (If you want to put in more records, Appendix A lists all 15 records for this table.)

CUST_ID: 4
SALEDATE: 8/21/94
TITLE: How to Write a Computer Book
AUTHOR: Obscurantis, Jargon
PRICE: 2.95

CUST_ID: 1
SALEDATE: 8/25/94
TITLE: In Praise of Idleness
AUTHOR: Russell, Bertrand
PRICE: 12.95

CUST_ID: 2
SALEDATE: 8/26/94
TITLE: Getting Your Husband Off His Lazy Butt
AUTHOR: Russell, Mrs. Bertrand
PRICE: 12.95

CUST_ID: 5
SALEDATE: 8/27/94
TITLE: How I Turned $25 Cash into a Successful Business
AUTHOR: Fleiss, Heidi
PRICE: 24.95

CUST_ID: 5
SALEDATE: 8/28/94
TITLE: dBASE for DOS for Dummies
AUTHOR: Palmer, Scott
PRICE: 19.95

That's it for now. You deserve a break. Hmmm . . . "90210" looks pretty good tonight. . . . Maybe Steve will hack into another computer! Naaah . . . he's turned into a regular good guy lately. Oh, well.

Chapter 12
Mastering Logical Operators and Replacing Data

In This Chapter
- What is a logical operator?
- Using logical operators for multiple-condition queries
- Doing calculations in a query
- Changing data by using the Query Design screen

*T*o create queries for your own database, read this chapter and follow the instructions to get the basics. If you want to work through the sample database in this book, you need to have created the Bookcust table (see Chapter 4) and the Sales table (see Chapter 11) and put data in the Bookcust table (see Chapter 5) and in the Sales table (see Chapter 11).

To get the most out of this chapter, you should know

- What a database is (see Chapter 1)
- What a table is (see Chapter 4)
- What a query is (see Chapter 11)

To create queries for your own database, read this chapter and follow the instructions to get the basics. If you want to work through the sample database in this book, you need to have created the Bookcust table (see Chapter 4) and the Sales table (see Chapter 11) and put data in the Bookcust table (see Chapter 5) and in the Sales table (see Chapter 11).

What Is a Logical Operator?

Logical operator may sound like someone who sits around answering phones all day while reading Aristotle. But in a database, logical operators are really just familiar words like *and*, *or*, and *not*. Logical operators were invented by George Boole, a mid-19th century English mathematician who had nothing better to do. They're sometimes called *Boolean operators*, in his honor.

Before Boole came along, people had trouble expressing ideas that required logical operators, wreaking havoc on the medieval judicial system, where someone could be sentenced to beheading and flogging in the same day. Because jailers executed the two punishments separately, this confusion caused some absurd situations when the beheading came first. If a person was sentenced to *either* beheading *or* flogging and tar-and-feathering, the jailers didn't have any idea where to start. So you can see, Boole's work was instrumental in furthering humanity.

Creating Multiple-Condition Queries

Logical operators are used in database management systems to create queries that look for more than one thing at a time (otherwise known as *searching for multiple conditions*). For example, you may want to identify every book sold before August 27th for more than $5. dBASE makes such a query simple.

Multiple-condition queries haven't always been this easy. In older versions of dBASE, as well as most other database managers, you had to type things like

```
Display fname, lname, city for zip = "20903" .and. lname =
         "tempchin".
```

But these days, almost all database managers have adopted the simple *Query by Example* (QBE) approach used by dBASE.

Using AND and OR

Creating a query with multiple conditions works just like creating a simple query. The only difference is that you put more than one condition in the table skeleton.

When you use multiple conditions, you use the logical operators AND and OR to combine the conditions. For example, if you're looking for every customer who lives in Chicago AND is named Smith, the query will not list anybody who is not named Smith, nor will it list anybody who lives outside of Chicago; a person must live in Chicago and be named Smith. On the other hand, if you look for people who live in Chicago OR are named Smith, your query will look for

- Any customer who lives in Chicago but is not named Smith
- Any customer who doesn't live in Chicago but is named Smith
- Any customer who lives in Chicago and is named Smith

That last bullet may surprise you. Normally, if you say you're going to the store OR going to the movies, you mean you plan to do one or the other, but not both. That's called an *exclusive* OR. But in dBASE, OR is *inclusive*; if you search for records that match A OR B, dBASE will find all the records that match A, B, or both A and B.

Combining conditions with AND

Using AND conditions is easy: enter each condition in the appropriate field *on the same line* of the Query Design screen's table skeleton, as shown in Figure 12-1.

Figure 12-1: Entering two AND conditions to find all sales records where the sale date is after August 22, 1994, and the price is greater than $3.

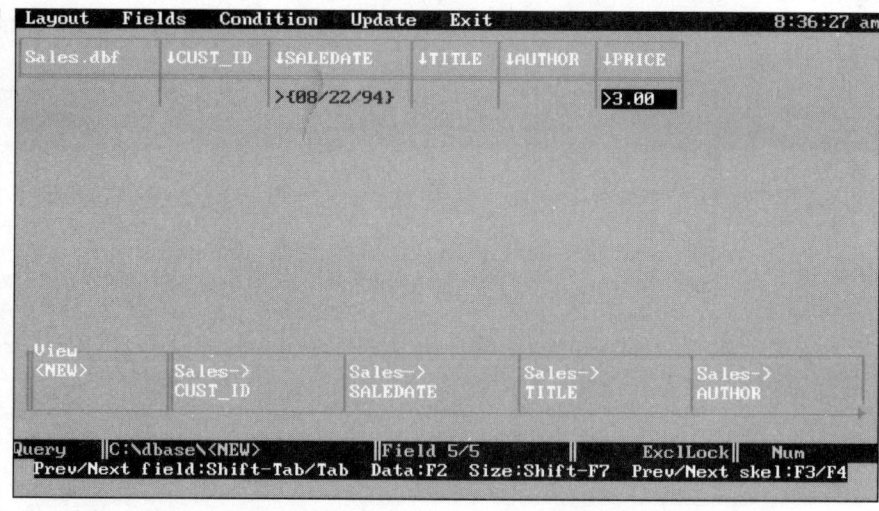

Everything else works the same as in the single-condition queries described in Chapter 11:

1. **Open the catalog that holds the desired database.**
2. **From the Control Center, use the arrow keys to highlight the word `<create>` in the Query column and press Enter.**

The Query Design screen appears, with the Add file to query option already highlighted.

3. Highlight the Add file to query option from the Layout menu and press Enter.

dBASE displays a small window on-screen that shows the tables you can choose from (see Figure 12-2).

4. In the window, highlight the table you want to use and press Enter.

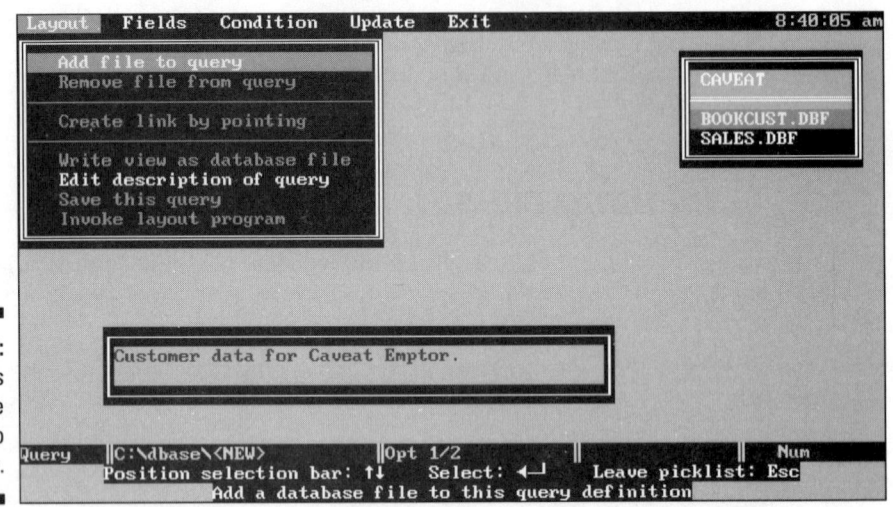

Figure 12-2: dBASE asks which table you want to query.

As soon as you select a table, dBASE displays the entire Query Design screen, which contains a skeleton of the table's structure at the top of the screen (this skeleton is basically just a horizontal field list). In the skeleton, pick the fields you want to include in the query. You also tell dBASE whether you want it to sort the records it finds in any particular order (for instance, by last name or account number).

5. Pick the fields you want to see in the query by using the Tab and Shift-Tab keys to highlight the available fields.

When you come to a field you want to add, press F5 to include it in the query. The field appears at the bottom of the screen in the view skeleton. dBASE will show the field on-screen when you execute the query.

6. To sort the records in the query answer, highlight the field you want to sort and select the Sort on this field option from the Fields menu.

A dialog box appears, asking which method you want to sort by. Table 12-1 describes what each choice does. Highlight the option you choose and press Enter. If you want, you then can tell dBASE to perform a secondary

Chapter 12: Mastering Logical Operators and Replacing Data

sort on the query by moving the highlight bar to a different field and selecting the Sort on this field option again. If you change your mind about the sort order, or whether to sort at all, you can reselect the Sort on this field option and change the sorting information.

Table 12-1 **Sorting Options**

If You Sort By This	You Get This
Ascending ASCII	Numbers, then capital letters, then lowercase letters.
Descending ASCII	Lowercase letters, then capital letters, then numbers.
Ascending Dictionary	Numbers and then all letters regardless of capitalization.
Descending Dictionary	All letters regardless of capitalization and then numbers.

7. Tell dBASE the AND conditions.

Tell dBASE what you're looking for by moving the cursor into the blank that's under the name of the field(s) you want to search, as shown in Figure 12-3. To get to a particular blank, use the arrow keys to move the highlight bar or just click on the blank. Refer to Chapter 11 for some important rules about how to enter values in field blanks. For example, if you were looking for a customer whose first name was Teri, you would enter **$"Teri"** into the first name (FNAME) field blank. The quotation marks tell dBASE you're searching for text; the dollar sign tells dBASE to search all records that contain Teri in the search field, no matter what else is also in the field.

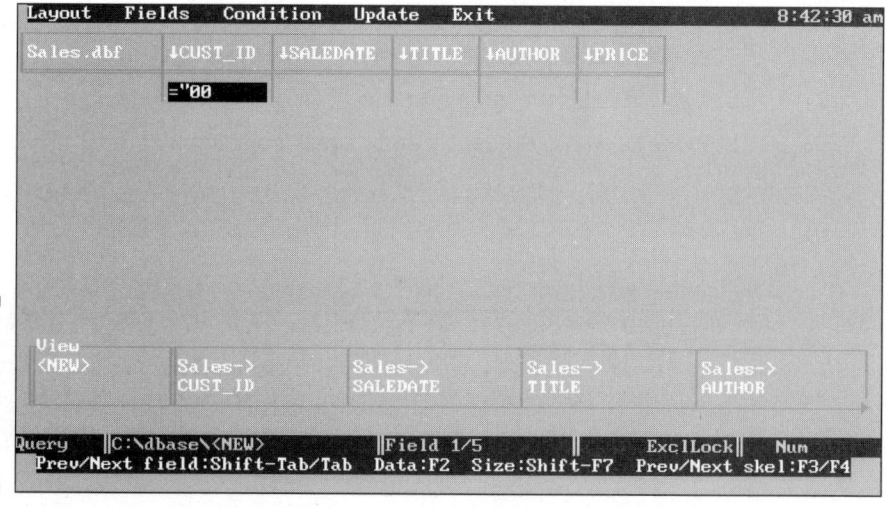

Figure 12-3: Adding search values to a query.

8. **Press F2 to run the query.**

   When you run the query, dBASE looks for the records that match the search values entered in Step 7 and displays the matching records on-screen. If there aren't any matching records, dBASE lets you know (actually, dBASE throws a hissy fit).

9. **Open the Layout menu and select the Save this query option.**

   dBASE responds with a cute little dialog box, asking you to name the query. The name must follow the same rules as the name for a table or any other DOS disk file.

Querying the Bookcust Sales table

If you took a break after the preceding chapter, get back into dBASE right now. What did you think you were doing? You rested last week.

Load the Caveat catalog. In this section, you create a sample query that searches for all records in the Sales table that have books sold after August 22 for more than $3. If you're doing a query with your own table, just follow along with the steps:

1. **Open the Query Design screen, selecting the Sales table for the query.**

2. **In the blank under SALEDATE, enter >{08/22/94}.**

   Don't include the period. Notice that you must surround the date with curly brackets.

3. **In the blank under PRICE, enter >3.00.**

4. **Move the highlight bar all the way to the left (under the filename) and press F5 to include all of the field in the view skeleton.**

   If all the fields are already selected, kindly disregard this step.

5. **Press F2 to run the query and display your answer.**

To simplify matters here, don't worry about sorting the records in the query answer.

Notice that you never typed the word AND anywhere. That's because dBASE automatically uses the AND operator when you put two (or more) search conditions in the same row.

If you want, save this query in the usual way (open the Layout menu and select Save this query). Then give it a name. Or, you can try to save this query in the unusual way (say cryptic voodoo chants to your hard disk).

Looking for a range of values

Another way to use AND is to look for a range of values — sounds like something a vice president would say. In dBASE, though, *range of values* is a term that means values that fall between a maximum and a minimum (which you specify).

Suppose, for example, that Janis wants to see all the records for sales that occurred between August 23 and 26. You can look for a range like this by combining two AND conditions in the same field, as shown in Figure 12-4. Here are the important points:

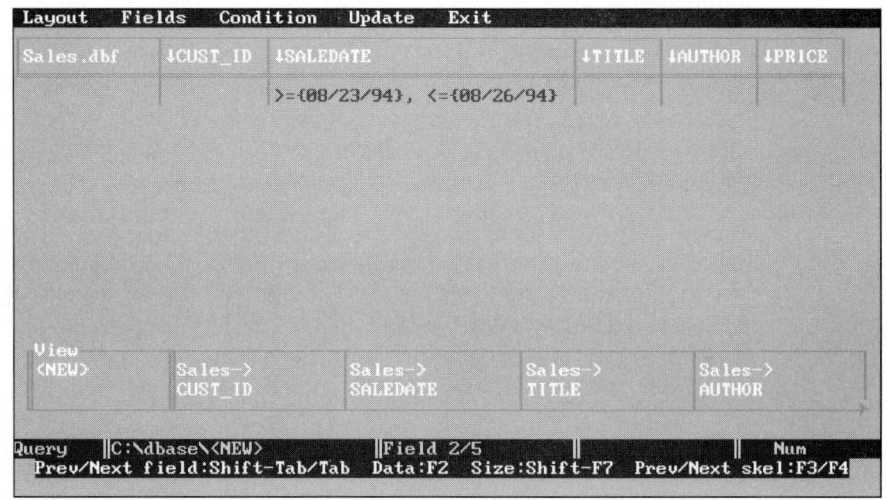

Figure 12-4: Entering multiple AND conditions for the same field.

- The first condition, >={08/23/94}, searches for all records with a sale date on or after August 23.
- The second condition, <={08/26/94}, searches for all records with a sale date on or before August 26.
- Because both conditions apply to the SALEDATE field, they both go in the SALEDATE column.
- Because both conditions are AND conditions, they both must go on the same line of the table skeleton.

When you have multiple AND conditions that need to go in the same column, put a comma between the conditions. In this case, the SALEDATE condition blank should contain >={08/23/94}, <={08/26/94}. See how easy that is?

You can use this technique with other values as well, including text values (such as ZIP codes) and numeric or float values (such as money). As an exercise, try setting up a query to find all customers with ID numbers between 00002 and 00004.

If you're still in the Query Design screen after creating the preceding query, you may want to save this one under a different name.

Combining conditions with OR

You enter conditions for the OR operator in exactly the same way as you do for the AND operator — except you enter the conditions on different rows. Yep, you may not have noticed it yet, but you can move the highlight bar down to separate lines while you're in the table skeleton. Go ahead and try: move the highlight bar underneath one of the field columns and press the down-arrow key. A new line pops into view (see Figure 12-5). If you want, you can press the down-arrow key again for more OR lines. Get crazy. Create ORs like nobody's business.

Suppose that you want to find records for all the sales made either before August 24 OR after August 26: On the first line in the SALEDATE column, enter the condition <{08/24/94}. On the second line, enter the condition >{08/26/94}. (As usual, don't include the periods.)

You run and save the query in exactly the same way as any other query.

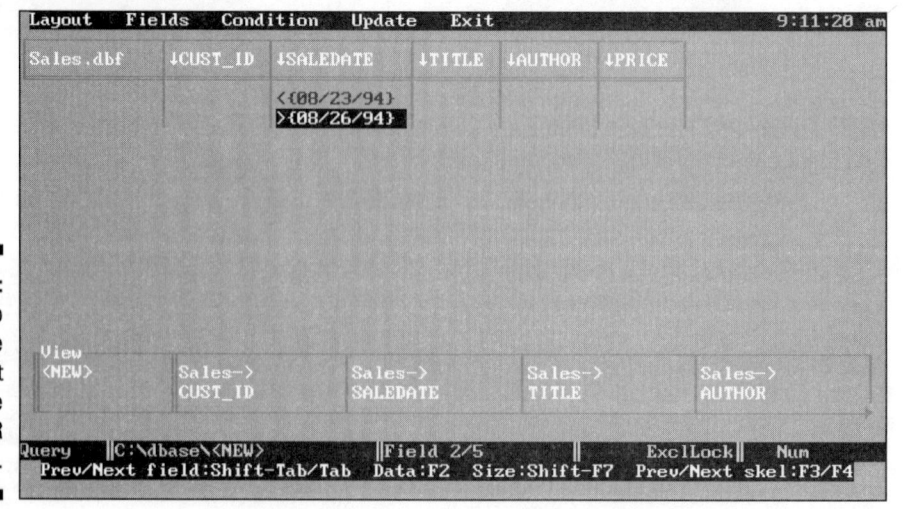

Figure 12-5: Opening up a new line and using it to combine multiple OR conditions.

Putting OR conditions in different fields

Believe it or not, you also can put OR conditions in different fields. Suppose that you want to find all the records for sales that either took place before August 24 OR were for more than $15. To do so, combine your OR conditions as before. The only difference is that because one condition applies to the SALEDATE field and the other applies to the PRICE field, the conditions go in different columns, as shown in Figure 12-6. Remember, each OR condition must be on a different line. If they're on the *same* line, dBASE will think you want them to be AND conditions.

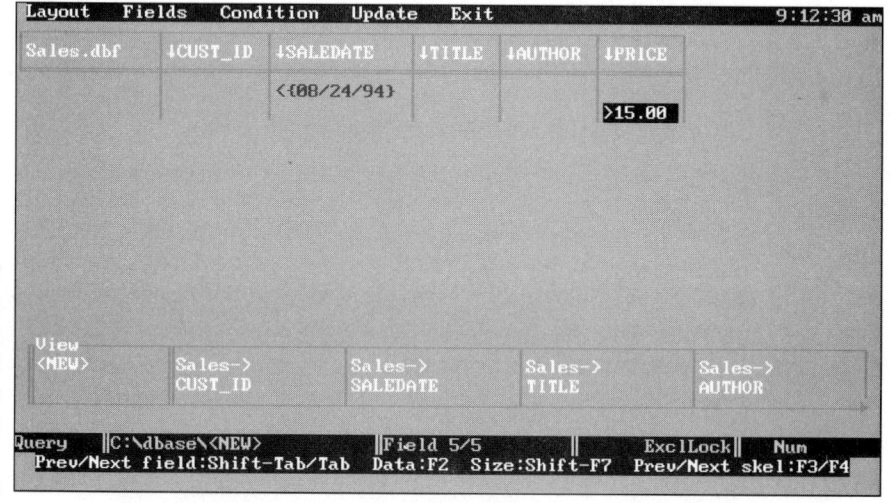

Figure 12-6: Combining OR conditions in different fields.

You run and save the query in exactly the same way as any other query.

Doing Calculations in a Query

Most people hate math. Heck, so does dBASE. But it's just a computer program, so it doesn't have any choice but to do the math that you give it. Of course, it can get back at you later by one day refusing to acknowledge the existence of the 5,000-employee database that you just spent a month entering. Computers can be so petty.

dBASE can do calculations inside a query. All you need to do is set up your query in the normal way and then add a *calculated field.* The basic steps are as follows:

1. Set up a query in the normal way.

Select the table and fields you want for the query answer, tell dBASE how to sort the data in the query answer, and enter any conditions you're looking for.

2. **Highlight the Create Calculated Field option from the Fields menu and press Enter.**

   dBASE adds a Calc'd Flds skeleton to the Query Design screen. This is where you can enter a name for the calculated field and a formula to do the calculation.

3. **In the highlight bar to the right of the Calc'd Flds column, enter the formula you want dBASE to calculate.**

   For example, suppose that you want to see how much money each sale would have involved if you had applied a 10-percent discount for longtime customers. In that case, you would need to take the original price (contained in the SALES field) and multiply it by 0.9. So enter as the formula **price * 0.9** (the asterisk means multiply).

   You can use any of the standard arithmetic operators in a calculation: + for addition, - for subtraction, * for multiplication, and / for division. You also can use other dBASE mathematical operators, but they're too numerous to discuss here, and you probably won't use them often, anyway. If you want more information about these operators, see your dBASE manuals.

4. **Make sure that the calculated field is marked to be displayed. If not, move under it and press F5.**

   The calculated field won't do you much good if it's invisible. dBASE prompts you to name the field.

5. **Enter a name for the field in the dialog box.**

6. **Run the query by pressing F2.**

   dBASE displays the query answer, including the calculated field, on your PC screen.

> **NOTE:** Adding a new field in a query has no effect at all on the table you're using in the query. The calculated field exists only in the query itself, not in the table.

Replacing Data in a Table

Unless you're a masochist, you won't go around replacing data by using the Browse screen. Browsing is a dreadful life; imagine trudging around with the arrow keys, replacing your data one record at a time. That kind of repetition is torturous to most. In fact, China switched from the water drum to the dBASE Browse screen as early as the late sixties.

A less painful way exists, however: you can use the Query Design screen to seek out and replace data in your database. Here are the basic steps:

1. **Open a catalog and load the table that you want to work with into the Query Design screen.**
2. **Highlight the Specify update operation in the Update menu and press Enter.**
3. **Select the Replace values in *filename*.dbf option from the submenu and press Enter.**

   Unless the name of the database that you're working with is filename, the word *filename* in this option is replaced by something else. A dialog box appears, warning you that you'll lose your views.

4. **Highlight Proceed and press Enter.**

   A table skeleton appears in the Query Design screen.

5. **Add any search conditions.**
6. **Type the word with in front of the value that you want to be placed in the database.**

   An easy way to envision this process is to start at the leftmost column on the screen, where the word *Replace* is written. The next word that you come to on that line is what dBASE uses as a search condition. It can be a string, a number, a date, and so on. (You also can have multiple-search conditions, just as you can in a regular query.) The condition that has the word *with* preceding it is the new data that will be placed into the field that it is under.

   For example, in a typical first name field, you may have the search criterion **"Robert", with "Bob"**, which tells dBASE to find all people with the first name Robert and replace their name with Bob.

   You also can do a search in one field to replace the data in another field. For example, you may search through a date field for all the people who have a birthday today. Then add 1 to the age field for each of those people.

7. **Select the Proceed to update option from the Update menu.**

   When dBASE finishes updating, you can press F2 to make sure that it changed the data in the way you wanted it to.

Up next: learn how to customize dBASE forms to make them even better! Stay tuned.

Chapter 13
Hot Stuff! Customizing Your Forms

In This Chapter
- Moving fields and text
- Changing and adding text
- Drawing boxes and lines on the screen
- Changing a form's colors
- Adding calculated fields
- Adding automatic error-checking for your data entry
- Using templates
- Saving your modified form design

*Y*ou may think you've reached database heaven, but that's just not the case. dBASE's Quick Layout (the thing you learned about in Chapter 9) does help a lot in designing your data entry forms, but it is far from omnipotent. This chapter shows you how to take your mere mortal form and transform it into a super form.

In this chapter, we present the basic ideas and skills for customizing and modifying forms. The good news is that dBASE makes it easy for you to change the features of a form. In this chapter, you'll learn how to move the fields and their captions around on the form. Then you learn how to change a field's caption. Finally, you learn how to change the color scheme and appearance of the form.

Before you can customize a form, you need to have

- Created a table (see Chapter 4) and put data in the table (see Chapter 5)
- Created a form that you intend to customize (see Chapter 10)
- Understood the concepts of a database (see Chapter 1), a table (see Chapter 4), and a form (see Chapter 9)

Part II: Playing with Your Data

If you're customizing a form from your own database, this chapter will give you the basic ideas and techniques. To practice on the form in this book, you need to have created the Bookcust table in Chapter 4, put data in it in Chapter 5, and created a form in Chapter 10.

A well-designed form is one of the signs of a true databaser. For the true databaser knows that a good form makes data entry much easier. And besides, a clear, easy-to-understand form just makes the world a happier place to be. You can use the following tools and tricks to make your forms the apple of everybody's eye.

Moving Fields and Text

Nine out of ten databasers agree: The simplest thing you can do to customize a form is to move around the fields and text that are on it. (Of course, *seven* out of ten databasers think that "Full House" is the best show on TV.) The basic steps for moving fields and texts on a form are:

1. **If you haven't already loaded it, open the form you want to modify.**

   From the Forms column in the Control Center, highlight the form you want, then press Enter. In the dialog box, select Modify layout. If you're using the book's example database, then select the form for the Bookcust table, which you created in Chapter 9.

2. **Select the field(s) and text(s) that you want to move.**

   To select a field (or any other item, such as captions) in the Forms Design screen, move the cursor to the item, press F6, and use the arrow keys to expand the highlight bar to include everything you want to move. If you want to select only one item (one field, one item, and so on), press Enter to complete the selection. If you want to select a group of fields or text captions, start with F6 as before, then use the arrow keys to increase the highlight bar to include as much of your form as you want to select. Then finally press Enter. If you make a mistake, press Esc to cancel the selection.

3. **Press F7.**

   F7 is the Move key in dBASE. You can now move the selected item to anywhere you want on the screen.

4. **Use the arrow keys to move the selected item(s).**

   The highlight bar attached to the cursor is an indicator of where the text will be put down. Notice that the Status Bar at the bottom of the screen lists your current position in the form. Knowing your current position can help you in lining up your fields.

5. **When the highlight bar is where you want the text to be, press Enter.**
6. **If you want to move more items, move the rest of the items into the places where you want them.**

   Repeat Steps 2 through 5 to place the rest of the items you want to move.

> **NOTE:** As with most other display tools in dBASE, nothing you can do in the Forms Design screen can mess up your actual database. If, however, you do begin to hear insane laughter coming from your computer's speaker, run away real fast.

Changing and Adding Text

Sometimes it seems that a big part of being a databaser (like yourself) is the need to create the most cryptic, incomprehensible fields names possible. For example, the book's example database Bookcust uses a field called MRMS to hold customers' titles (such as Mr., Mrs., and so on). To the average person who hasn't read this book, however, MRMS probably means nothing. For this reason, dBASE allows you to change the look of your field names to something more descriptive. This can be a big help to other people who are trying to use your database and who don't know what each field does.

To change a field name in the Forms Design screen, follow these steps:

1. **Move the highlight bar to the field name you want to change.**

   Make sure that you're on the field name, and not the field itself. The field itself is something like XXXXXX, or 9999999. The field name is just simple text like MRMS, or CUST_ID.

2. **Delete the field name.**

   Use the standard editing keys: Delete, Backspace, and so forth.

3. **Type the new text that you want to add.**
4. **Save the new form layout.**

   From the Exit menu, select Save changes and exit. If it's a new form, dBASE prompts you to enter a name for it, so type in a name that complies with the MS-DOS dogma for filenames (eight letters or fewer, no spaces or punctuation except for underscores).

Drawing Boxes and Lines on the Screen

dBASE lets you add boxes and lines to the forms you create. Boxes and lines can help make your form easier to read and can even cut down on data entry error.

Adding a box

To add a box to your form, get to the Forms Design screen. If you're already there, fine. If not, in the Control Center, highlight the form you want and press Enter. In the dialog box, select Modify layout. Then, follow these steps:

1. **Choose the Box option from the Layout menu.**

   A submenu appears as in Figure 13-1.

2. **Select the kind of box you'd like to draw.**

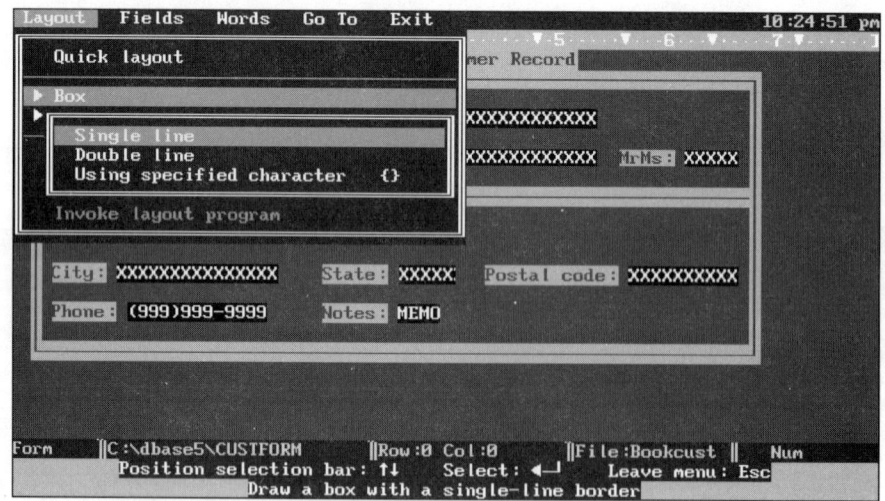

Figure 13-1: The Box submenu.

If you're using the book's example database, select the Double Line option.

3. **Move the cursor to where you want the upper-left corner of the box to be.**

   Use the Status Bar to see where your current position is. For the Bookcust database, move the cursor to position Row 1 : Column 2.

4. **Press Enter.**

   This starts the box.

Chapter 13: Hot Stuff! Customizing Your Forms

5. Move the cursor to where you want the lower-right corner of the box to be.

If using the Bookcust database, move the cursor to Row 15 : Column 68.

6. Press Enter.

This finishes the box. You can then use the arrow keys to move elsewhere on the form and make additional modifications if you wish.

Adding a line

To add a line to your form, start in the Forms Design screen and follow these steps:

1. Move the cursor to the position where you would like the line to start.

If adding a line to the Bookcust form, move the cursor to Row 7 : Column 3. Look at the Status Bar at the bottom of the screen to check your current position.

2. Select the Line option from the Layout menu.

A window appears with options for different kinds of lines.

3. Select the kind of line you want from the Line submenu.

For the book's example database, select the Single Line option.

4. Move the cursor to the position where you would like the line to end.

For the example database, move the cursor to Row 7 : Column 67. It's easiest to use the arrow keys for this.

5. Press Enter to complete the line.

Figure 13-2 shows what the Form screen may look like after adding a box and a line.

TIP: If you ever mess up and make a line or box too large, just position the cursor on the line or box and press the delete key until it shrinks to the size you want. You can also use this trick to completely erase a line or box that you've decided you don't want anymore.

Changing a Form's Colors

Changing colors on a form is easy. You can change the colors of the fields and the text captions. With the form displayed in the Forms Design screen, the basic steps are:

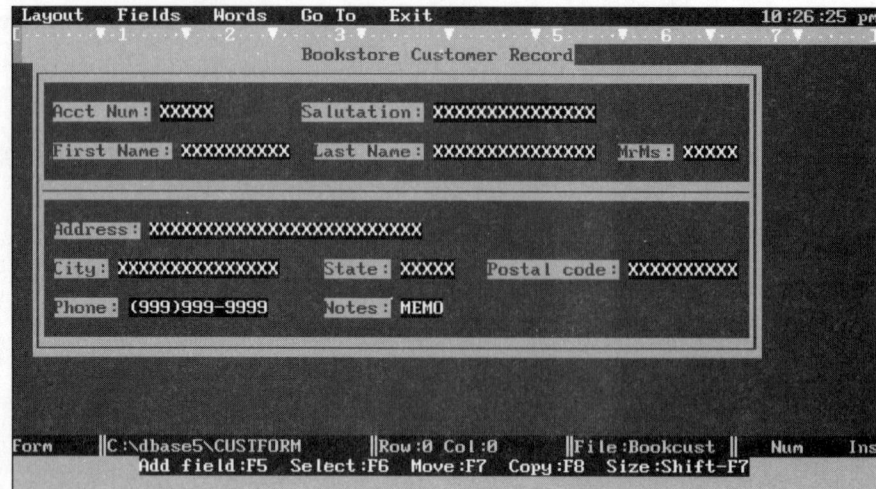

Figure 13-2: The Form screen after adding a box and a line.

1. **Select the fields and texts whose colors you want to change.**

   To select them, press F6, then use the arrow keys to highlight the fields and texts you want to change, then press Enter.

2. **From the Words menu, select Display.**

   The Display window appears.

3. **Select the color to use in your foreground.**

   Use the up- and down-arrow keys to do this. The color next to the little white box is the current color. You can also look at the box with the words Blink OFF in it. This box gives you a sample of what the currently selected foreground and background colors look like together.

4. **Press the right-arrow key to move over to the background colors.**

5. **Select the color to use in your background.**

   You select the background color in the same way that you select the foreground color. If, after seeing the colors together in the Blink OFF box, you decide to change the foreground color, simply press the left-arrow key to move back.

6. **Press Ctrl-End to accept the color scheme.**

7. **Select the Save changes and exit option from the Exit menu.**

   The next time you use the form to enter data, your new colors will be displayed.

Adding Calculated Fields

Calculated fields in a form are a lot like calculated fields in a query. They're fields that perform a mathematical operation on two or more of your fields and display the results, but they do not add any data to your database. A calculated field is for show only; it does not become a real field on your table. To add a calculated field to your form, follow these steps:

1. **Position the cursor where you want the calculated field to be.**
2. **Select the Add Field option from the Fields menu.**

    A window appears with a pick list in it.

3. **Select the <create> option.**

    A dialog box appears (as in Figure 13-3), asking you for information about the field.

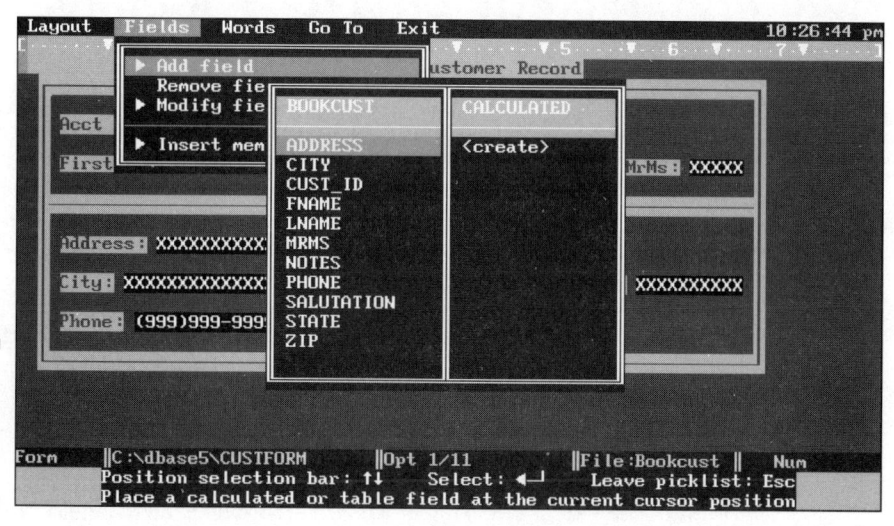

Figure 13-3: The Add Field submenu.

4. **Fill in the dialog box.**

    NAME: Enter a name for the field.

    DESCRIPTION: Enter a brief description of what the field does.

    EXPRESSION: Enter the mathematical formula for the field (that is, field 1 + field 2). You can do calculations on fields that are of the numeric or float data types. Some of the calculations you can do are '+' for addition, '-' for subtraction, '*' for multiplication and '/' for division. Other operations are available, but they're not used very often. There's a complete list of available operations in the dBASE manual.

TEMPLATE: Enter place holders for the number that will be generated by the field. Type a '9' for each digit that will be displayed. For example, if you know that none of the answers that will be shown in the calculated field is going to need five digits (10,000 or over) then you should enter four 9s (like this: **9999**). You should also enter 9s for decimal points if the field will have answers of the float data type, which is used for numbers with decimals. Enter the 9s like this: **9999.99.** (Ignore the period at the end of the sentence.) The 9s after the decimal point will be used to hold digits in the answer that come after the decimal point.

PICTURE FUNCTIONS: This is a submenu that lets you do things like pad a number with zeroes, adjust margins, things like that.

5. **Press Ctrl-End to save the field.**

   The field appears on the form.

Adding Automatic Error-Checking for Your Data Entry

Error-checking, or range-checking (in some states), is a feature you can use to help reduce data entry error. What is data entry error? Data entry error is what happens when you intend to enter **12/25/94** into your Sales form's date field, but your finger slips and you enter **13/25/94** instead. What's worse is that this kind of error may occur without you even noticing. That's very bad — you'll have faulty data in your database.

As an example, suppose that you want to see all of the sales transactions for the imaginary bookstore *Caveat Emptor* that occurred in the month of December. Since the date you just entered had 13 for the month, there's a good chance (depending on how you do your search) that dBASE won't find that sale. That means that you'll make more money in December than your records said you did. And that means the IRS will be at your door within 24 hours. So you can see how important error-checking is. To add error-checking to a field from the Forms Design screen, follow these steps:

1. **Place the cursor on the field you want to error-check.**
2. **Select Modify field from the Fields menu.**

   A submenu appears.

3. **Select Edit Options from the Fields submenu.**

   Another submenu appears with several choices. Here's what each does:

Chapter 13: Hot Stuff! Customizing Your Forms *155*

EDITING ALLOWED: When set to NO, this choice prevents a person from editing the information in a field.

PERMIT EDIT IF: This choice lets you enter a condition that will enable editing if the data in the field matches the condition (if you don't know what a condition is, Chapter 12 talks all about that stuff).

MESSAGE: When you enter a message here, this choice displays your message at the bottom of the Form screen whenever the cursor is on the selected field.

CARRY FORWARD: When set to YES, this choice takes the data from the field in the previous record and copies it to the same field in every subsequent record that's entered.

DEFAULT VALUE: Selecting default value lets you type in the data that you want to have in the selected field for every record in the database.

SMALLEST AND LARGEST VALUE ALLOWED: This choice lets you enter the lowest or highest value (date or number) that can be entered in the selected field. dBASE will beep and refuse any data that's outside of the range. You can specify only a SMALLEST value, only a LARGEST value, or even both.

RANGE MUST ALWAYS BE MET: When set to NO, this choice turns off error-checking.

ACCEPT VALUE WHEN: This choice rejects any data that doesn't meet the requirements you set; it's basically the same as the SMALLEST and LARGEST VALUE ALLOWED command.

VALUE MUST ALWAYS BE VALID: This choice turns off error-checking when set to NO.

UNACCEPTED MESSAGE: This choice lets you type a message here that will be displayed if the user tries to enter invalid data.

4. **Fill out the Edit Options menu.**

   Use the list above to add the error-checking features that you want the selected field to have.

5. **Press Ctrl-End twice to save the error-checking setup for this field.**

Using Templates

A template in dBASE is a special kind of filter for your data. It takes the raw data that you type and automatically transforms it into polished data. An example of how templates are useful is the STATE field in the book's example database. Normally, state letters are capitalized (such as CA for California, MD for Maryland, and so on). If you are entering state abbreviations into a database then, you have to press the Shift key to capitalize the state letters for every record that you enter. That gets old real quick. A better way to do it would be to just type in the state abbreviation, let a template capitalize it for you, and forget about it. The next steps will show you how to do just that:

1. **Move the cursor to the field to which you want to add a template.**

    If using the book's example database, then move the cursor to the STATE field.

2. **Select the Modify field option from the Fields menu.**

    A submenu appears.

3. **Select the Template option from the Modify field submenu.**

    A window appears, describing what each of the various template symbols does, and what kinds of data each accepts (digits, letters, punctuation, and so on). The cursor is on the current template.

4. **Use the backspace key to delete the current template.**

5. **Enter the template symbols that you want.**

    Each symbol holds one keystroke. You can use the window that has the symbol descriptions in it to determine which symbols you want use in your template. If you're doing this for the example STATE template, then enter five !'s, like this: !!!!!. The exclamation point is the symbol that tells the template to capitalize what the user enters (which is what we want it to do). And since the STATE field is five characters long, it needs five symbols in its template to hold five possible keystrokes. Your Forms Design screen now may look something like Figure 13-4.

6. **Press Ctrl-End to save the new template.**

Now, when you use the Form screen to enter data into that field, the data will be automatically polished by the template.

You can save a form design by selecting the Save changes and exit option from the Exit menu. Or you can save it by crossing your fingers, and wishing really, really hard, but the first way is recommended.

If you're using the book's example form, save it as CustForm. Then relax for a bit. Feel yourself floating in the air. You're a feather. Go on. Float.

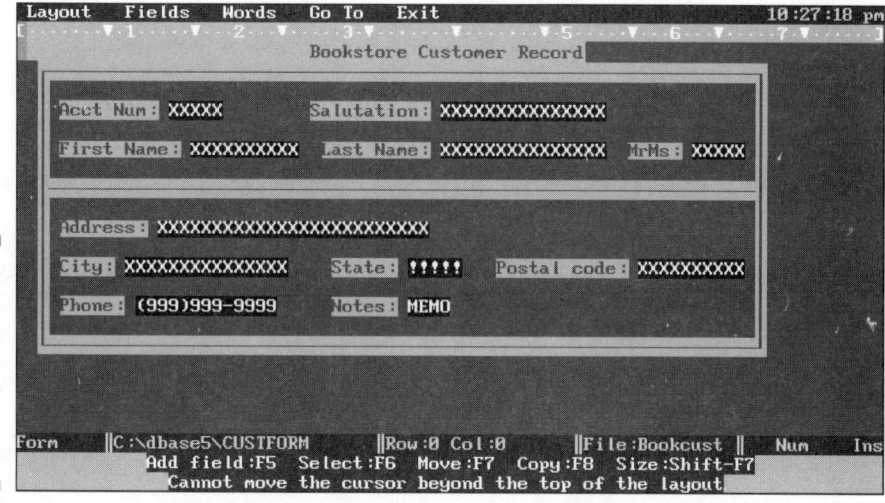

Chapter 13: Hot Stuff! Customizing Your Forms *157*

Figure 13-4: A typical Forms Design screen after changing a template.

Part III
Organizing and Printing Your Data

The 5th Wave　　　　By Rich Tennant

"MISS LAMONT, I'M FILING THE CONGREGATION UNDER 'SOULS', MY SERMONS UNDER 'GRACE' AND THE FINANCIAL CONTRIBUTIONS UNDER 'AMEN'."

In this part ...

*P*utting data into a database is one thing. Parts I and II covered all the ways to do that. Organizing data and getting it *out* of a database are something else. This part shows you how to sort the data in your database in any way you like.

This part also shows you how to print out your data: either the easiest way, with Quick Layout, or with the more sophisticated way, by using advanced report features.

Chapter 14
Sorting, Indexing, and Other Apodictic Truths

In This Chapter
- Two ways to order data
- Sorting different kinds of fields
- Sorting on more than one field at a time
- When to use indexes
- Indexing on more than one field at a time

Think about a dictionary. In fact, think about all the dictionaries you've ever seen. They all have one thing in common: they're in alphabetic order. If you're like me, you've probably spent hours wondering why all dictionaries are alphabetized. You've also probably gone for a solid week with eating nothing but Tabasco sauce, but that's another story.

The reason that all dictionaries are alphabetized is because it's much easier that way to find the word that you're looking for. If you have some idea how to spell the word, then you can flip through the pages of the dictionary, eventually narrowing your search down to the page that the word is on. Just imagine what it would be like if dictionaries weren't alphabetized. *Platypus* could come immediately after *freckle*, and just before *light bulb*. You'd never be able to find anything that you needed. The dictionary would be useless. In fact, before alphabetization was invented, many dictionary companies went bankrupt for just this reason.

In this sense, your dBASE database is much like the dictionary. It really won't do you much good unless it's in some kind of order. In this chapter, you learn about two different tools you can use to put your data in order: the *Sort* and the *Index*. If you have a dBASE table of names and addresses, like this book's example Bookcust table, you'll be able to see your records not only by the order in which they were entered, but also by last name, city, Zip code, or any other field you choose to order them by. You have the power.

Part III: Organizing and Printing Your Data

To understand the ideas in this chapter, you should know the concepts of a database (see Chapter 3) and a table (see Chapter 4). To do the exercises with the example database in the book, you need to have created the Sales table (see Chapter 11). To sort records in your own database, read this chapter to get the basic ideas. Then, use the ideas and techniques in the chapter to customize your own form.

Doing Simple Sorts

When you see the term *simple sort,* you may think of Jethro Clampett or Ernest P. Worrell. But though these fictional characters are indeed simple sorts, they're a different kind of simple sort from those you do in dBASE. In dBASE, a simple sort puts data in order by one field, such as a Sale Date field or a Last Name field. You can also sort your records with more than one field, but don't worry about that right now. It'll be covered later in the chapter.

When dBASE sorts the records in a table, it creates a totally new table with the records in the order you want. The original table isn't changed at all, as you can see in Figure 14-1.

TIP

The only type of field you *can't* use to sort your records is a memo field, because there's no way to compare memo fields to decide which should come first, which should come second, and so on.

Figure 14-1: Sorting the records in a table leaves the original table undisturbed. dBASE creates a completely new table with the records in the order you want.

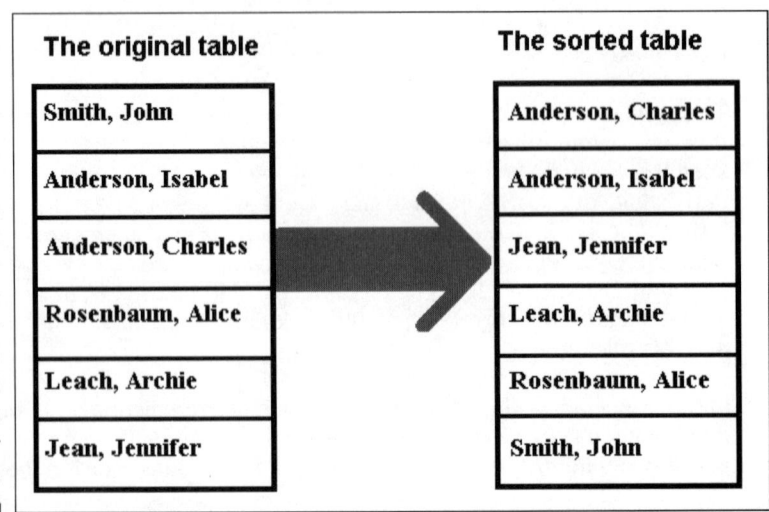

The original table	The sorted table
Smith, John	Anderson, Charles
Anderson, Isabel	Anderson, Isabel
Anderson, Charles	Jean, Jennifer
Rosenbaum, Alice	Leach, Archie
Leach, Archie	Rosenbaum, Alice
Jean, Jennifer	Smith, John

You can sort records in two directions: ascending and descending.

- An *ascending* sort puts the records in order from lowest to highest, such as A to Z, 1 to 10, and January 1, 1995, to December 31, 1995.
- A *descending* sort puts the records in order from highest to lowest, such as Z to A, 10 to 1, and December 31, 1995, to January 1, 1995.

The basic steps for sorting records

Sorting records in dBASE is no sweat. Simply open the table you want to sort, then tell dBASE which field to use for ordering the records. Just follow these steps:

1. **In the Browse screen, open the Organize menu and select Sort Database on Field List.**

    A dialog box, amazingly similar to the one in Figure 14-2, lets you tell dBASE which field you want to sort on and what kind of sort you want to do.

Sorting by ASCII

It's not usually something you need to worry about, but dBASE sorts character-type fields by what are called *ASCII codes*. Every letter, digit, punctuation mark, and other key on your keyboard has an ASCII code, which is a whole number from 0 up through 255. The codes 0 to 31 are for special characters, such as the Enter key (which is ASCII 13). The codes 32 to 127 are mostly punctuation marks, digits, and letters (uppercase letter codes are 65-90, lowercase letters are 97-122).

When you're sorting (or indexing) a table that has upper and lowercase letters, punctuation marks, digits, and so on, you occasionally need to know about the ASCII codes to predict what order the records will be in. If you do an ascending sort, for instance, the name *John* would be put before the name *john* because uppercase letters have lower ASCII codes than lowercase letters.

The reason it's not usually a problem is that names and other text items should normally be typed the same way in every record. Thus, you wouldn't have customer records with the first names JOHN, joe, jiM, JOsiaH, and so on. The reason that it sometimes IS a problem is that occasionally there might be more than one person entering data into your database. When this happens, you may have one person who likes to leave Caps Lock on all the time, and another person who has dust collecting on the Shift key. The best way to avoid this problem is to have a standard method for entering data that anyone who even breathes near the computer knows about.

And if you really *must* know, *ASCII* stands for *American Standard Code for Information Interchange*. It's designed to let different computers use the same codes for letters and other characters so that you can send data from one type of computer to another.

Part III: Organizing and Printing Your Data

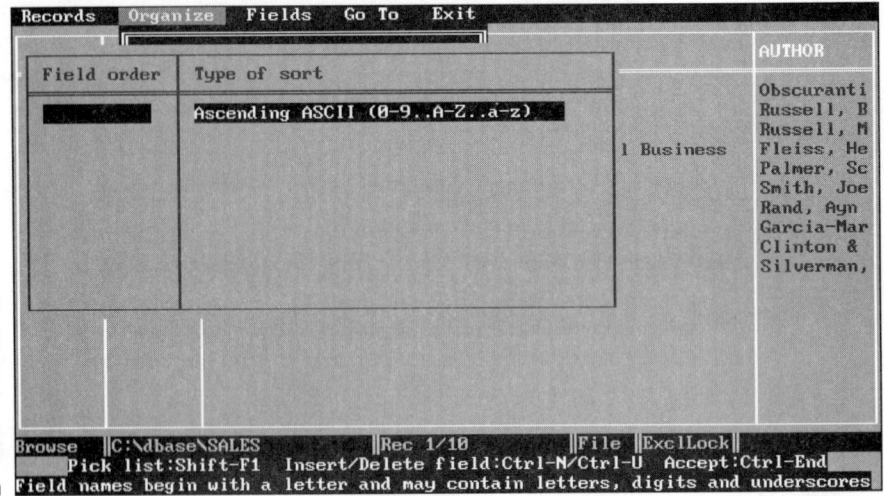

Figure 14-2: The dialog box for picking a sort field.

2. **Press Shift-F1 to see a list of the fields.**

   At the right side of your screen, dBASE shows you a list of the fields by which you can sort your records.

3. **Highlight the field you want to use in the sort and press Enter.**

   If you're using the book's example database, select the CUST_ID field. Notice that the field you select will appear under the Field order column in the Sort dialog box. If you ever make a mistake by adding the wrong field to your sort list, you can press Ctrl-U to deselect the field.

4. **Select the type of sort you want dBASE to do.**

   Press Tab to move the highlight bar to the right half of the window, then use the spacebar to cycle through the available sorting methods. There are four different kinds of sorts. dBASE briefly describes each one right there on the screen. Table 14-1 gives you an idea of what each kind of sort does.

5. **Press Ctrl-End to create the new, sorted table.**

   If you forget to specify the field you wanted to sort on, or anything else important like that, then dBASE will beep jeeringly at you and refuse to do the sort. If everything's OK, then a dialog box appears asking you to name the sorted table. If you're using the book's example table, Sales, then name the new table *Sales2*. Otherwise, type in any name you want, just so long as it follows the general rules for MS-DOS filenames (up to eight letters long with no spaces or punctuation).

6. **Enter a description for the sorted table.**

Yet another dialog box appears, asking you to describe the table. If you're using the Sales2 table, then type "The table I created while learning how to do sorts." If using your own database, then type anything you want. But don't abuse that power.

7. **Return to the Control Center.**

   Open the **E**xit menu and select **S**ave changes and exit. dBASE returns you to the Control Center.

Table 14-1   Items Sorted by the Four Kinds of Sorts

Ascending ASCII	*Ascending Dictionary*
10	10
20	20
Ark	ant
Zoo	Ark
ant	zipper
zipper	Zoo
Descending ASCII	*Descending Dictionary*
zipper	Zoo
ant	zipper
Zoo	Ark
Ark	ant
20	20
10	10

Sorting on more than one field

If you haven't done much of this sorting stuff, you probably have two questions at this point:

- What the heck is "sorting on more than one field?"
- Why the heck would any sane person do something like that, what with all the traffic jams and pollution and bad Top 40s music that's already in the world?

The answer is simple. Suppose that you sorted the records in a customer table by the customer's last name. Does that mean that all's well with the world? No.

For one thing, Pauly Shore makes a lot more money than you do. And if that isn't enough to convince you that something is seriously wrong in the universe, consider what might happen if you have several customers with the same last name. Although the records are in order by last name, they're almost certainly out of order by *first* name. In other words, you've got

Last Name	First Name
Jones	Sarah
Jones	Ed
Jones	Tim
Jones	Andy

When what you *want* is

Last Name	First Name
Jones	Andy
Jones	Ed
Jones	Sarah
Jones	Tim

That's why you often want to sort on more than one field. One-field sorts don't always organize your data as much as multiple-field sorts can. For instance, in the example above you want the customer records in order by last name. But if two or more customers have the same last name, you want *their* records in order by last name plus first name. So when you do the sort, you tell dBASE to look at both the Last Name and First Name fields.

You begin to do a multiple-field sort in exactly the same way as you do a single-field sort. The difference comes at Step 5. Just follow these steps:

1. **In the Browse screen, open the Organize menu and select Sort Database on Field List.**
2. **Press Shift-F1 to see a list of the fields.**
3. **Highlight the field you want and press Enter.**
4. **Select the type of sort you want.**

    Press the Tab key to move the highlight bar to the right half of the window, then use the spacebar to cycle through the available sorting methods.

5. **Press the down-arrow key to move the cursor to the next line.**

    Then, enter the second field you want to sort on in the same way that you entered the first field. Keep pressing the down-arrow key to add as many fields as you want (up to ten).

Chapter 14: Sorting, Indexing, and Other Apodictic Truths

6. Press Ctrl-End to create the new, sorted table.

If everything's okay, then a dialog box appears asking you to name the sorted table. Type in any name you want, just so long as it follows the general rules for MS-DOS filenames (up to eight letters long with no spaces or punctuation).

7. Enter a description for the sorted table.

Yet another dialog box appears, asking you to describe the table. Type anything you want, as long as you keep it clean.

8. Return to the Control Center.

Open the Exit menu and select **S**ave changes and exit. dBASE returns you to the Control Center.

REMEMBER: Be careful when you're entering more than one field into a sort. The order that you enter them in is the order by which dBASE will sort them. For example, if you're sorting a customer database by last name, but within each last name you want to alphabetize the first names, then you'd sort on the more important field first (the Last Name field) and on the less important field second (the First Name field). That way, the data will be *primarily* organized by last name, and it will be *secondarily* organized by first name. The First Name field will be used only if two or more people have the same last name. This rule applies for all sorts that use more than one field. dBASE will *primarily* sort the new table by the first field that you enter, then by the second field, then the third, and so on.

Sorting character fields that contain numbers

Sorting character-type fields that contain numbers, such as account numbers or Social Security numbers, is a special problem. If dBASE (or any other database manager) thinks it's dealing with text, then it will sort the numbers wrong unless you pad them with zeroes.

Here's why. Suppose that your records have a character field containing the numbers 1, 2, 3, 4, 10, and 20. A sort begins with the first "letter" of a character field — in this case, the letter is a digit. Now, the way dBASE is *supposed* to sort the numbers is

    1
    2
    3
    4
    10
    20

But remember: dBASE doesn't know these are numbers. And if they're not numbers, then the first letter of 10 is "1," while the first letter of 20 is "2." So how dBASE will *actually* sort the numbers is

1
10
2
20
3
4

There are two ways to solve this problem. The first way is to make the field a number field instead of a character field. The drawback is that number fields take more disk space than character fields, though if your database is small, it doesn't make much difference.

The second solution is to keep the field a character field but pad the numbers out to the left with zeroes. Then, dBASE sorts the numbers correctly, and you get

0001
0002
0003
0004
0010
0020

Indexing: Usually Better than Sorting

The reason we talked about sorting first is that it's easier to understand than indexing. Moreover, indexing is a special, more efficient kind of sorting — so unless you understand sorting, you can't really understand indexing.

In the non-computer world, an index usually helps you find information, as shown in Figure 14-3. The index of a book, for example, lists topics and has a page number for each topic — a kind of pointer to the place where you can read about the topic.

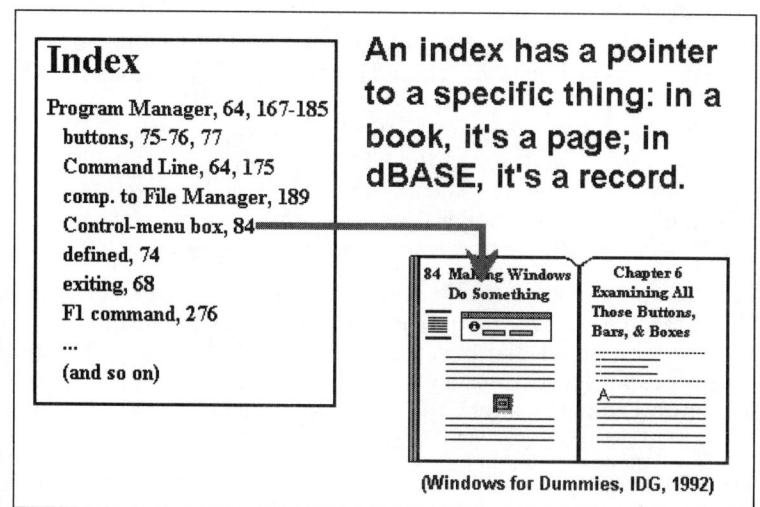

Chapter 14: Sorting, Indexing, and Other Apodictic Truths   *169*

Figure 14-3: How indexes work.

> **Index**
> Program Manager, 64, 167-185
>   buttons, 75-76, 77
>   Command Line, 64, 175
>   comp. to File Manager, 189
>   Control-menu box, 84
>   defined, 74
>   exiting, 68
>   F1 command, 276
>   ...
>   (and so on)

An index has a pointer to a specific thing: in a book, it's a page; in dBASE, it's a record.

(Windows for Dummies, IDG, 1992)

An index in dBASE works almost exactly like a computerized book index. When you tell dBASE to index a table on a certain field, you can then view the table records in order by that field. But unlike sorting, indexing doesn't physically rearrange the records in a new order, nor does it create a new, sorted version of the table. Instead, it simply *displays* the records in order by that field.

If you ever need to search for data in a particular field — such as searching for a customer's last name, or a particular account number — the search goes faster with an indexed field. When dBASE searches for a value in an indexed field, it simply looks in the index to find the location of the records that have that value.

But the biggest advantage of indexing is convenience. Because indexing doesn't physically rearrange the table's records, you can quickly switch between different "sorted" views of your data. With sorting, you have to load a completely different file every time you want to see your data in a different order. Moreover, if you add new records to a sorted table, you must re-sort the table to get the new records in their proper sorted positions. With an indexed table, dBASE updates the order automatically: you don't need to worry about it.

> **TIP**
>
> When you index a field, dBASE can find stuff in that field faster than it can in a non-indexed field. *However* — and it's a big however — in smaller databases, indexing makes very little difference. If you have only a few hundred records in a table, indexing *slightly* speeds up search operations and queries, but not enough to notice.

Stuff you need to know before you index

The exact steps of creating an index will be described a little bit later. Here are some of the basic things you should know about how indexes work in dBASE:

- To index a table, you go into the Table Design screen. That's the place where you first designed the table, remember? If you don't, zoom back to Chapter 4. You have to position the cursor in the row that has the field you want to index, and under the column that says *Indexed*, you need to put a Y. This tells dBASE to create an index for that field.

- As soon as you index a field in a table, dBASE creates a *master index file* for that table. This file holds all the indexes for all the fields in that table. The master index file has the same name as the table, but ends with the extension .MDX. Thus, if you had a table called BOOKCUST.DBF (dBASE always adds the letters .DBF to the table name), the master index file would be called BOOKCUST.MDX.

- When you open a table, the master index file is opened automatically. This is a *big* advance over older versions of dBASE, in which you had to remember to open each index file yourself. If you ever forgot to open an index file before changing the data in your table, then the index file would get out of date, and you'd have to index again.

- Within the master index file, each individual field has its own index called an *index tag*. To index your records by a particular field, you tell dBASE to make that field's *index tag* into something called the *master tag*. The field that's selected as the *master tag* is the field that dBASE uses to organize your database by first.

If indexing helps dBASE find stuff more quickly, why not just index every field? The reason is that every index you create makes dBASE do more work to manage your records, and that takes more time. If you're entering records in a table that has a *lot* of indexed fields, it can take dBASE longer to save new records because each time it saves, it has to update all the index tags in the master index file.

If a table has one indexed field, dBASE must create a new entry in the index tag every time you enter a new record. If the table has ten indexed fields, dBASE has to create *ten* new entries in *ten* different index tags for each new record. Even with a fast program like dBASE and a fast PC, the slowdown can become significant. So you shouldn't automatically index every field. If you know that you'll be searching a particular field often or that you need to use it to link up with other tables (as you'll learn in Chapter 19), indexing is a good move. Otherwise, don't do it.

Making sure that the right fields are indexed

Undoubtedly, it helps to make sure that a field is indeed indexed *before* you try to use that field's index for your database. To make sure that a field is indexed, follow these steps:

1. **From the Control Center, highlight the table you're going to index. Then press Enter.**

   A dialog box appears, asking what you want to do with the table.

2. **Select Modify Structure/Order.**

   The Table Design screen appears with the Organize menu open.

3. **Press Esc to get rid of the menu.**

   The Organize menu goes away. Notice the Index column on the far right of the table. This column is where you tell dBASE whether or not to index a field. If there's an N in the column, then the field that's on the same line as the N is not indexed. If there's a Y, then the field is indexed. If a field that you want to index has an N in the Index column, move the cursor to that N and press Y. The letter will change to a Y and the field will now be indexed. You can index any kind of field except a memo field.

   If you're using the book's example database, index the CUST_ID field.

4. **Open the Layout menu and select Save this database file structure.**

   A dialog box appears, asking you to name the table. Unless you say otherwise, dBASE saves the table under the name it already had. If you want to save the table under a different name, type the new name in the blank.

5. **Press Enter to save the table.**

6. **Press F2 to view your indexed data.**

   The Browse screen appears with the records placed in order according to the field you just indexed. Aahhhh.

Displaying your records in indexed order

Once you index the fields you want, you can use their index tags to display your table's records in order by those fields. The basic steps are as follows:

1. **Get to the Browse screen.**

2. **Open the Organize menu and select the Order Records by Index option.**

   A list of available index tags will appear.

3. Highlight the field you want to use as the master index and press Enter.

The records will be displayed in order by the field and index you selected.

> **NOTE:** As you use the arrow keys to scroll through your data, you might notice that the record numbers displayed in the Status Bar do not change in an orderly fashion. That's because the records are actually in a different order than what's on your screen. Indexing only changes the order in which your records are displayed — not their physical order in the table. That way, if you ever want to display your records in their original order, simply follow the steps above and choose *Natural order* at Step 3.

> **TIP:** It doesn't happen often, but if your master index file gets damaged somehow — maybe your electric power jumps just as you're entering a record, or your spouse has been fooling around with your PC when you *explicitly told him or her* that it was "hands off" — then your records may not display in the correct indexed order.

If your records are not displayed correctly, whether or not you blame your spouse, don't despair. Instead, press Esc to exit from the Control Center and go to the Command window. In the Command window, enter **use filename**, where *filename* is the name of the table whose index has been damaged. Then enter **reindex**. This rebuilds the index file for your table. Close the file by entering **use** all by itself, then press F2 to return to the Control Center.

Indexing on multiple fields

You'd want to index on multiple fields for the same reason you'd want to sort on multiple fields. If your customer records are in order by last name, for example, you want each group of records with the same last name to be in order by first name. If your sales records are in order by date, you might want each day's records in order by the name of the item sold, or by the dollar amount of the purchase.

Unfortunately, indexing on multiple fields isn't *quite* as easy as sorting on multiple fields. Oh, yes, it's easier than getting a straight answer out of a politician; it's easier than finding a good video on MTV; but it's still a little harder than it should be.

To do it, you need to create a new index that includes *all* the fields you want to use. If you want records in order by last name and first name, these would be the fields you use. Notice that multiple-field indexes are a lot different from the single-field indexes you create. Here, you gotta do some typing.

Chapter 14: Sorting, Indexing, and Other Apodictic Truths

So if you're adventurous, if you're pumped, if you're *ready*, here's how to do it. Just so these instructions don't get too abstract, assume that you want to index the book's example Bookcust table on last name and first name. If you're following these instructions with your own table, just make the appropriate substitutions.

1. **From the Browse screen, open the Organize menu and select Create New Index.**

   A menu box appears. The highlight is already on the choice for **Name of index**.

2. **Press Enter to name the index.**

   The cursor moves to the brackets on the right.

3. **Type a name for the index and press Enter.**

   If using the book's example database, name the index ID_PRICE.

4. **Highlight the Index Expression option and press Enter.**

   The cursor jumps over to the brackets on the right. You enter a multiple-field index by putting a plus sign (+) between the field names that you want to index on. The first field that you enter will have top priority, the second field will get second priority, the third will get third, and so on.

5. **Type the index expression that you desire, and press Enter.**

   If you're using the book's example Bookcust table, then type LNAME + FNAME. If you want a little extra help, press Shift-F1 and dBASE displays a box with a list of fields and operators you can use. (Don't worry about the operators: you only need the plus sign for this.) You select stuff in this box in the usual way: by highlighting it and pressing Enter.

6. **Move the highlight bar to the Order of Index option and press Enter.**

   Press the spacebar to cycle between Ascending and Descending order. You probably want Ascending, so select that one.

7. **Press Ctrl-End to create the index and display the records accordingly.**

   The records appear according to the index you just made. Unless, of course, they're being stubborn about it. (Just kidding. dBASE records are never stubborn. Now, dBASE users, that's another story. . . .)

> **TIP**
>
> Indexes are always sorted according to the ASCII standard of sorting. That's the kind of sort described earlier in this chapter where uppercase letters come before lowercase letters. In an ASCII sort, for example, Z would actually be listed *before* a. Can you take the insanity? To get around this little problem, you can trick dBASE into using what's called the Dictionary standard of sorting. Just add the function UPPER( ) to the field name you want to index. For example, UPPER(LNAME) + UPPER(FNAME) is a typical expression that can be used to index people's last and first names by the Dictionary standard.

You can also use this feature if you've been entering data into your database in lowercase letters, while Sally down the hall has been using all uppercase letters. Normally, this would cause a big problem when you index. With the UPPER( ) command, however, the data you entered would be temporarily converted to uppercase so that it would be consistent with Sally's data.

Your eyes look tired. Why don't you go take a break? Do some Thighmaster for awhile. You deserve it. But stay tuned. Next chapter: easy ways to print out reports of your data. Or at least they're easy if you have a printer. That would help.

Chapter 15
Organizing Stuff with dBASE's DOS Utilities

In This Chapter
- The basics of dBASE's DOS utilities
- Using the utilities to keep your files organized
- A guide to dBASE file extensions

*I*f you are reading the chapters of this book in order, then you've probably created a lot of new files on your hard disk by now. For example, if you've done ALL of the exercises for the book's example *Caveat Emptor* database, then you have created at least six new files. This rapid creation of files can become a real problem in dBASE. If you're not careful, you can quickly wind up with three or four databases that have six or more files in each. That many files can be quite difficult to search through. If you want to erase, edit, move, or do anything else to any particular file, then you have to remember the file's name and change the file in the desired way from DOS. That causes a second problem: dBASE takes a decent amount time just for your computer to load it. If you need to go back to DOS every time you want to manipulate a file, then you'll be wasting a lot of time due to the load-up time required by dBASE.

An easy way around these problems is simply to do your DOS commands directly from within dBASE. DOS commands within dBASE, you ask? Yep. And in fact, in many cases, the DOS functions that you do will be easier to execute in dBASE than they are in DOS. This chapter takes you through the DOS features that are available from within dBASE, and shows you what each can be used for.

To understand the basic ideas in this chapter, you should have:

- Some knowledge of basic MS-DOS workings such as directories, file extensions, etc. If you're fuzzy on DOS, check out IDG's *DOS For Dummies*.
- An idea of the basic parts of a database, like the table (see Chapter 4) and the form (see Chapter 9).

The Basics of dBASE's DOS Utilities

dBASE's DOS utilities come in two basic groups: the preprogrammed DOS commands and the DOS shell. Each of these groups has its advantages and disadvantages.

dBASE's preprogrammed DOS commands

dBASE comes with a "preprogrammed" list of a few of the most common file management commands: delete, copy, move, rename, view, and edit. The preprogrammed commands are useful because they're fast, they can be executed from menus on-screen, and they make use of powerful marking techniques that we talk about later. The biggest disadvantage to preprogrammed commands is that *six commands* are available. In other words, if you want to execute a DOS command that isn't one of the preprogrammed six, then you're just out of luck. Unless....

The DOS shell

The DOS shell (yes, you can hear the ocean in it) is the comprehensive part of the DOS utilities. If the command that you want to execute isn't available from the preprogrammed command list, then you can execute it from the DOS shell. The biggest advantage of the shell is that it allows you to execute all DOS commands without having to leave dBASE. That way, you can get back to what you were working on relatively quickly. The DOS shell has two basic tools: Perform DOS command, and Go to DOS. We describe both a little later in the chapter.

Catalogs vs. utilities

Why do you need DOS to manage your database files? Isn't that what catalogs are for anyway? No. Catalogs are tools that dBASE uses to help you keep track of which files go with which database. However, a catalog only has an effect while you're using it inside of dBASE. It has absolutely no effect on the actual physical state of your files on your hard disk. That means that you may have files from several different databases, all floating around in the same directory (dBASE's main directory). This can be hazardous to your data. Suppose that one of your catalog files becomes corrupted. That could lead to serious errors in your data if all of your data files are kept in the same directory.

Chapter 15: Organizing Stuff with dBASE's DOS Utilities   *177*

How to Use the Utilities

This section walks you through the hands-on, down-and-dirty part of using the DOS utilities. Don't be nervous, they can smell that. These are the absolute, need-to-know things that you indeed need to know before you try to use any of the DOS utilities. If you don't know them, you won't get the full pleasure and joy that's been associated with DOS utilities for generations.

The DOS utilities screen

To reach the DOS utilities screen, simply select the DOS utilities option from the Tools menu in the Control Center. dBASE shows you the utilities screen, which looks amazingly like Figure 15-1. Notice the Status Bar at the bottom of the screen. That's where dBASE gives you important on-screen information about the operation that is currently highlighted on the screen.

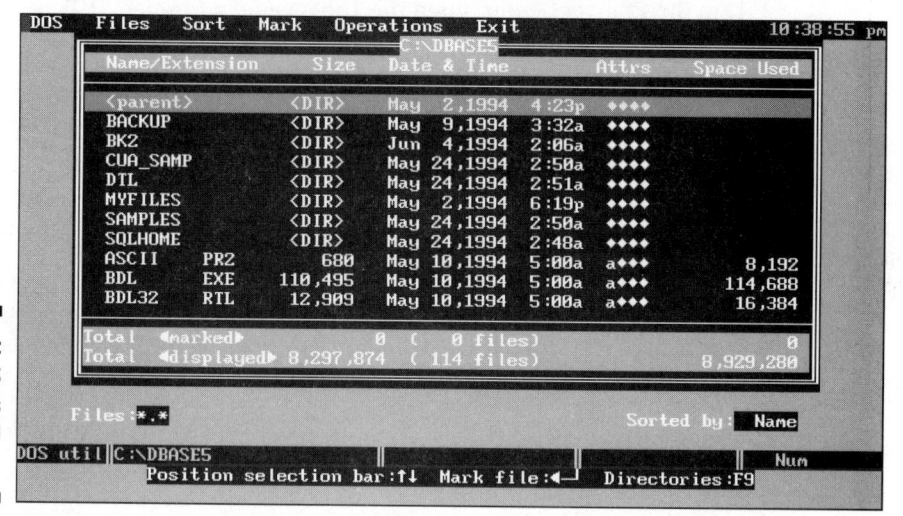

Figure 15-1: The DOS utilities screen in all its glory.

Also, notice the *Files:* and *Sorted by:* blocks located halfway down, on the left and right sides of the screen, respectively. The Files: block shows what a file has to be in order for it to be displayed on the screen. Files: is usually set to *.* in order to display all of the files in the current directory, but you can make it whatever you want. Sorted by: tells you the order that files on the screen are currently being displayed by (name, date, extension, or size). We talk more about these features later on in the chapter.

How to mark a file and why you'd want to

To *mark* a file means to tell the computer to make a note to itself that says "this file is important." Marking a file is a useful feature of many programs because it allows you to go through a long list of files and "mark" only the ones that you want the computer to act on. You can then give the computer a command that will affect all of the marked files. If you don't use marking, you have to issue the command for every file that you want the action to be performed on. With 50 files, that could take awhile.

Marking a file has come a long way. Back in the dark ages of computers, marking a file meant that the file's time on this Earth was short. If you marked it, you were going to delete it. In these modern times, however, you can mark a file for just about anything. Sure there's still the purpose of deleting it, but you can also mark files for renaming, copying, moving, or even just for the fun of it. Mark it because it smells bad, get crazy. To mark a file with dBASE's DOS utilities, follow these steps:

1. **In the Control Center, open the Tools menu and select DOS utilities.**

    The DOS utilities screen appears.

2. **Highlight the file(s) that you want to mark and press Enter.**

    A small arrow appears to the left of the file, and the *Total marked:* line near the middle of the screen changes to show the number of files marked (see Figure 15-2). If the file that you want to mark is in a different directory from the one that's currently displayed, try selecting <parent> in the file list. That moves you back one directory. You can then move into the subdirectory that has the file you want to mark. If you accidentally mark the wrong file, simply highlight it and press Enter again to unmark it. You can mark all of the files in a directory by opening the Mark menu and selecting Mark all.

Deleting a File

Files don't mind when they're deleted. It's like the Place of Happy Relief to them. In fact, that's why it's just so darn easy (often far too easy) to delete them. You can delete files from everywhere. Deleting a file is probably the most common thing that you will do with your DOS utilities. Or, at least, it will have become the most common after you've accidentally deleted every file on your hard disk — so be careful when you delete stuff. You can't always get it back. Normally, you'll delete file(s) in one of two ways:

- Delete a single file.
- Delete marked files.

Chapter 15: Organizing Stuff with dBASE's DOS Utilities *179*

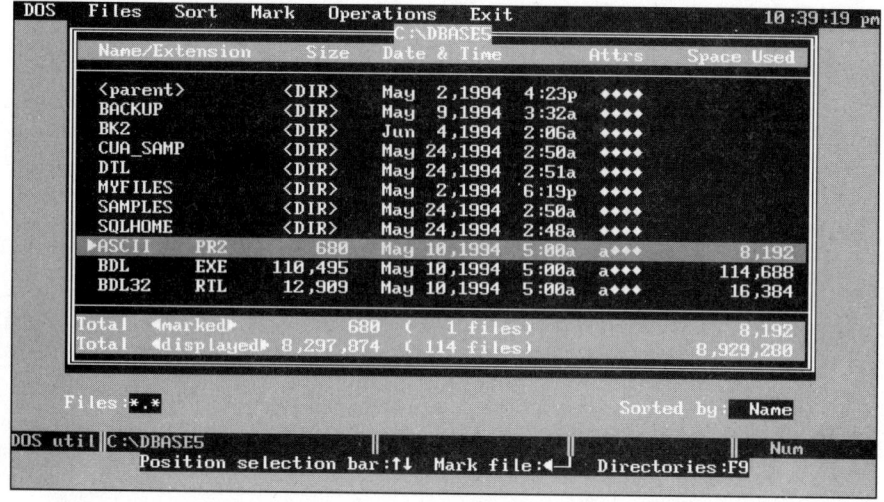

Figure 15-2:
The DOS utilities screen with the file ASCII.PR2 marked.

To use the DOS utilities screen to delete a single file from your disk, follow these steps:

1. **Move the highlight bar to the file you want to delete.**
2. **Select the Delete option from the Operations menu.**

    A submenu appears in the upper part of the screen.

3. **Select Single File.**

    dBASE prompts you to proceed if you want to delete the file or cancel if you don't.

4. **If you're sure that you want to delete the file, select Proceed.**

    The file is deleted from your disk. It also disappears from the file list on the screen.

Deleting marked files

To delete more than one file from the DOS utilities screen, follow these steps:

1. **Mark the files that you want to delete.**

    Mark the files you want to delete by highlighting them and pressing Enter (if you're not sure how this works, then check out the section on "How to mark a file and why you'd want to"). If you're deleting all of the files displayed in the directory, then just make sure that the correct directory is displayed on the screen. You can switch to a different directory by selecting Change drive: directory from the Files menu, and entering the name of the directory you want to delete.

2. **Select the Delete option from the Operations menu.**

   A submenu appears.

3. **Select the kind of delete you want to perform.**

   If deleting marked files, then select Marked Files. If deleting an entire directory, select Displayed Files.

   The Displayed Files option is misleading. If you select this option, it will delete *all of the files* in the currently displayed directory — not just the files that are physically visible on the screen.

   dBASE prompts you to proceed if you want to delete the files or cancel if you don't (see Figure 15-3). Stop and think carefully before deleting the files. Are all the desired files marked? Are *only* the desired files marked? Are you *sure* that you want to delete them?

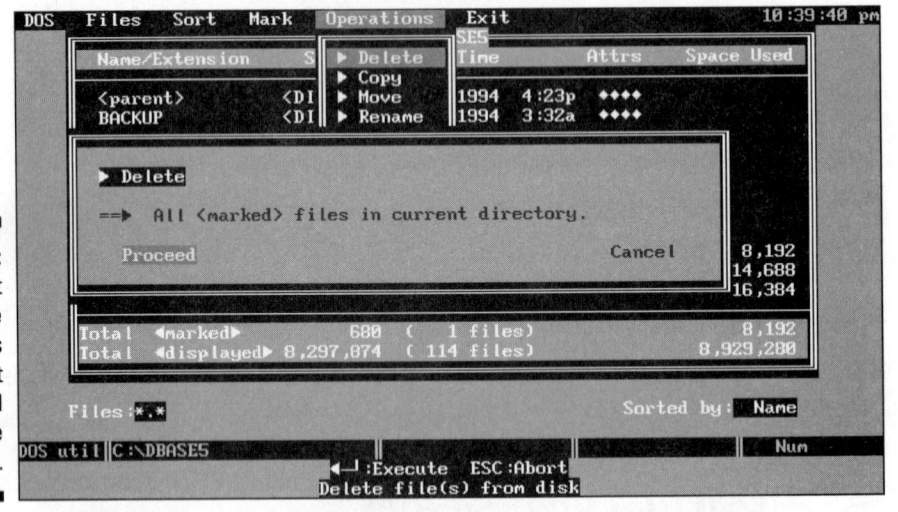

Figure 15-3: The prompt where dBASE asks if you want to proceed to delete the files.

4. **If you're sure that you want to delete the files, then select Proceed. Otherwise choose Cancel.**

   The files will be deleted from your disk and will disappear from the file list on the screen.

Moving and copying a file

Moving and *copying* files do basically the same thing: create a new file that's a copy of a previously existing file. The difference is that moving erases the already-existing file, while copying leaves it alone. This section covers moving and copying at the same time, so be sure to keep that difference in mind when you're choosing whether to move a file or to copy it. To move/copy a file (or files) follow these steps:

1. **Mark the file(s) you want to move/copy.**

   You can mark the files by highlighting them and pressing enter. An arrow appears to the left of the file to tell you it's been marked.

2. **Open the Operations menu and choose Move or Copy.**

   As you may have guessed, choose Move if you want to move files or Copy if you want to copy them. dBASE prompts you for the directory and filename that you want to move or copy the marked files to (see Figure 15-4).

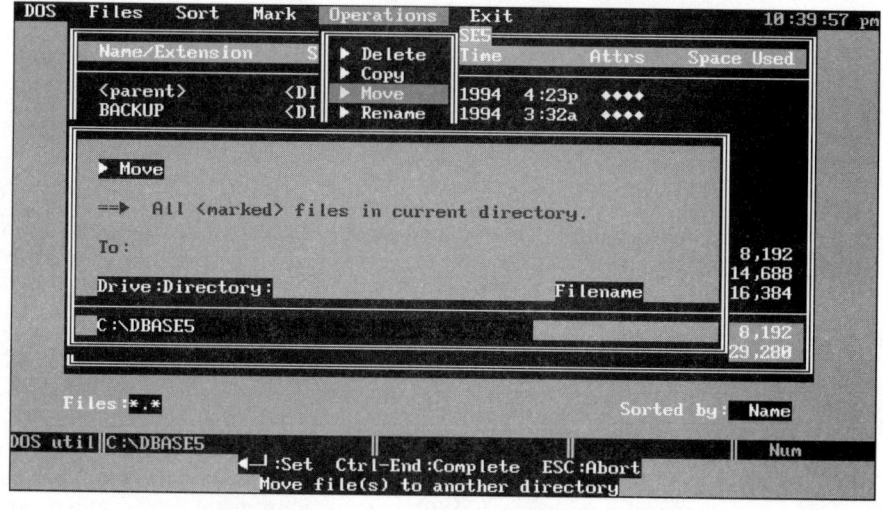

Figure 15-4: dBASE prompts you to enter the directory and file you want to move/copy to.

3. **Select the directory that you want to move or copy the marked file(s) to.**

   To do this, type the name of the directory you want into the Drive: Directory: blank near the bottom of the dialog box, and press Enter. The cursor will move to the Filename blank on the right.

4. **In the Filename blank, type the name for the new (copied or moved) file.**

Part III: Organizing and Printing Your Data

You can enter any standard MS-DOS filename, and you can even use wild cards for moving/copying more than one file. For example, if you enter ***.*** into the Filename blank, then the file(s) you marked will be copied with the same names that they currently have. To contrast, if you enter ***.jjj** into the Filename blank, then all of the files you move/copy will be given the extension .jjj. Or if you enter **test.***, then all of the files that you move/copy will have the filename "test.", and whatever extensions they originally had.

5. **Press Ctrl-End to move/copy the files.**

   Your marked files will be moved/copied. If you change your mind, press Esc to cancel the operation.

Renaming a file

Renaming a file works just like moving a file, except that you can put a moved file into any directory that you want, while a renamed file will only be saved to the same directory that the original file is already in.

On the Menus: Other Important File Utilities

The preprogrammed commands and the DOS shell are the most important DOS file management utilities in dBASE. However, the dBASE File Manager has other features that can help you make sense of your files. The best way to learn about these is to look at them menu by menu.

The DOS menu

Normally, if you want to do stuff in MS-DOS (the software that runs your PC while you're working in dBASE), you just shut down dBASE and exit to the C:\ prompt. Then you can change directories, rename files, and use weird DOS commands like ATTRIB and MODE to your heart's content. However, you don't need to quit dBASE to do DOS commands. The DOS menu lets you do stuff in MS-DOS without quitting dBASE:

- ✔ **Perform DOS command:** Lets you do a single DOS command quickly, from within the dBASE screen.

- **Go to DOS:** Temporarily suspends dBASE and displays a blank screen (called a DOS window) with the DOS C:\prompt. Then, you can enter as many DOS commands as you like. To return to dBASE, type **exit** and press Enter.

- **Set default directory:** Lets you set the disk directory that dBASE uses automatically unless you say otherwise. The default directory is fully explained in Chapter 22.

If you're running dBASE inside Microsoft Windows, be very, *very* careful when entering DOS commands, especially when using the Go to DOS menu choice. Microsoft Windows expects to have full control of your PC. If you interfere with that control by something you do in a DOS window, your PC may crash and you may lose at least some of your data. If you want to be completely safe, just don't use DOS commands when you're running dBASE under Windows.

The Files menu

The Files menu lets you control how files and directories are displayed in the dBASE File Manager. Its menu choices are:

- **Change drive/directory:** Lets you display files in a different directory or on a different disk drive.

- **Display only:** Lets you tell dBASE to display only certain files. For example, to display all files whose names begin with the letter 's', press Enter at this menu choice. Then type **s*.*** (an 's', followed by an asterisk, a period, and an asterisk) and press Enter. The dBASE File Manager then displays only those filenames that begin with 's.' The other files are still there, just hidden. To see all files ending in .DBF (that is, all the table files in the directory), you enter ***.dbf** and, to go back to displaying all the files, you enter ***.***. (Don't type the final period.)

In the Display only menu choice, the asterisk is what's called a *wild card*, because it stands for anything at all.

The Sort menu

The Sort menu lets you control the order in which the dBASE File Manager displays your files. The options are **N**ame (display files in order by their names), **E**xtension (by the file type, such as .DBF, .QBE, etc.), **D**ate & Time (by the date and time the file was last changed), and **S**ize (by the amount of space the file takes up on your disk).

To choose a particular sorting option, just highlight the option in the menu and press Enter. The word ON appears next to the option.

The Mark menu

No, this has nothing to do with the second of the synoptic gospels. The Mark menu lets you mark groups of your files for doing other things. For example, if you want to move all your table files to a different directory, you just mark all the files ending in .DBF, then use the **Operations** menu to move them. The choices are:

- **Mark all:** Marks all files that are currently displayed. If you previously used the **Files** menu to display only certain files, only these files will be marked.
- **Unmark all:** Unmarks all files that are currently marked.
- **Reverse marks:** Marks all files that are unmarked and removes the marks from all files that are currently marked.

The Operations menu

The **Operations** menu lets you do, well, *operations* on the files displayed in the File Manager. Its menu choices are:

- **Delete:** Lets you delete one or more files. When you press Enter, you get a submenu that lets you select a single file, all marked files, or all displayed files.
- **Copy:** Lets you copy one or more files. When you press Enter, you get a submenu that lets you select a single file, all marked files, or all displayed files.
- **Move:** Lets you move one or more files. When you press Enter, you get a submenu that lets you select a single file, all marked files, or all displayed files.
- **Rename:** Lets you rename one or more files. When you press Enter, you get a submenu that lets you select a single file, all marked files, or all displayed files.
- **View:** Lets you view the contents of a file.
- **Edit:** Lets you edit a file. It works *only* with text files (files with words in them), not with tables or other kinds of dBASE files.

The Exit menu

This menu has only one job: it takes you back to the dBASE Control Center.

A Guide to dBASE File Extensions

dBASE adds extensions for each of its files that tell you what kind of file each file is. Table 15-1 decodes these extensions to help you sift through the vast multitudes of dBASE files. As a refresher, extensions are the last three letters of a filename. They come after the period. For example, in BOOKCUST.DBF, the .DBF is the extension.

Table 15-1	Decoding dBASE Extensions
If the Extension Is This	The File Is This
.DBF	The data for your database.
.QBE	A saved query.
.UPD	A program that updates a query (usually the query with the same filename).
.FMT	A user-made form for data entry.
.SCR	A form design, that is used to *create* forms for data entry.
.FRG	A saved report.
.LBL	A saved mailing label layout.
.PRG	A user-created dBASE application.

That's all there is to organizing your files, so take a break. Learn to Lambada. Or to speak Swahili. Or do other interesting things.

Chapter 16
Creating Simple Reports with dBASE

In This Chapter
▶ What are reports?
▶ Creating a row-and-column report
▶ Changing column names and other formatting tricks
▶ Saving and printing a report

*H*ave you ever noticed that the word *report* almost always seems to mean something bad? There's the report *card,* which usually means no TV for a month; the *credit* report, which recounts in loving detail the $11.75 dry cleaning bill you forgot to pay six years ago; the *gunshot* report, which you usually hear a split-second after you accidentally propel a bullet through your foot; and, of course, the ever-popular *tax* report, by which you render unto Caesar everything you earned since his last April 15 payday.

The good news is that in dBASE *report* means something *good.* A report is a printout of your database data. It can be plain or fancy. It can have all your data or just some of it. It can be grouped and organized, include totals and summaries, use boldface type and other printing effects — or not. You can have it any way you want it. And the *great* news is that dBASE makes it easy for you to create these reports.

Here are some examples of reports you can produce from the example Caveat Emptor bookstore database:

✔ A name, address, and phone number list of all customers

✔ A list of all sales for a given month, with sales broken down by state

✔ A customer list that includes the items each customer purchased and the total amount spent by each customer

✔ A summary of sales for the entire year, with revenues broken down by quarter

Before you can create a report, you need to have

- ✔ An understanding of basic database concepts like *catalog*, *table*, and *record* (see Chapter 4).
- ✔ Created a table (see Chapter 4) and put some data in it (see Chapter 5).
- ✔ Taken a shower. You've been in front of the computer for far too long. Your friends are starting to complain.

To create a report for your own real-life database, just read this chapter to get the basic ideas. To use the book's example database, you need to have created the Bookcust table (see Chapter 4) and put data in it (see Chapter 5).

Different Kinds of Reports

All the different variations of reports really boil down to two main categories. First, you can create a *formal report*. A formal report is what you'd normally think of as a snazzy business report. It can present your database information in rows and columns, and include page numbers, footers, totals, and so on. The report doesn't have to use a row-and-column format: if you're ambitious, you can hand-craft a different layout.

Second, you can create a *special-purpose report*. This type of report lets you create mailing labels and form letters.

In this chapter, you learn how to create formal reports. You learn about form letters in Chapter 17 and mailing labels in Chapter 18.

> For most of the exercises in this chapter, you may want to use your printer. Make sure that your printer is turned on, has plenty of paper, and is ready to print. If you see the word *online* (or *select*) somewhere on the front of the printer, the little light next to it should be turned on — it means that the printer is ready to go.

Creating a Simple Report

dBASE comes with an extremely useful report tool called the Quick Layout. A Quick Layout's basic job is to take any table or query that you throw at it, and convert it into a row-and-column report. All you do then is a little bit of tweaking, and you're set.

Chapter 16: Creating Simple Reports with dBASE 189

Creating a report with a Quick Layout is extremely easy. To prove it to yourself, follow these steps to create one:

1. **Start dBASE and get to the Control Center.**
2. **In the Data panel, highlight the table you want and press Enter.**

   dBASE asks what you want to do with the table.

3. **Select Use file.**

   The file you select is open for use.

4. **In the Report panel, highlight** <create> **and press Enter.**

   The Report Design screen appears, as shown in Figure 16-1. The Layout menu is open with Quick layouts already highlighted.

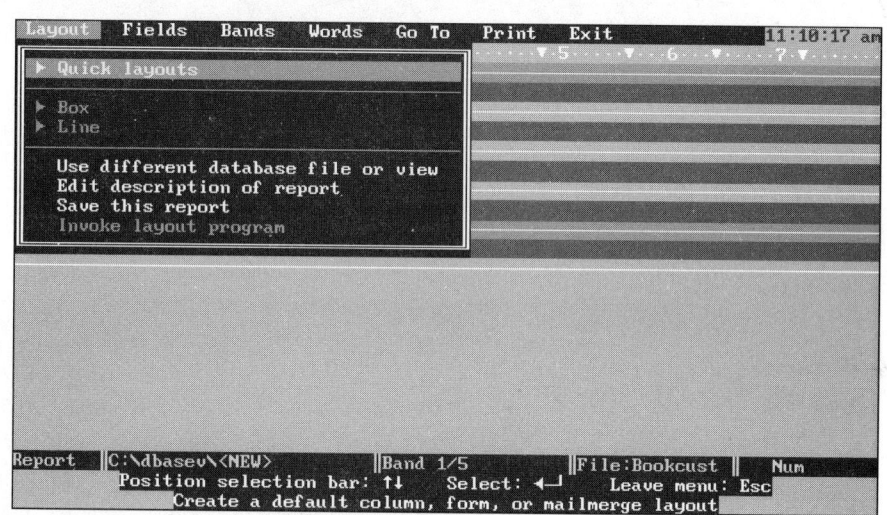

Figure 16-1: The Report Design screen.

5. **Press Enter to select Quick layouts.**

   dBASE displays a submenu asking which report format you want to use.

6. **Select Column layout.**

   The screen will look somewhat cryptic, similar to Figure 16-2. Don't worry about the screen right now, we'll explain it in just a minute.

7. **Open the Print menu and select View report on screen.**

   dBASE displays your report on-screen, as shown in Figure 16-3. You can move down through the report by pressing the spacebar.

Part III: Organizing and Printing Your Data

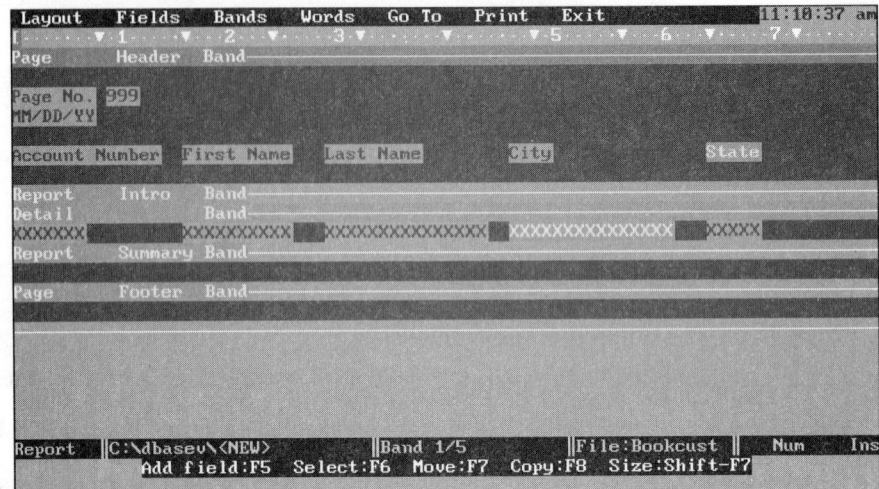

Figure 16-2: The Column Layout report.

> **NOTE:** In dBASE, every three computer screens of data equal one printed page of data. Other than that, a printed report will look the same as it does on the screen.

   8. **Press Esc to return to the report screen.**

Figure 16-3: A Quick Report for the Bookcust table as seen in print preview. Fortunately, it looks a lot better when it's actually printed.

   9. **To print the report, open the Print menu and select Begin printing.**

   dBASE sends the report to your printer. If your printer isn't printing, and you're sure that it's connected properly and turned on, then select the

Destination option from the Print menu, and make sure that it says Printer. If it says File, press Enter to change it to Printer.

10. **Select the Save this report option from the Layout menu.**

    A dialog box appears, asking you to name the report's layout.

11. **Type a name for the report's layout and press Enter.**

    The name you type will be a DOS filename, so it must follow the rules about eight letters or less, no spaces, and no punctuation except underscores. If you saved your report data to a disk file instead of printing it, then dBASE will also prompt you with a second dialog box. Don't worry about that now, just press Enter to accept the default.

> **TIP:** It's a good idea to save a report layout once you've created it. That way, if you need to print a similar report again (for example, a weekly sales report), you already have the report form set up. All you have to do is enter the new data into your table and then print it.

What are bands and what are they good for?

Bands are those weird things that you see on the screen when you create the report. A band is what dBASE uses to show you nicely everything that's going into your report. To illustrate why bands are needed, just hold a standard piece of printer paper next to your monitor. Unless your monitor is extremely large, you notice that the paper is considerably taller than the screen. Obviously, this size difference causes a problem for dBASE when it's trying to show you on your monitor what your printed paper will look like. To solve this problem, dBASE breaks up the report layout into sections, called bands, which it can then display on your screen. All you have to do is decide what kinds of information you want to have in each band, and you'll be set.

The different things that you can put in a band are

- ✔ Text that you can type right in from the keyboard (such as a form letter)
- ✔ Fields from the database you were working on when you opened the Report screen
- ✔ Fields that you create from within the Report screen that do math problems and hold the results
- ✔ Lines and other drawing objects that can make your report look much nicer

dBASE comes with five bands that you can put stuff into. Each band starts where the band's name is written and continues downward to the horizontal line that is immediately underneath the band's name (see Figure 16-4).

Part III: Organizing and Printing Your Data

The five bands of a simple dBASE report are

- **Page Header Band:** This band is at the top of the page. It usually contains the date, the name of the report, the names of the data columns, and the page number.
- **Report Intro Band:** This band usually holds some explanatory information that is needed for a reader to understand the report.
- **Detail Band:** This is where the database's actual data appears.
- **Report Summary Band:** This band holds calculated fields for totals, summaries, and other ending information.
- **Page Footer Band:** The Page Footer Band is similar to the Page Header Band, except that it's at the bottom of the page instead of the top.

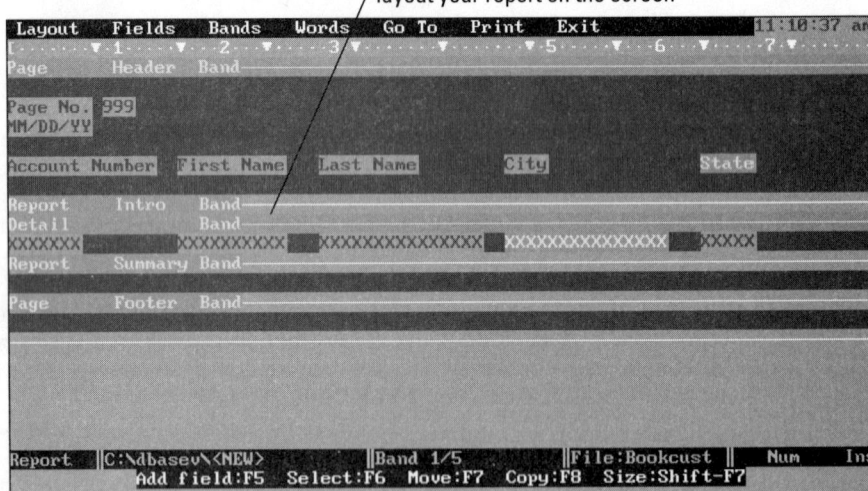

Figure 16-4: A dBASE band.

A band used by dBASE to help layout your report on the screen

> If you don't need all of the bands for a particular report, you can turn any band "off" by moving the cursor onto it and pressing Enter. The band will still be displayed on the screen, but you won't be able to use it. If you change your mind, you can turn it back "on" by moving to it again and pressing Enter. Turning off bands you don't need may help you make sure that you're putting the correct data into the correct band.

By putting lines, text, and calculations into the various bands, you can create some slick reports. The exact procedures for how to do this will be covered in Chapter 20.

Chapter 16: Creating Simple Reports with dBASE   193

What are all those Xs and 9s on my screen?

Those Xs and 9s on your screen are called place holders. dBASE uses them as symbols that show you where your data is going to be put. Each series of Xs or 9s represents a field from your table. There are quite a few place holders other than X or 9 as well, but X and 9 are by far the most common, so don't worry about the others right now. They don't like the spotlight anyway. Xs represent text, and 9s represent numbers. That's all you need to know at the moment.

Changing the Look of Your Report

You can do several things to make your report more clear without doing any major band work. Here are a few tricks that are usually quick and easy to do, yet have a significant impact on the way your report looks. Just remember that the easier your report is to understand, the better your report will be, and the bigger your promotion will be.

Undeleting and deleting columns

Believe it or not, most of your database will probably be useless to you much of the time. Even if you're an expert databaser and you're working with the simplest database in the world, you will someday need to do a report using only a few of the fields in your database. So you'll want to delete some columns. Fortunately, like most things in the computer world, deleting a column is easy. Unfortunately, it's far too easy. In fact, it's so easy that this section will start by showing you how to add a deleted field back to a report. Just follow these steps to add a field you've accidentally deleted:

1. **Move the cursor to the screen position that it was at when you deleted the field.**

    If you've been holding your breath since you deleted the field and you haven't touched the keyboard at all, then you're already in the right place.

    If you have moved the cursor, do your best to put it back where it was. It doesn't have to be perfect.

    If you have no idea where the cursor was, scream. Then, look for the column name that goes with the field. For example, if you see the CUST_ID column name and the field that you're trying to add is the CUST_ID field, then it's a good bet you should put the CUST_ID field under the CUST_ID column name. Remember, though, that the CUST_ID column name is in the Header Band. The cursor should be in the Detail Band underneath the

CUST_ID column name before you add the field. If you've accidentally erased the column name, too, and thus have no idea where the field was before it was deleted, then just put the field anywhere within the Detail Band.

2. **Open the Fields menu and select the Add field option.**

   A window appears with a pick list of the available fields.

3. **Highlight the field you just deleted and press Enter.**

   A menu appears on the screen, asking you to enter the field's options. You can use this menu to resize the field's template, or change the way it will print. For now, though, don't worry about the options. You can always change them later with Modify field in the Fields menu.

4. **Press Ctrl-End to accept the default options.**

   The field's place holders appear on the screen.

Now that you know how to bring back the column that you delete accidentally, you can delete one on purpose. Follow these steps to delete a field:

1. **Open the Fields menu and select Remove Field.**

   A window appears with a pick list of the fields you can delete.

2. **Highlight the field you want to remove and press Enter.**

   The field magically disappears from the report. You can repeat the procedure to delete more fields. And like most other display tools in dBASE, removing a field from a report does *not* delete the field from your database. The field will still be nice and cozy on your hard disk. So delete away. You can always add the fields again. If you're using the book's example Bookcust database, then delete the ADDRESS, MRMS, SALUTATION, ZIP, and NOTES fields.

3. **Move the cursor to the Header Band and delete the column name(s) that matches the field(s) you just deleted.**

   Use the standard editing keys (like Backspace and Delete) to erase the column name.

Changing column names

To the average person, the term CUST_ID may not mean much. However, to that same average person, the concept of an Account Number is easily understood. So dBASE allows you to change the names of your columns from the standard field names (which can sometimes be rather cryptic) to something that's more easily understood. To change the column name(s) of a report, simply follow these steps:

1. **Load the report layout that you want to change into the Report Design screen.**

   If you haven't created the report layout yet, you may want to check out the section above on "Creating a Simple Report." If you're loading a saved report, highlight it in the Report column of the Control Center and press Enter. Then select Modify Layout in the box that appears.

2. **Move the cursor to the column name you want to change and use the standard editing keys (Backspace, Delete, and so on) to change the name.**

   If you're using the book's example database Bookcust, then change the CUST_ID field to Account Number, the FNAME field to First Name, the LNAME field to Last Name, the STATE field to State, and the CITY field to City. You can now view, print, or save the report as you normally would. The column names will be changed to the text that you entered.

Changing column widths

If you have problems fitting all of the report's fields onto paper or the screen, you may want to try resizing the column widths. It takes several steps to resize a column width, but the result can be well worth the effort. Here are the steps:

1. **From the Report Design screen, move the cursor down into the Detail Band.**

   Remember, the Detail Band is the band that holds your actual data. The Xs and 9s in the band are place holders. They hold the place where your data will go (Xs hold characters, and 9s hold numbers). You can shrink or enlarge a column width by adding or subtracting Xs or 9s.

   Resizing the column width has no effect on the data that goes in the column. All the data is still safely in your database. However, be careful not too shrink a column's width too much. If you make a column too small, some of the bigger records in your database won't fit, and some of your data will get cut off.

2. **Within the Detail Band, move the cursor onto the series of Xs or 9s that serve as place holders for the field you want to resize.**

   You can estimate which series of Xs or 9s goes with which field by looking at the Header Band and seeing which field name is above the series. To make sure that you have the correct series, move the cursor onto the series and look at the Status Bar near the bottom of the screen (see Figure 16-5). The Status Bar will tell you which field the series goes with. If you're using the example Bookcust database, then move the cursor to the City field.

Part III: Organizing and Printing Your Data

Figure 16-5: The Status Bar displaying information about a field.

The Status Bar

3. **Open the Fields menu and select the Modify Field option.**

   A window appears with a pick list for you to choose from.

4. **Highlight the field you want to resize and press Enter.**

   A box appears with several options.

5. **Highlight the Template option and press Enter.**

   A window appears, asking you to make the column width the size that you want. At the bottom of the window is a list of possible place holders that you can put into the field. It's usually a good idea to stick with the more common ones like X or 9.

6. **Add or Subtract Xs and 9s as you see fit.**

   Use the standard editing keys (Backspace, Delete, and so forth) to change the number of Xs or 9s. The number of Xs or 9s that you include in your field is the number of spaces that the field will be able to display. If you're using the Bookcust table, subtract 4 Xs from the City field by pressing Delete.

   The column length will now be changed to match the number of place holders that you entered.

   Keep in mind that resizing may be completely useless if you're not careful. If the field you resize has a column name that's longer than the number of place holders you enter, then dBASE will still need to make the column wide enough to fit the column name. Suppose, for example, that you have a field that holds three characters. If the column name for that field (in the Header Band) is ten characters long, then dBASE will still print out the entire field at a width of ten characters. To fix this, change the column name to something shorter (the procedure is described in the section "Changing column names").

Saving and Printing Your Report

Yes, it's fun just looking at a report on your monitor, but eventually you'll probably need to print it out. You'll also want to save your report layout, so that the next time you need to print out your data, you won't have to create the report layout all over again.

Saving a report layout

To save a report layout, follow these steps:

1. **Open the Layout menu and select Save This Report.**

   A dialog box appears, asking you to enter a filename.

2. **Enter a filename that conforms to MS-DOS rules for filenames.**

   The name can have no more than eight letters, and cannot include spaces or punctuation except for underscores.

Opening a saved report

To open a report that you've already saved, follow these steps:

1. **Get to the Control Screen.**

   You can do so by starting dBASE and pressing F2.

2. **Highlight the report's name under the Reports column and press Enter.**

   A dialog box appears, asking what you want to do with the report.

3. **Select the Modify Layout option from the dialog box.**

   The Report Design screen appears in all its glory, with your report already loaded.

Printing a report

You can print out a report easily from either the Control Center or the Report Design screen. The menus and commands associated with printing are the same for either screen.

To get to the print menu from the Report Design screen,

1. **Open the Print menu by pressing Alt-P.**

   The Print menu appears.

To get to the print menu from the Control Center,

1. **Highlight the report you want to print in the Report Column and press Enter.**

   A dialog box appears, asking what you want to do with the report.

2. **Select the Print Report option.**

   The Print menu appears.

From the Print menu, follow these steps to print your report:

1. **Select the Begin Printing option.**

   If the printer doesn't start printing, then give it a minute. If it still doesn't start printing, then give it another minute. If (after the first few minutes) it still doesn't start printing, and you're sure that it's connected properly, and turned on, then you might need to change the destination of the report.

2. **To change the destination of the report, select the Destination option from the Print menu.**

   A submenu appears with various destination options. Check the Write To part of the submenu, and make sure that it says Printer and not File. If it says File, change it to Printer.

3. **To change the Write To part of the submenu, highlight it and press Enter.**

   The Write To will change to whatever it wasn't (either File or Printer). If you want to print out the report, then make the Write To say Printer.

If you're wondering what happens when you Write To a file, it may interest you to know that dBASE can "print" your report to a file on your hard disk. This feature can make transporting your report to a word processor much easier. The procedure is covered in detail in Chapter 23.

That's all there is to reporting for now, so go on, take a break. Take that shower you've been wanting. Please.

Chapter 16: Creating Simple Reports with dBASE **199**

The 5th Wave By Rich Tennant

"I ALWAYS BACK UP EVERYTHING."

Chapter 17
Form Letters for Fun and Profit

In This Chapter
- What is a form letter?
- Creating a form letter
- Form letter printing tricks
- Printing the form letter

Mr. John Doe
123 Fifth Ave.
New York, NY 10101

Dear Mr. John Doe:

You have been chosen to be the lucky recipient of a $10 check from Walter's Hay and Feed Co. of Surripere, Kansas. To receive your check, just fill out the enclosed form and send it back to us with your order for a six-month supply of Walter's World-Famous Swine Feed at the low, low price of just $4,000. Within four to six weeks, you'll receive both your $10 check and this outstanding hog feed (known for producing the finest, healthiest pigs on Earth). But don't delay, John. We can't hold a deal like this forever. Only a very few people in New York will have the opportunity to cash in on this great deal and the $10 check. So send in your form today.

Sincerely,

Claudius Iago
President

You get them all the time: personalized form letters. Your mailbox is stuffed with them. Even your dog gets them. And although some are just junk mail, others are really important.

Part III: Organizing and Printing Your Data

Because you may need to send out the *important* kind of form letters — whether to customers, to patrons of charitable groups, or even to family members (if you have a very large family!) — dBASE lets you create them from your table data.

Before you can go gallivanting away on a wild, form-letter-creating spree, you need to have

- A name and address table that you created (see Chapter 4) and put some data into (see Chapter 5)
- An understanding of basic database concepts (see Chapters 1 and 2)
- A small idea of what a report is and how to create one (see Chapter 16)
- Ed McMahon's home address

To create form letters for your own real live database, read the chapter to get the basic idea and follow the instructions. If you want to print form letters for the book's example database, then you need to have created the Bookcust table (see Chapter 4) and put data into it (see Chapter 5).

Form Letter Basics

A form letter is a document that combines standard "boilerplate" text with data from your database (which dBASE plugs in for you). This concept is illustrated nicely in Figure 17-1.

Figure 17-1: Take a data source, such as a dBASE table. Add a document with slots for the data. Mix, stirring gently. Bake 20 minutes. Cover with candy and gumdrops. Chill. Serves thousands.

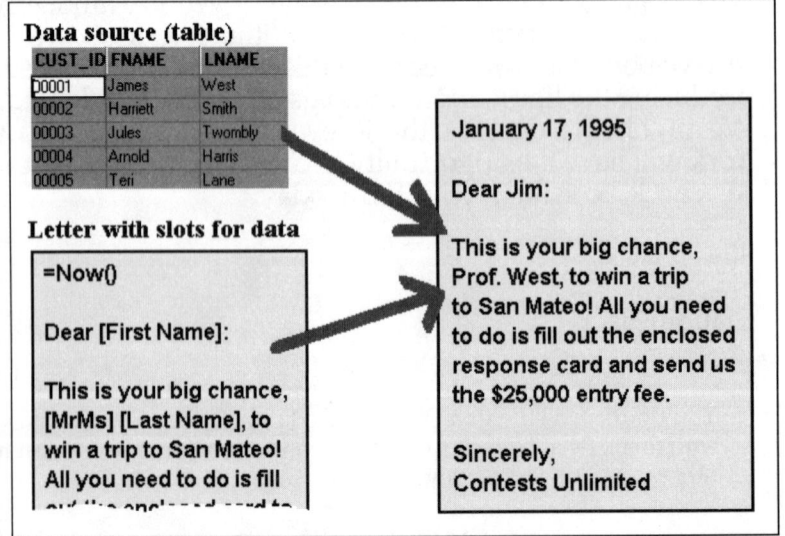

Data source (table)

CUST_ID	FNAME	LNAME
00001	James	West
00002	Harriett	Smith
00003	Jules	Twombly
00004	Arnold	Harris
00005	Teri	Lane

Letter with slots for data

=Now()

Dear [First Name]:

This is your big chance, [MrMs] [Last Name], to win a trip to San Mateo! All you need to do is fill

January 17, 1995

Dear Jim:

This is your big chance, Prof. West, to win a trip to San Mateo! All you need to do is fill out the enclosed response card and send us the $25,000 entry fee.

Sincerely,
Contests Unlimited

REMEMBER All form letters begin with a table. For example, if you want to send form letters to the customers in the book's Bookcust database, then you use the data in the Bookcust table to fill the slots in your form letter.

A form letter is nothing more than a glorified report

If you remember what a report is (see Chapter 16), then you already know what a form letter is . . . just about. That's because a form letter is a glorified report. Nothing more. And a report is simply what dBASE uses to print your data onto paper.

The difference between a report and a form letter is in *how* dBASE prints your data. For example, in a report, your data may be printed out something like this:

Mr. James   West

Ms. Harriett Stowe

Mr. Jules   Twombly

Notice the nice, neat, dull columns that dBASE puts your data into. When you create a form letter, dBASE goes through all kinds of behind-the-scenes gyrations to format your data in a more interesting and useful fashion. The key is dBASE's special kind of report layout: the Mailmerge layout.

Creating a form letter with a Mailmerge layout

A Mailmerge layout automatically eliminates dead space from your form letters, lets you edit the letters easily, and lets you print them just as easily. All for no extra charge. To create a form letter, just follow these steps:

1. **In the Control Center, highlight and select the table of your choice from the Data panel.**

    Then select Use File from the dialog box that appears. The table that you selected moves above the horizontal line in the Data panel, letting you know that it is, indeed, in use. You also can use a query (see Chapter 11) to print form letters.

Part III: Organizing and Printing Your Data

2. **Select <create> from the Reports panel.**

   The Report Design screen appears with the Layout menu open and the Quick Layouts option already highlighted. Quick Layouts is the option you want.

3. **Select Quick Layouts from the Layout menu.**

   A submenu appears, asking you for the kind of layout that you want to use.

4. **Select Mailmerge Layout from the Quick Layouts submenu.**

   The Report Design screen changes to look like Figure 17-2. Notice that all of the bands are turned off except for the Detail band. dBASE turns off the other bands because you're creating a form letter and the data that you enter will most likely need to go into the Detail band. If you need to turn a band back on, just move the cursor onto it and press Enter.

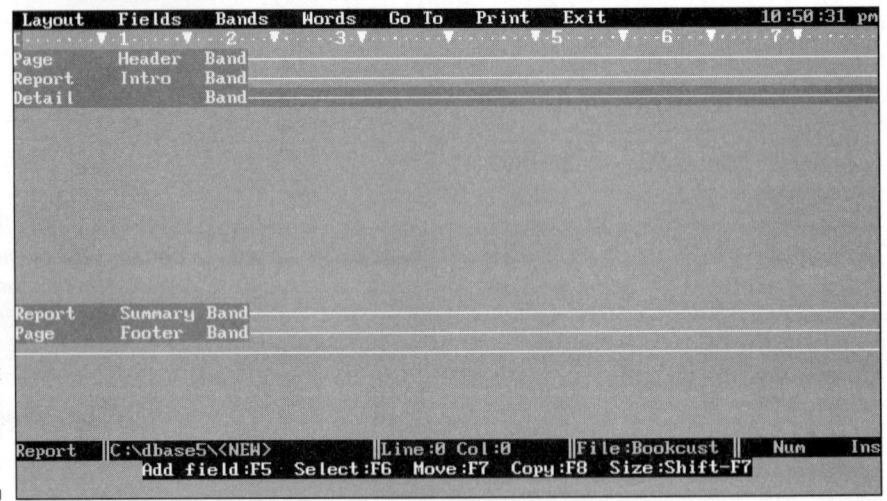

Figure 17-2: The Report Design screen after you select the Mailmerge layout.

5. **From the Words menu, select Enable Automatic Indent.**

   Set this option to NO before you enter anything into your form letter so that the Report Design screen will handle Tabs and Indents like a word processor. After you select this option, the Words menu disappears from the screen. You can check to make sure that you did, in fact, set the option to NO by opening the Words menu again and looking at it. But do not select Enable Automatic Indent again: if you do, you set it back to YES. Just press Esc to close the menu.

Chapter 17: Form Letters for Fun and Profit *205*

6. **Add the fields and text that you want your form letter to include.**

   On the layout screen, type the text you want in your form letter. Wherever you need to insert data from your table, press F5 to insert a field. dBASE handles all the details. Inserting a field into a form letter works exactly the same way as it does in any other kind of report.

   Figure 17-3 gives an example of a form letter made with the book's example Bookcust database. If you want to design this form letter for the Bookcust database, then set it up with the fields in the locations where you see them in the figure. However, you can't tell from the figure *which* field is which, so enter the fields in the following order: MRMS, FNAME, LNAME, ADDRESS, CITY, STATE, ZIP, SALUTATION.

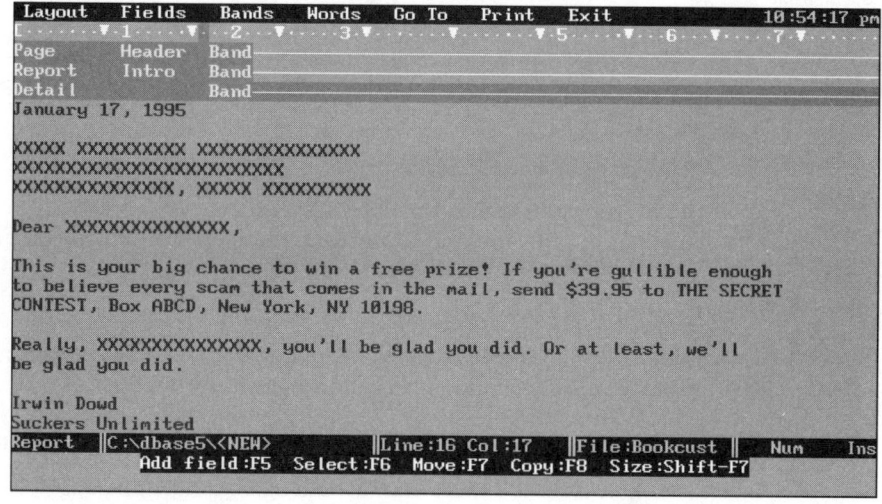

Figure 17-3:
A typical Mailmerge layout after adding some fields and text.

7. **Select view report on screen from the Print menu.**

   The screen changes to look something like Figure 17-4. You can use this screen to get an idea of what your form letter will look like before you print it. Press the spacebar to move down through the form letter. When you're done, press Esc. If you don't like something, you can change it in the Report Design screen.

8. **To save the form letter layout, select Save This Report from the Layout menu.**

   dBASE prompts you to name the form letter. If using the book's example database, then enter the name Letters. dBASE saves the form letter (from certain doom).

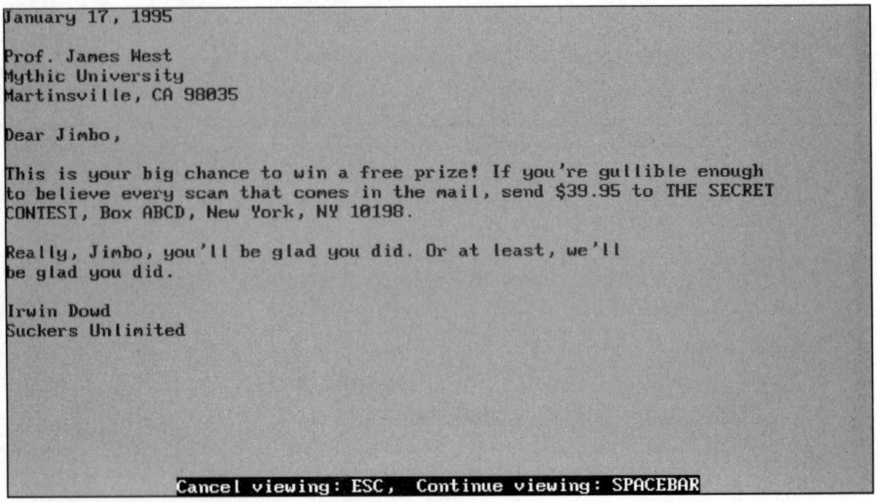

Figure 17-4:
The first record of the Bookcust database, displayed using the View Report on Screen option from the Print menu.

```
January 17, 1995

Prof. James West
Mythic University
Martinsville, CA 98035

Dear Jimbo,

This is your big chance to win a free prize! If you're gullible enough
to believe every scam that comes in the mail, send $39.95 to THE SECRET
CONTEST, Box ABCD, New York, NY 10198.

Really, Jimbo, you'll be glad you did. Or at least, we'll
be glad you did.

Irwin Dowd
Suckers Unlimited


Cancel viewing: ESC,   Continue viewing: SPACEBAR
```

9. **Preview your form letter.**

   Before you print your form letter, it's a good idea to preview it on the screen. You preview your form letter just as you would any other report: open the **P**rint menu and select **V**iew records on screen.

10. **Print your form letter.**

    Open the **P**rint menu and select **B**egin printing. Make sure that you have enough paper! You also can print form letters from the Control Center:

    - From the Reports panel, select the form letter that you want to print.
    - Select Print Report from the dialog box that appears.
    - Select **B**egin printing from the menu that appears on the left.

Form letter tricks, such as changing margins and tab stops

Here are a few tricks you can use to help set up your form letter.

- To set the left margin for your form letter, position the cursor in the Detail band of the layout screen. Then open the **W**ords menu and select **M**odify ruler. The cursor will jump up to the ruler at the top of the screen, just under the Menu Bar. Using the arrow keys, move the cursor to the location you want for the left margin. Then press the left square bracket ([) key. A left square bracket appears, marking the new location of the left margin. You can set the right margin in the same way: just use a right square bracket (]) instead of a left square bracket. When you're finished changing the ruler, press Enter. dBASE will return you to the Detail band.

- To set tab stops for your letter, open the **Words** menu and select **Modify ruler**. The cursor will jump up to the ruler. To set new tab stops, press the equal (=) key. A dialog box will appear asking for the interval at which you want tabs to appear, such as every five spaces. Enter the number of spaces you want between tabs. If you enter **0** (zero), it will clear all the current tab stops. If you want to set an individual tab stop, use the arrow keys to move the cursor to the place you want to insert a tab stop. Then type **!** (an exclamation mark). This inserts a tab stop at the cursor location. When you're finished fooling around with the ruler, press Enter. dBASE returns you to the Detail band.

- To trim extra space from a field, highlight the field and select Modify field from the Fields menu. In the submenu, select Picture Functions and then, in the next submenu, select Trim. The Trim option should be ON; if it isn't, turn it on. This option causes dBASE to eliminate any dead space from the beginning or end of the field.

- So that everything on your form letter prints properly on your printer, make sure that the text that you enter does not run over the right edge of the screen. To keep your text from running over, press Enter to move the cursor down to a new line (just as you would in a word processor).

Adding a calculated field to a form letter

Just as in any report, you can have dBASE do calculations in a form letter. To add a calculated field to a form letter, follow these steps:

1. **Select Add Field from the Fields menu.**

    A submenu with lists of available fields appears.

2. **Select <create> from the Calculated column.**

    In the Name option, enter the name of the field. In the Formula option, enter the formula that you want dBASE to calculate and display in the field. For example, suppose you want to see how much money each of a certain number of sales would involve if you applied a 10 percent discount for long-time customers. To do the calculation, you need to take the original price and multiply it by 0.9. So the formula you enter is **price * 0.9**, with the asterisk meaning multiply. The operators you use in a formula are explained in the next paragraph.

You can use any of the standard arithmetic operators in a calculation: + for addition, - for subtraction, * for multiplication, and / for division. You also can use other dBASE mathematical operators, but they're too numerous to discuss here, and you probably won't use them often. If you want more information about these operators, see your dBASE manuals.

Using Type Styles and Other Printing Tricks

If you want to make your form letters more readable, and generally more attractive to other form letters, then adding various typefaces is the way to go. To add a typeface, just follow these steps:

1. **Select the text whose typeface you want to change.**

   If you want to change the typeface of a field, simply move the cursor onto the field to select it. If you want to change text, move the cursor to the beginning of the text and press F6. Then use the arrow keys to highlight the text you want to select. When you're done highlighting, press Enter.

2. **Select the style that you want to use.**

   You can select from boldfacing, underlining, italics, subscripting, or superscripting. The typefaces you select won't be apparent on the screen, but they will show up on the paper when you print it.

That's enough for now, kemosabe. So go take a break. Play with some wild horses or something.

Chapter 18
Designing and Printing Mailing Labels

In This Chapter
▶ What you should know about mailing labels
▶ How to design, save, and print labels
▶ How to change a label

The printing of mailing labels is one of the most classic and widely used features of database managers. This chapter describes computerized mailing labels and then shows you how to create, save, and print labels. And we do it all for one low price.

To understand the ideas in this chapter, you should already have

✔ A basic understanding of database concepts (see Chapter 3)
✔ Some knowledge about tables (see Chapter 4)
✔ A good idea of how to create reports (see Chapter 16)

If you're blatantly ignoring the book's example database and creating labels for your own database, read this chapter to get the basic ideas. Then, follow the steps with your own table. To create labels for the book's example Bookcust database, you should have created the Bookcust table (see Chapter 4) and put some data in it (see Chapter 5).

dBASE Label Basics

If you receive junk mail, then you know exactly what mailing labels are. They're those little pieces of paper with your name and address on them that are glued onto the mail. Nowadays, almost all mailing labels are printed by computers.

Computers are extremely good at printing labels. By taking a standard *label design* and plugging data from the individual records into that design, computers can print large numbers of mailing labels quickly and accurately.

Labeling with dBASE is flexible and feature-filled. You can choose from various text styles and label styles. You can make labels extremely large or very small. The possibilities are almost endless.

Labels do not always have to be mailing labels. They can be videocassette labels, food container labels, clothing labels, any labels.

More sizes fit all

So that your labels can be the exact size you need, dBASE uses predefined size descriptions in three categories:

- Avery
- Rolodex
- Measured

Avery labels are labels that use the Avery system of classifying label sizes. For each different label size, there is a corresponding Avery number that identifies that size. If your labels have an Avery number written on the box that they came in, just find the matching Avery number in the Predefined Size window and select it.

The two Rolodex sizes are used for printing on Rolodex cards. They can be either 3 inches by 5 inches, or 2.25 inches by 4 inches.

The remaining seven sizes are displayed by the actual measured dimensions of the labels. The first number in the measurement is the label's height. The second number is the label's length, and the third number specifies how many labels each row of labels contains.

Strike out the bands

Adding data to a label is much easier than adding data to a regular report. Because an entire mailing label fits easily on your screen, dBASE doesn't need to use bands to break up the screen. Not having bands makes the label much easier to design because you can see everything that you do just the way it will appear when you print it.

How to Design, Save, and Print Labels

The basic steps for creating and printing labels are similar to the steps for creating any other kind of report. First, index your database on the field by which you want to organize your labels.

Indexing your database

To index your database, follow these steps:

1. **Start dBASE and get to the Control Center.**
2. **Highlight the table you want use for printing labels. Then press Enter.**

   A dialog box appears, asking what you want to do with the table.
3. **Select Modify structure/order.**

   The Table Design screen appears with the table that you selected.
4. **Make sure that you indexed the field by which you want to order your labels.**

   Look at the Index column of the field you want to index on. If it says N, then the field is not indexed. Move the highlight bar to the Index column of the field you want to Index on and press Y. If you're printing actual *mailing* labels, as opposed to labels for videocassette recorder tapes or leftover jars, then index your table on the ZIP field. The U.S. Post Office requires bulk mailings to be ordered by Zip code. If you're using the book's example database, then you should Index on the ZIP field as well.
5. **Select the Save this database file structure option from the Layout menu.**

   dBASE prompts you to name the file.
6. **Press Enter to save the table under the same name as before.**
7. **Select the Order records by index option from the Organize menu.**

   A window appears (see Figure 18-1), asking which field you want to index on.
8. **Select the field by which you want to organize your labels.**
9. **Highlight the Save changes and exit option from the Exit menu. Then press Enter twice.**

   You're back in the Control Center.

Part III: Organizing and Printing Your Data

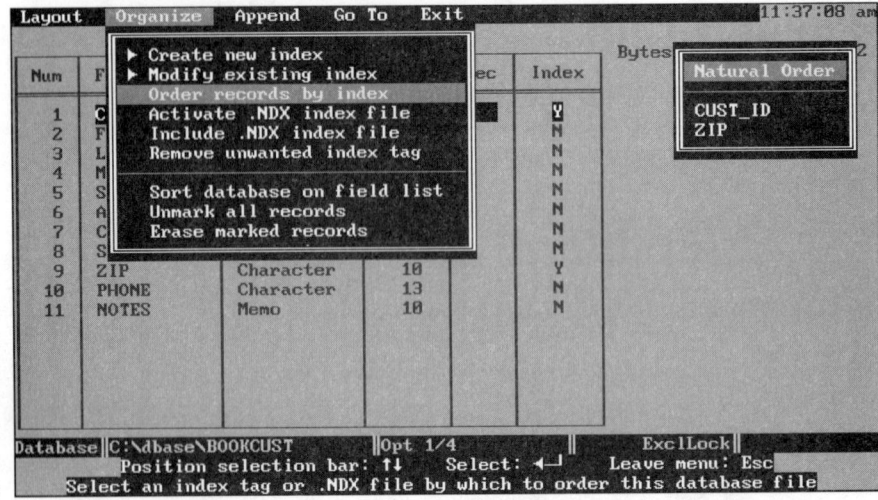

Figure 18-1: The window where you select the field to index on.

Creating your labels

To create your labels, follow these steps:

1. **From the Control Center, highlight the word** <create> **in the Labels column and press Enter.**

   Your screen changes to look like Figure 18-2. This is the Label Design screen.

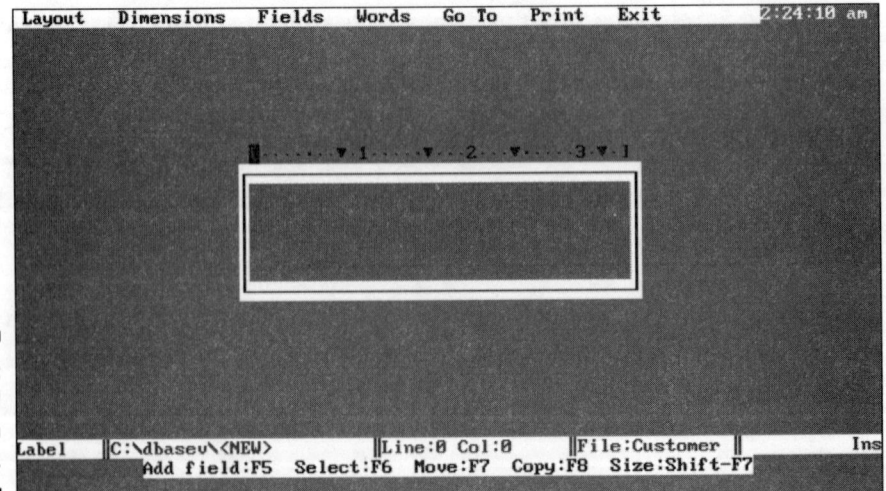

Figure 18-2: The Label Design screen.

Chapter 18: Designing and Printing Mailing Labels

2. **Select the Predefined Size option from the Dimensions menu.**

   dBASE opens a window that lists about 80 of the most common sizes for mailing labels. See Figure 18-3. Cycle through the available sizes by using the up- and down-arrow keys. You can choose from the Avery, Rolodex, or measured dimensions.

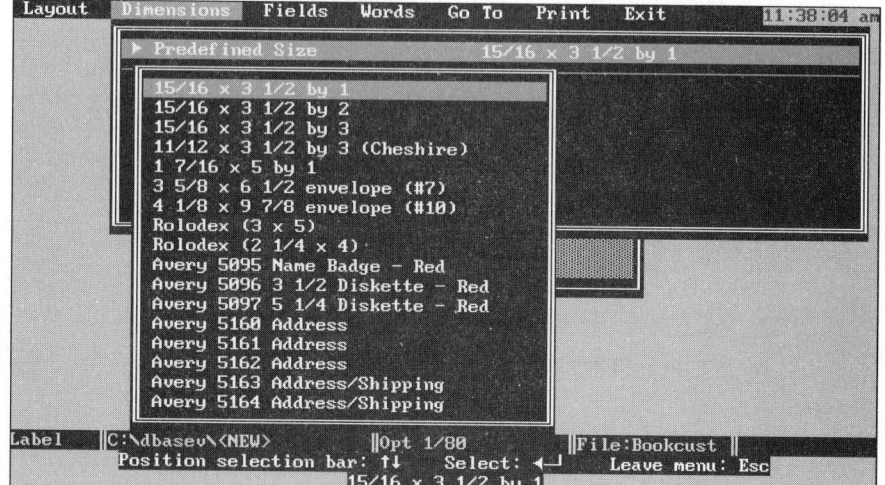

Figure 18-3: The Predefined Size window.

3. **Select the predefined size that matches your label.**

   If the predefined size that you need just isn't available, then you need to create a custom label size (see the "Creating custom label sizes" section elsewhere in this chapter).

4. **If using a measured or Rolodex label, then open the Dimensions menu and change the Rows Per Page option.**

   Rows Per Page is initially set at zero. To change it, type the number of rows your label paper has per page and press Enter.

5. **To add data, type some simple text into the top line of your label.**

   If you're using the Bookcust database, then type **IMPORTANT MAIL FOR:**. Notice that any text you type is displayed on the label just as you typed it. You can use text to help flesh out your label and make it easier to read. Or don't.

6. **Move down to the first space in the second line of the label.**

7. **Open the Fields menu and select Add field.**

   A list appears, asking for the field you want to add to your label. If using the Bookcust database, add the MRMS field.

Part III: Organizing and Printing Your Data

8. Select the field you want to include in your label.

A dialog box appears with two available options: Template and Picture Function. Template works just like a report template, where Xs or 9s serve as place holders for your data. You can expand or shrink a field blank by adding or removing place holders. Picture Function controls things like text alignment and converting letters to uppercase.

> **NOTE:** The most important option from the Picture Function submenu is the Trim option. Unless you turn it off, Trim is automatically turned on. With this option on, dBASE eliminates blank spaces from your data. To see why this is important, consider what happens when field widths are bigger than the names and addresses that you are printing on the label. These extra-large field widths cause problems, as you can see in the following mailing label mockup:

    Mr.   James   West

    Mythic University

    Martinsville   ,   CA   98035

The field widths cause big gaps to appear in the printed text. Because the FNAME field has a width of ten, the field takes up ten spaces in the first address line of the letter even though there are only five letters in the name *James*. Obviously, that's not how you want the label to look. It should look like this:

    Mr. James West

    Mythic University

    Martinsville, CA 98035

Getting rid of those pesky trailing spaces is what the Trim option does for you — automatically, with no effort on your part!

9. Press Ctrl-End to put the field on the label.

Your label looks something like Figure 18-4.

10. If you want, you can now type other text on your label.

11. Repeat Steps 7 through 10 to add another field to your label.

If you're doing this for the Bookcust database, then add the FNAME field this time, and then add another space.

You can continue adding fields in this way until your label is just the way you like it. If you're making a label for the Bookcust database, then add the remaining fields and text as follows:

    1. LNAME, then carriage return

    2. ADDRESS, then carriage return

Chapter 18: Designing and Printing Mailing Labels 215

3. CITY, then a comma and a space
4. STATE, then a space
5. ZIP

WARNING! If your label isn't big enough to hold a field that you put into it, dBASE beeps at you and tells you it's going to truncate the field. To truncate the field means that dBASE will cut off the part of the field that it can't fit on the label. If the truncating isn't too bad (one or two letters), then you may want to let it slide. If you're losing a lot of important data (like Zip codes for example), however, then you may want to restructure your label or buy bigger labels.

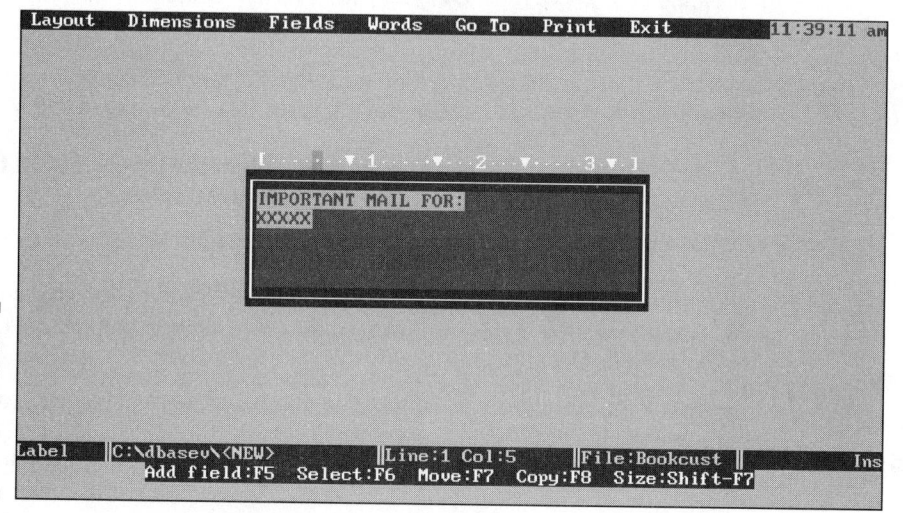

Figure 18-4: A label design after entering a field.

Creating custom label sizes

All of the commands for customizing a label's size can be found in the Dimensions menu. You can do six different things to customize a label for your label paper:

- **Change its Width of Columns:** Width is the number of characters that can fit across your label in pica pitch.

- **Change its Height of Columns:** Height is the number of lines that you can fit on a label, based on the assumption of six lines of text per inch.

- **Change the Indentation:** Changing the indentation tells the printer how many spaces to leave between the margin and the leftmost column of text.

- ✓ **Change the Lines Between Labels:** This controls the number of lines between the bottom of one label and the top of the label beneath it.
- ✓ **Alter the Space Between Columns:** If your label paper has more than one column of labels on it, altering the space between columns specifies the number of spaces from the right edge of one label to the left edge of the next.
- ✓ **Change the Columns of Labels:** This specifies the number of labels in each row.

Adding special style to your text

dBASE comes with a few standard styling options (such as boldface, italic, and so on) that you can include right on your mailing labels. To select a special style for some of the text in your mailing label, just follow these steps:

1. **Press F6 and use the arrow keys to highlight the text you want to style. When you're done highlighting the text, press Enter.**
2. **Open the Words menu and select the Style option.**

   A list of various styles is displayed in a submenu.

3. **Go through the styles you want to add to your text and press Enter to turn them ON.**

   When you print out your labels, the text will have the styles you added. If you decide later that you don't want the style, simply go back to the Style option of the Words menu and turn the style OFF by pressing Enter.

Saving mailing label designs

After you enter all the fields and text that you want to include in your label, it's time to save the label. To save the label, follow these steps:

1. **Select the Save this label design option from the Layout menu.**

   dBASE prompts you to name the label design.

2. **Enter a name for the label, adhering to MS-DOS rules for filenames.**

   If this label is for the Bookcust database, go ahead and name the label Bookcust as well.

3. **Select the View labels on screen option from the Print menu.**

   This gives you an idea of what the mailing labels will look like when you print them.

Printing mailing labels

To print your mailing labels, follow these steps:

1. **From the Label Design screen, choose Generate sample labels from the Print menu.**

   dBASE prints a series of XXXs as sample labels. If the sample labels don't line up with your label paper, press Esc to get back to the Label Design screen. Check your printer alignment and make sure that the proper label size is selected. When you're done checking, run the sample labels again. If they still don't line up, try printing a few of the real labels anyway. With some printers, the sample labels are just screwy.

2. **When you believe the printer is aligned with the label paper, select the Begin printing option from the Print menu.**

   dBASE begins printing your labels.

Changing a Label Design You've Already Created

If, after creating your Label Design, you realize you made a mistake, you can go back and change the design without too much hassle. The first thing to do is open the label in the Label Design screen. To open the label, follow these steps:

1. **From the Control Center, highlight the label design you want to open in the Labels column and press Enter.**

   A dialog box appears, asking what you want to do with the design.

2. **Select the Modify Design Layout option.**

   The Label Design screen appears with the label you selected in it.

To remove a field from the label

To remove a field from the current label, simply

1. **Move the cursor onto the field you want to remove.**
2. **Select the Remove field option from the Fields menu.**

   The field disappears from the Label Design screen. The field will also be gone from the labels that you print.

To add a field to the label

To add a field to the label,

1. **Position the cursor where you want to add the field.**
2. **Select the Add field option from the Fields menu.**

    A window appears, asking for the field you want to add.

3. **Select the field that you want to add.**

    A menu appears, asking if you want to change the Template or the Picture Function.

4. **If you want to change the template, then select the Template option and add or delete place holders as you see fit.**
5. **Press Ctrl-End to add the field.**

    The field appears where your cursor was in the Label Design screen.

To move a field

To move a field from one place in the label to another, follow these steps:

1. **Move the cursor onto the field you want to move and press F6, then press Enter.**
2. **Press F7.**
3. **Use the arrow keys to move the field to where you want it to be.**
4. **Press Enter to set the field down where you want it.**

To add or remove text

To add or remove text from a label, just use standard editing keys (such as Backspace, Delete, and so on) and type the text that you want.

To switch to a different label size

If you want a different label size, do the following:

1. **Select the Predefined Size option from the Dimensions menu.**

    A window appears, with a list of the available label sizes.

2. **Select the size you want to switch to.**

   The display of the label changes to reflect the new size.

> **WARNING!**
>
> Switching from one label size to another after you enter your fields may result in damage to the label design. You can fix this simply by creating a new label design, but after all the work you already put into it, why would you want to?

That's it for labels, so go on, get out of here. Leave your computer all alone by itself. It'll get back at you by crashing later.

Part IV
Really Advanced Stuff to Impress Your Friends

The 5th Wave   By Rich Tennant

"I THINK 'FUZZY LOGIC' IS AN IMPORTANT TECHNOLOGY TOO. I'M JUST NOT SURE WE SHOULD FEATURE IT AS PART OF OUR TAX PREPARATION SOFTWARE."

In this part ...

This part shows you how to divide up your database so that it's as efficient as possible. In addition, you learn how to create really sophisticated reports that group your data, do calculations, and draw information from more than one table. You also learn how to use dBASE to create form letters and mailing labels in case you want to do one of those annoying mass mailings.

Chapter 19
Divvying Up Your Database and Putting It Back Together

In This Chapter
- Reasons to use more than one table in your database
- Relating tables to combine their data
- Different ways that tables can be related
- Using a common field to relate tables

*T*ables are the building blocks of a database. When most people design a database for the first time, they try to cram everything into a single table: customer records, sales records, Bob Dylan records, and even world bungee-jumping records.

But that's not the right way to do it. One of the great strengths of dBASE is that it lets you divide your data into different tables. That way, you have one table for customer records, another for sales records, and so on. Each table contains data about a different subject.

Dividing up your data is pretty useless, however, unless you can put it back together when necessary. And that's just what you do when you link two or more tables: by combining them in a query, you can tell dBASE to treat them temporarily as a single table.

Before you can combine data from two or more tables, you need to have

- Created two tables that have a common field (see Chapter 4)
- Put data in the tables (see Chapter 5)
- Learned how to use the Query Design screen (see Chapter 11)

To use the book's sample database, you need to create the Bookcust table (see Chapter 4) and the Sales table (see Chapter 11) and then put data in the two tables (all the data is in Appendix A). If you're working with your own real-life database, you can follow along and learn the basic concepts and techniques. Then apply them to your own database.

The Basic Idea: Divide and Conquer

REMEMBER

You can put all your data in one table. But remember from Chapter 4 that all the records in a table must be the same size. If you put all your data in a single table, some records contain a lot of information and others contain very little. Every record, however, takes up the same amount of disk space, so records with little information take as much disk space as those that are packed to the gills.

This concept is pretty abstract, so consider the example Bookcust and Sales tables. Each customer record must have the customer's name, address, account number, and a few other pieces of information. Each sales record must have the buyer's account number, the date, a description of the item, and the amount of money received for the item.

Suppose you put all the data from these two tables into a single table. Some customers may make 25 purchases a month, while others may make only one or two. The records for customers who buy 25 times a month need 75 extra fields to hold their monthly sales data (25 purchases x 3 fields per purchase). But because all records in a table have to be the same size, the records for customers who buy once or twice a month *also* need 75 extra fields — and most of those fields remain empty. That's incredibly inefficient.

This approach presents another problem, too. What if a customer makes 26 purchases in a month? In that case, you're simply out of luck. There are no more fields in which to record the data for the 26th sale. You can add more fields, but that requires you to restructure the table (see Chapter 7), which is a waste of time.

Dividing your data into different tables

As you learned earlier in this book, dBASE enables you to divide your data into different tables. Instead of creating one big Customer/Sales table, you can create a Bookcust table and a Sales table. Each customer record includes the same information (account number, name, address, and so on), and each sales record includes the same information (account number, sale date, book title, and so on). No disk space is wasted, and customers can make as many purchases as their probably over-the-limit credit cards allow.

But suppose you want to print a report showing each customer's name and purchases for the month. The customer information is in one table, and the sales information is in another. You need a way to bring the two together. And that's what linking tables is all about, as the next section shows.

Linking tables with a query

You bring tables together by combining them in a query. A query, as Chapter 11 explains, is a question you ask about your database. One question you can ask is, "What would happen if I combined the data from two or more tables? Would it be, like, *totally bogus,* or would it actually do some good?"

The answer is that most of the time, it does you some good. Only rarely is combining tables in a query totally bogus, and even then it can't hurt unless your name is Bill or Ted.

In Chapter 16, you learn how to use a table as the data source for a printed report. If you want to create a report that combines data from two or more tables, you simply base it on a multitable query instead of a single table. Because all the data in the tables is available in the query, you can use the same data in the report.

You see the actual mechanics of creating a multitable report in Chapter 20. Here, you learn how to combine data from different tables by using a query, called setting up a *relation* between the tables.

Different types of relations between tables

In dBASE, you can set up two different types of relations between tables: *one-to-one* and *one-to-many*. In a one-to-many relation, the "one" table (such as Bookcust) is often called the *parent* table, and the "many" table (such as Sales) is called the *child* table.

An example of a one-to-one relation is that of husband and wife. In Western countries (at least in theory), each husband has only one wife, and each wife has only one husband. An example of a one-to-many relation is that of a customer to a purchase: each customer may make many purchases, but each purchase can be made by only one customer. Figure 19-1 illustrates this type of relation.

Figure 19-1: An example of a one-to-many relation.

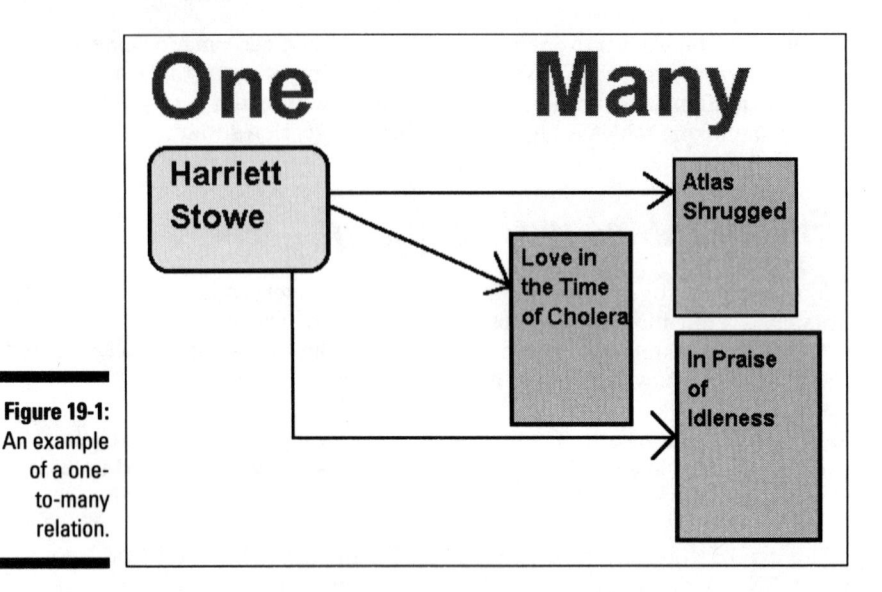

One-to-one relations between tables aren't that common. Most of the time, you set up one-to-many relations, as in the example of the Bookcust table: each customer record can have many sales records associated with it. Many-to-many relations are possible, but again, they're much less common than one-to-many relations.

> You should realize that for a one-to-many relation, each "one" record need not have many records related to it. When you set up a one-to-many relation between a customer records table and a sales table, some customers may have only one sale, while others may have many or none at all.

To be related, tables must share a field

For two tables to be joined or related, they must have a common field, such as an account number field. You need to know four main things about this shared field (some of them are a little technical, so don't sweat the details too much).

- The field does not need to have the same name in both tables, but it must contain the same data. In other words, it doesn't matter if the account number field is called *Cust ID* in the Bookcust table and *Madonna* in the Sales table, as long as both fields contain account numbers.
- dBASE works faster when the common field is indexed in both tables. In a one-to-many relation, the common field must be indexed in the "many" table.

- The shared field must be the same data type in both tables.
- Usually, the common field is the first field in the table.

The Practical Part: Here's How You Do It

In the following exercise, you set up a relation between two tables. We use the Bookcust table and the Sales table, but you can follow along and make the same moves with your own tables. To begin, make sure that the appropriate catalog is open and displayed in the Control Center. If you're following along with the book's example, use the Caveat catalog.

Checking the "many" table

First, you must make sure that a field in the "many" table is indexed. Because the Sales table is going to be the "many" table in the example, you must index its Cust_ID field. If you're at all unsure about whether you indexed that field when you set up the table (if you followed instructions for the example in Chapter 11, you did), make sure that the field is indexed by following these steps:

1. **In the Control Center's Data panel, highlight the "many" table and press Enter.**

    For the example, highlight the Sales table. A dialog box appears, asking what you want to do with the table.

2. **Select Modify structure/order.**

    The Table Design screen appears.

3. **Press Esc to close the Organize menu.**

4. **In the first row, make sure that the Index column says Y.**

    The first row in the example is (CUST_ID).

    If the Index column for the row does *not* say Y, move the cursor to that column and press Y.

5. **Open the Exit menu and select Save changes.**

    Doing so saves the table design.

6. **Close the Table Design screen.**

Setting up the relation

To link the two tables, you set up a multitable query that includes all the fields from both tables. You use this query when you create multitable reports.

Back in the good old days, when MTV was young and Madonna was still fairly interesting, a multitable query required you to type all kinds of awful stuff, like **set relation from "customer" into "sales" on "custID"** or a variation on that theme. But in dBASE, establishing the relationship is as easy as typing **dbase:** and performing these steps:

1. **In the Control Center, close any open tables.**

   If a table is open, its name appears above the horizontal line near the top of the Data panel. To close a table, highlight its name and press Enter. Then select **C**lose file in the dialog box.

2. **In the Control Center's Queries panel, highlight** `<create>` **and press Enter.**

   The Query Design screen appears. The Layout menu should already be open. If not, open it.

3. **In the Layout menu, select Add file to query.**

   At the right side of your screen, dBASE displays a list of available files for the query.

4. **Select the first table you want to use.**

   To select a table, highlight it and press Enter. The table skeleton for that table appears. In the book's sample database, this is the Bookcust table.

5. **Select the second table you want to use.**

   Reopen the Layout menu and again select **A**dd file to query. In the file list, select the table you want. If you're following the book's example, select the Sales table.

   Your screen should look something like Figure 19-2.

   Now you need to get ready to add the link between the two tables. Remember that the two tables must share a common field, such as account number. In the "many" table, the field must be indexed. Here, the Cust_ID field is the common field and is indexed in the "many" (Sales) table.

6. **To set up the link, enter the same value in the Cust_ID field of both table skeletons.**

   The value must fit in the field, but it also has to be a value that you won't actually use as a real value in that field. Because the Cust_ID field is a character field that contains values like 00001 and 00015, you're pretty safe entering a word, such as **dbase**.

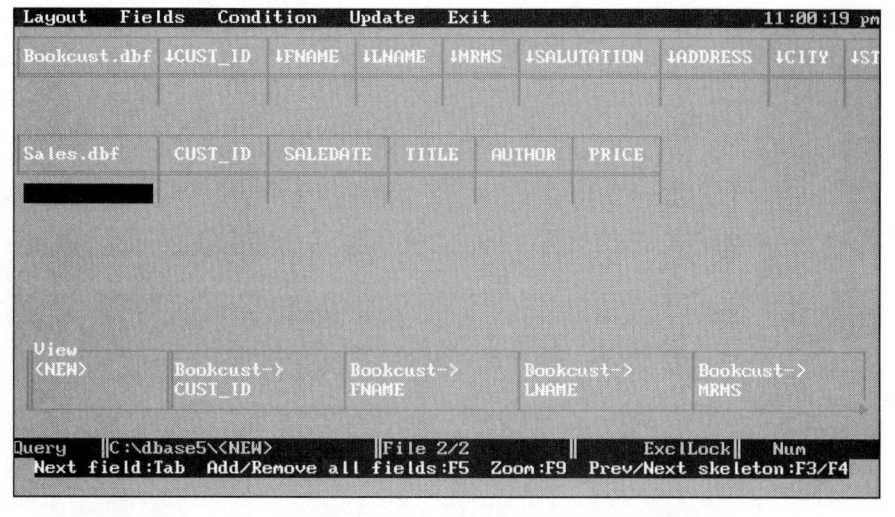

Figure 19-2: The Query Design screen with two tables added to the query.

7. **Press F3 to move the cursor from the second table skeleton to the first table skeleton.**

   The cursor should be in the first column under the table name. In the example, you're moving from the Sales table to the Bookcust table.

8. **Press F5 to select all the fields in the first table.**

   A down arrow should appear next to each field name.

9. **Tab to the common field and type a value in the blank.**

   The word itself is completely arbitrary, as long as it fits in the field and is something that you don't plan to use as a real value in the field. And keep it clean in case your mother ever uses the database. In the example, tab to the Cust_ID column and type **dbase** in the blank.

10. **Press F4 to go back to the second table skeleton.**

11. **Tab to the common field and type the same value or word you entered in Step 8.**

    In the example, tab to the Cust_ID column and type **dbase**. The link should now be established.

12. **Select the fields in the second table.**

    You don't want to select *all* the fields, which would include the common field twice. Instead, tab to each field other than the common field. In each column, press F5 to select the field, and do so until all fields except the common field are selected. In the Sales table, select all the fields except for the Cust_ID field.

13. Press F2 to make sure that the link is set up correctly.

You see a Browse screen of the answer to this query, in which you can verify that the link has been established. When you tab to the right, you should see all the fields in both tables, as shown in Figure 19-3.

Figure 19-3: The query answer combines fields from the two tables.

ZIP	PHONE	NOTES	SALEDATE	TITLE
98035	(415)555-4678	MEMO	08/25/94	In Praise of Idleness
10087	(212)555-2345	memo	08/26/94	Getting Your Husband Off His Lazy Butt
23413	(321)555-9876	memo	08/21/94	How to Write a Computer Book
93101	(805)555-1234	memo	08/27/94	How I Turned $25 Cash into a Successfu
93101	(805)555-1234	memo	08/28/94	dBASE for DOS for Dummies

You're done! Save the multitable query by opening the Exit menu and selecting Save changes and exit. If you're saving the query for the book's example database, call it *Custsale*. Otherwise, call it whatever you want, remembering that (a) it's an MS-DOS filename, so it can have up to eight letters, digits, and underscores; and (b) dirty, filthy query names will not be tolerated — you could get detention for a month.

Deleting a relation

You don't really ever need to delete a relation. The only time it becomes active is when you use the query as the basis for a Browse screen, form, or report. But if you ever *want* to delete a relation, it's easy. Simply highlight the multitable query and press Enter. When the Query Design screen appears, delete the common word from the common fields in the table skeletons. Then save the modified query. Zap! It's history! You're going to use the relation between the Bookcust and Sales tables in the next chapter, so don't delete it. But if you ever want to delete a relation, you know how to do it.

Chapter 20
Hot Stuff! Creating Sophisticated Reports

In This Chapter
- Constructing a grouped report
- Creating a really jazzed-up report
- Basing a report on a query instead of a table
- Creating a multitable report

When most people hear the term *sophisticated reports,* they naturally assume that it has something to do with tea and crumpets, watching "Masterpiece Theatre" on public television, or putting on a tie and jacket before they sit down at the computer.

Not true! It certainly *helps* to wear a tie and jacket while using dBASE — at least, it helps the people who sell ties and jackets — but sophisticated reports are just another way for dBASE to print out your database information. Chapter 15 covers the simple Browse screen, and Chapter 16 covers simple reports. This chapter shows you how to create and print fancier reports that organize your database information in a variety of ways.

So make yourself a nice cup of tea (Earl Grey, hot), eat a crumpet (whatever the heck *that* is), and get ready to create some kick-it reports. Formal dress is optional.

Before you can create a super-sophisticated report, you need to

- Know basic database concepts, such as *catalog, table,* and *field* (see Chapters 1 and 2).
- Know basic report concepts and parts of reports (see Chapter 16).
- Create a table (see Chapter 4) and put data in the table (see Chapter 5).

To do the steps in this chapter with the sample database, you need to create the Bookcust table (see Chapter 4) and Sales table (see Chapter 12); data for these tables is in Appendix A. For the multitable report, you also need to create the multitable query (see Chapter 19). If you're creating a report for your own real-life database, follow along with the example and learn the ideas and techniques. Then use them to create and modify your own report.

The Basic Ideas

The basic ideas behind creating a report are the same for every kind of report. A report is just a printout of the information in your database. You can print all the information or just some of it; put the information in alphabetical order or not; and include groups and totals or not.

Before you can print a report, you first have to create the *report layout.* The report layout shows where the parts of the report appear on the printed page. When you create the layout, you also can *format* the parts of the report to control the type style, text alignment, and so on.

dBASE makes it easy to create several different types of report layouts:

- **Row-and-column** arranges your data with records in rows and fields in columns, similar to the way you see it in a Browse screen. You can learn how to create this kind of report in Chapter 16.

- **Grouped** enables you to group your records by any field. For example, you can use this layout to create a report that groups sales transactions by state and includes a subtotal of the money from each state and a grand total of all sales revenue at the end of the report.

- **Form letter** inserts each person's name and address from a dBASE table. Everything else stays the same, even if you print 10,000 copies of the letter; only the name and address information changes.

- **Mailing Label** enables you to design and print name-and-address labels to put on envelopes.

After you create the report layout, you can use Print Preview to see how it will look on paper. Then you can switch back to the Design screen and change the layout. You go back and forth from Print Preview to the Design screen, adjusting the layout until it's exactly the way you want it. Then you save the report layout to disk. Any time you want to view or print the report, double-click on its icon in the Catalog menu.

The Basic Steps

The steps for creating a report are the same, whether you want a simple row-and-column report, a grouped report, or another other kind of report. Just do the following (and for full details, see the next section):

1. **Open the catalog for which you want to do a report.**
2. **In the Control Center, highlight the table you want to use and then press Enter.**
3. **In the dialog box, select Use file.**
4. **In the Control Center's Report panel, select <create>.**

   dBASE takes you to the Report Design screen. The Layout menu should be open.

5. **If you want to do a Quick Layout, press Enter. If you prefer to do a customized layout, press Esc to close the menu.**

   The screen should look like Figure 20-1.

6. **Position each field in the Detail band of the report layout.**
7. **Add column captions and other niceties in the Page Header band.**
8. **Tell dBASE how to sort and group records.**

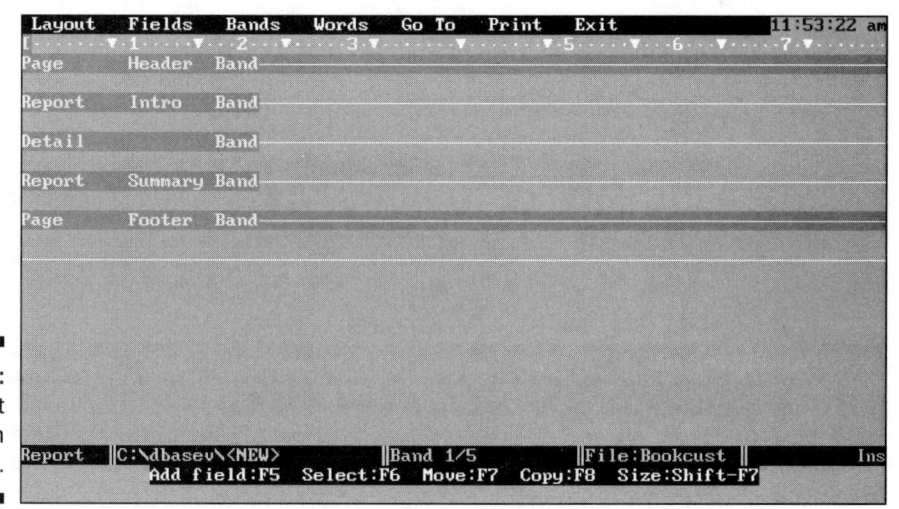

Figure 20-1: The Report Design screen.

9. **Open the Print menu and select View report on-screen.**

   This step gives you a preview of how the report will look on paper. When you're finished viewing the report, press Esc to return to the Report Design screen.

10. **If needed, modify the report layout.**

    Switch back and forth between the Report Design screen and Print Preview until the report looks exactly the way you want it.

11. **From the Report Design screen, open the Exit menu and select Save changes and exit.**

    Do so to save the report layout to disk.

12. **Name the report.**

Whenever you want to use the report layout — to view it, print it, or modify it — just highlight the report name in the Control Center and then press Enter. To print the report from the Report Design screen, open the **P**rint menu and select **B**egin printing.

> **TIP:** Notice that at the bottom center of the Report Design screen, the Status Bar shows you the current cursor position on-screen. The first number is the line number (up and down), and the second number is the column number (right and left). This is a big help when you position fields and text on a report layout.

Creating a Grouped Report

A grouped report is similar to the row-and-column report you learn to create in Chapter 16, but it lets you divide the records. If, for example, you want a report that lists customers by state and also includes the total number of customers in each state, use a grouped report.

Indexing the grouping field

One thing that dBASE's Report Design screen *doesn't* do for you is put records in order. When you first design your table (as in Chapter 4), you should make sure to index any fields that you want to use for report groups. That's why, for instance, you index the State field when you set up the book's example Bookcust table in Chapter 4. When you print the report, the index for the grouping field must be the *controlling index*. If you don't make it the controlling index (see Chapter 14 for a full explanation), then the records print either in the order they were entered or in the order dictated by some other index.

Before you begin setting up a grouped report, therefore, make sure that you've indexed the field you want to use for grouping and that its index is the controlling index. To index the field, go to the Table Design screen, move the cursor to the line for the field you need to index, and enter a **Y** in the Indexed column. Once you index the grouping field, you need to check that records are in order by the grouping field. Follow these steps:

1. **In the Control Center's Data panel, highlight the table and press Enter.**

   If you're creating the example report in this chapter, select the Bookcust table. A dialog box appears, asking what you want to do with the table.

2. **Select Modify structure/order.**

   The Table Design screen appears.

3. **Press Esc to close the Organize menu.**

4. **In the row for the group field, make sure that the Index column says Y (for yes).**

   For the example report, look at the row for the *State* field.

   If the Index column for the row does *not* say Y, move the cursor to that column and press **Y**. Doing so tells dBASE to index the field.

5. **Open the Layout menu and select Save this database file structure.**

   This command saves the new table design that includes the index.

6. **Open the Organize menu and select Order records by index.**

   At the right side of your screen, dBASE displays a list of indexed fields, as shown in Figure 20-2. At the top, Natural Order isn't an index; it refers to the order in which you first entered records into the table.

7. **In the list, highlight the grouping field and press Enter.**

   Doing so makes the index for the grouping field the controlling index.

8. **Open the Exit menu and select Save changes and exit.**

   The grouping field is now indexed, and records are displayed in order by that field.

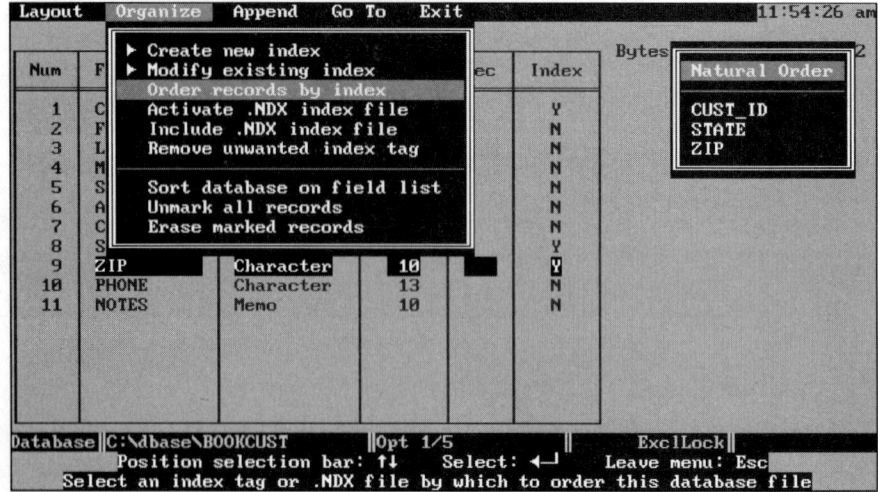

Figure 20-2: Selecting an index to order records in the report.

Setting up a basic report

The following steps walk you through the process of creating a grouped report. First, get to the Control Center. In the Data panel, highlight the table to use and press Enter; then select Use table. If you're doing a grouped report with the book's sample database, use the Bookcust table: you create a report in which customers are grouped by state. Then follow these steps:

1. **In the Reports panel, highlight <create> and press Enter.**

   The Report Design screen appears. The Layout menu is already open.

2. **Press Esc to close the Layout menu.**

3. **Press the down arrow on your keyboard to move the cursor to the Detail band.**

   The cursor should be in the line under the word *Detail* at the left end of the Detail band.

4. **Open the Fields menu and select Add field.**

   A list of available fields appears, as shown in Figure 20-3. For the moment, you can ignore all the columns except the one labeled with the name of the table you're using.

5. **Highlight the field you want and press Enter.**

   This is normally the field you're using to group the records. If you're doing a report with the book's example database, select the State field. A boxed menu appears.

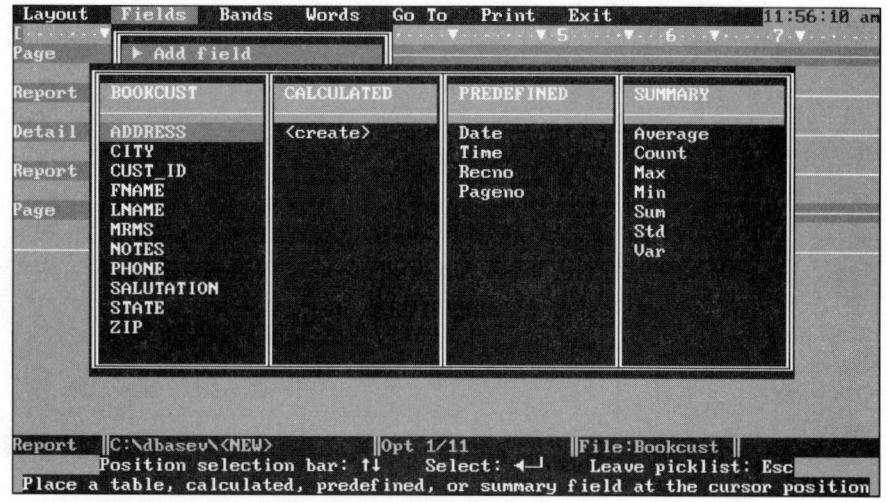

Figure 20-3: A list of fields that you can place in the report.

6. **Press Ctrl-End to bypass the menu.**

   The field blank appears at the left end of the Detail band.

   The menu which you so rudely bypassed lets you put templates into a field, much like the templates you can use with an on-screen form (see Chapters 9 and 13). Here you don't use it, so don't worry about it.

7. **Using the arrow keys, move the cursor to the Page Header band.**

8. **Type a column label for the field.**

   You want the label to be directly above the field, so position the cursor accordingly. In the book's example, type **State** for the column label.

9. **Repeating Steps 4 through 8, add more fields to the Detail band.**

   For the book's example, add FNAME (at column 8), LNAME (at column 26), and CITY (at column 44).

10. **In the Page Header band, type column labels directly above the fields you just entered.**

    For the book's example, type **First Name**, **Last Name**, and **City**.

11. **In the Report Intro band, type the title of the report.**

    Whatever you put in this band prints at the top of the report's first page. For the book's example report, type **Customers by State** in column 27 of the Report Intro band. When you're finished, your screen should look something like Figure 20-4.

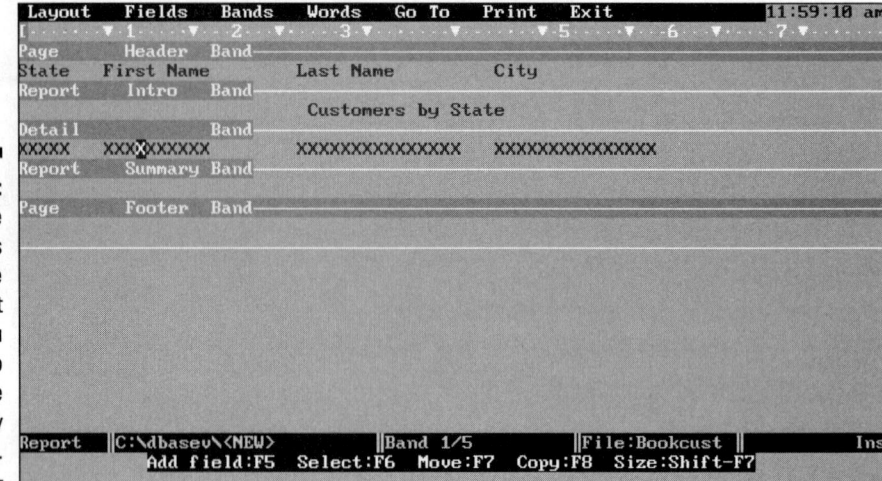

Figure 20-4: The Customers by State report layout. You still need to group the records by state.

```
Layout    Fields   Bands    Words    Go To    Print    Exit              11:59:10 am
[·····▼·1···▼·····2··▼······3·▼·······▼·5·······▼·6·····▼·····7·▼······
Page      Header   Band
State     First Name          Last Name            City
Report    Intro    Band
                              Customers by State
Detail             Band
XXXXX     XXXXXXXXX            XXXXXXXXXXXXXX       XXXXXXXXXXXXXX
Report    Summary  Band
Page      Footer   Band

Report    ||C:\dbasev\<NEW>          ||Band 1/5      ||File:Bookcust ||           Ins
          Add field:F5  Select:F6  Move:F7  Copy:F8  Size:Shift-F7
```

> You can move things around in the report layout by using the same keys as you did in a form layout. To select a field blank in the Detail band, just position the cursor on the field and press F6 (Select). To move the field, press F7 (Move) and press the arrow keys until the field blank is in its new location. Then press Enter.
>
> To move text, position the cursor on the first letter of the text and press F6. Press the right-arrow key until all the text is highlighted, and then press Enter. As with a field, press F7 to move the text, press the arrow keys until unitl the text is in position, and press Enter. Finally, press Esc to remove the highlight from the text.

12. **Finally, preview the report by opening the Print menu and selecting View report on screen.**

    An approximate preview of the report appears on-screen, as shown in Figure 20-5. When you're finished looking at the print preview, press Esc to return to the Report Design screen.

Adding group sections

The report looks okay so far, but the records from different states are squashed together like people in line for tickets to a Streisand concert. It helps to separate them with a little more space. *No problemo!* Follow these steps:

1. **Position the cursor on the last line of the Report Intro band.**

    This line is just above the line that marks the top of the Detail band.

Figure 20-5:
The Customers by State report without any grouping.

```
State    First Name      Last Name          City
                         Customers by State
CA       James           West               Martinsville
CA       Teri            Lane               Santa Barbara
CA       Susan           Brown              Los Angelos
CA       Harris          Harrison           Goleta
CA       Tracy           Dancer             Zuma Beach
CA       Diane           Walker             San Francisco
ID       Arnold          Harris             Boise
IN       Shirley         Edison             Bloomington
IN       Don             Wilds              Bloomington
IN       Jack            Stein              Bloomington
IN       Irwin           Jones              Bloomington
LA       Thomas          Baker              Shreveport
NV       Jules           Twombly            Las Vegas
NY       Harriet         Stowe              New York
WA       Janet           White              Redmond

Cancel viewing: ESC,  Continue viewing: SPACEBAR
```

2. **Open the Bands menu and select Add a group band.**

   A submenu appears.

3. **In the submenu, select Field value.**

   Doing so tells dBASE that you want to group the report based on the value in one of the fields. When you select Field value, a list of possible grouping fields appears.

4. **In the list, select the State field.**

   Notice that two new bands immediately appear in your report layout: a Group Intro band and a Group Summary band. Anything you put in the Group Intro band prints at the top of each group in the report. Anything you put in the Group Summary band prints at the bottom of each group. You often use the Group Summary band to calculate totals and numbers of records in each group. Group bands are also a good place to put horizontal lines that separate the groups in a report.

   You don't have to select *any* fields to group your report. If you don't select grouping fields, the report is the same as a simple row-and-column report, like the one in Chapter 16.

5. **Preview the grouped report.**

   When you open the **Print** menu and select View report on screen, you see that the records are now grouped by state. However, two things are still wrong. First, if more than one record is in a particular group, the name of the grouping field repeats; the report looks better if it appears only once per group. Second, a line between the groups makes the report easier to understand at a glance. When you're finished looking at the print preview, press Esc once or twice to return to the Report Design screen.

6. **Position the cursor in the grouping field blank in the Detail band.**

   In the book's database, this is the State field.

7. **Open the Fields menu and select Modify field.**

   The Modify field submenu appears, as shown in Figure 20-6.

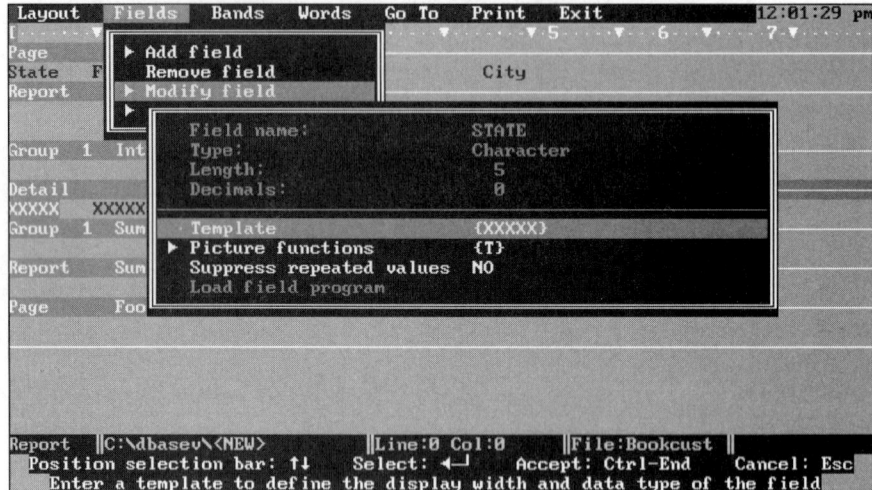

Figure 20-6: The Modify field submenu.

8. **In the submenu, highlight Suppress repeated values.**

   Currently, this choice probably says No.

9. **Press the spacebar to change the choice to Yes.**

10. **Press Ctrl-End to save the change.**

    dBASE closes the menu and returns you to the Report Design screen.

Remember that almost any time you change your mind about doing something, you can back out by pressing Esc. This trick applies to submenus, designs, and pretty much *anything* you do in dBASE.

Prettying up report section breaks

If you stop right now, the report looks much better. The State field's value no longer repeats when several records come from the same state. But you can do one more thing to pretty up the report layout: add a line between the group sections. To use horizontal lines to separate the report groups, follow these steps:

Chapter 20: Hot Stuff! Creating Sophisticated Reports 241

1. **Position the cursor at the left end of the Group Intro band.**
2. **Open the Layout menu and select Line.**

   The Line submenu appears. In the menu, you have three choices:

   - **Single line** draws a single horizontal line to separate the groups.
   - **Double line** draws a double horizontal line to separate the groups. The two lines are drawn very close together.
   - **Using specified character** {} lets you choose the letter, punctuation mark, or other character you want to use for the line. To use this option, press Enter. dBASE displays a list of characters you can use, as shown in Figure 20-7. Use the arrow, PgDn, and PgUp keys to highlight the character you want.

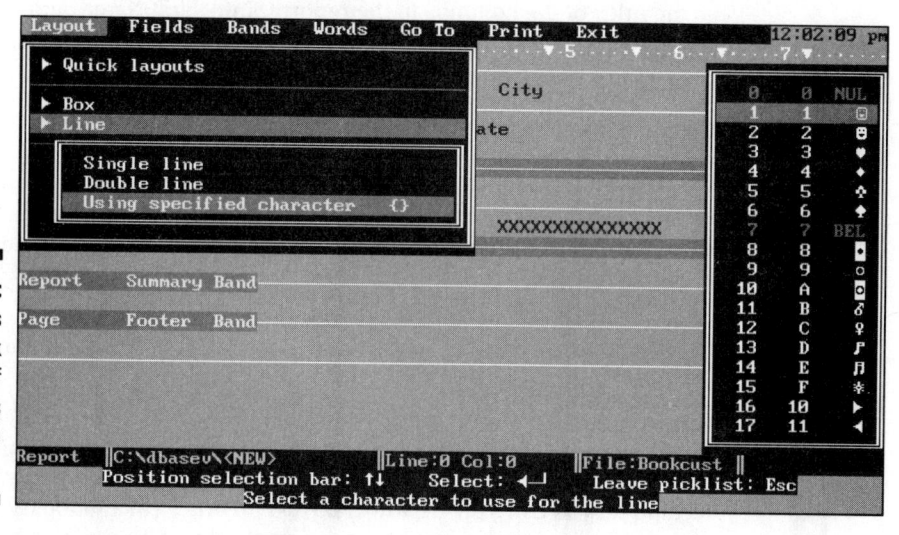

Figure 20-7: dBASE lets you pick from a list of characters for line drawing.

3. **Highlight your choice and press Enter.**

   dBASE returns you to the Report Design screen. As before, the cursor is the left end of the Group Intro band. If you're drawing a line with the book's sample report, make it a single line. No need to get too fancy your first time out.

4. **Press Enter to mark the left end of the line.**
5. **Repeatedly press the right-arrow key to draw the line.**

   When the line extends as far as you want it to go, stop.

6. **Press Enter to mark the right end of the line.**

   You're done!

When you now open the **Print** menu and select **View** records on-screen, you see that your records are nicely grouped by state, with a horizontal line separating each group from the one before it. In a table like this one, with only a few records, groups don't really help a lot. But you can imagine how much they help in a table with 1,000 records in 50 different groups.

Parts of the grouped report design

Take a look at the Report Design screen, shown in Figure 20-8. This report design, just like the simpler one you see in Chapter 16, consists of horizontal bands. Each band contains a different kind of information to print on the page.

- **Page Header band** contains stuff that prints at the top of each page, such as the titles of the columns in the report (State, First Name, and so on).

- **Report Intro band** contains stuff that prints at the beginning of the report, such as the report title.

- **Group Intro band** contains stuff that prints at the top of each group in the report. In the figure, the report is grouped by state, so dBASE prints the name of the state for each group of records. In the example report, it actually says *Group 1 Intro Band,* because there's only one group. If you have more than one group — suppose that within each state group, you group the records by city — then you have a Group 1 Intro Band, a Group 2 Intro Band, and so on.

- **Detail band** contains the actual data from the Bookcust table: names, account numbers, and so on.

- **Group Summary band** contains stuff that prints at the bottom of each group. You can tell dBASE to count the number of customer records for each state (you learn how to do so in the next section). Using the same technique, you can also create totals and do other calculations that appear at the bottom of each group. Here, it actually says *Group 1 Summary Band,* for reasons explained in the paragraph about the Group Intro Band.

- **Report Summary band** contains stuff that prints at the end of the report, such as grand totals and items that have to be in the report but that you don't want anyone to read.

- **Page Footer band** contains stuff that prints at the bottom of each page, such as the page number.

- **New Trier High School Marching Band** contains immensely talented but sometimes out-of-step high school students. If it appears on your screen, you are in serious trouble and should call 911 immediately.

Saving the report

To save the report, open the Layout menu and select **S**ave this report. In the blank, give it a name — if you're saving the book's example report, type the name **by_state** in the blank. Then press Enter.

Doing Calculations in a Report

The grouped report you created in the preceding section looks pretty good. You can see that the records are grouped by state: you have two customers in California, one in Idaho, and so forth. The grouping field is in the first (left-most) column of the report.

You can improve the report in one other obvious way. It would be nice if, at the end of each state group, dBASE told you how many customers are in that state. That's surprisingly easy to do, and you can pick up a few other tricks along the way.

Changing the height of a report band

Before you can put a total of each group's records in the Group Summary band, you probably need to make it a little taller. It's easy — move the cursor to the left end of the Group Summary band, right under the *G* in the word *Group*. Then press Enter a few times. As you do, the band gets taller.

WARNING! If pressing Enter doesn't make the Group Summary band get taller, then your keyboard has the Insert key set to off. To turn Insert on, just press the Insert key. If Insert is on, the letters *Ins* are visible at the lower-right corner of your screen in the Status Bar.

You can use the same technique to increase the height of any band in the report. When you want to *decrease* a band's height, position the cursor on empty lines in the band and press Ctrl-Y to delete the extra lines.

With the book's example by_state report, press the Enter key twice so that the Group Summary band now has three lines in it.

Inserting a summary field

Counting records in a group is one way of *summarizing* information about the group. You do so by having dBASE put a summary field in the Group Summary band. In addition to counting records, a summary field can do other kinds of calculations. When you create a sales report with the records grouped by date, for example, a summary field can give you a total dollar amount for the books sold on each day.

To insert a summary field that counts the records in each group, follow these steps:

1. **In the Group Summary band, type a caption for the summary field.**

   If you're using the book's example report, move to Line 1, column 21 and type **Number in this state:**.

2. **With the right-arrow key, move the cursor one space to the right of the caption.**

   In the example report, it should be at Line 1, Column 43.

3. **Open the Fields menu and select Add field.**

4. **Use the arrow keys to move to the Summary column and highlight Count.**

5. **Press Enter.**

   The Template menu will appear. Press Ctrl-End. dBASE inserts the record-counting field at the cursor position.

When you open the **Print** menu and select **View** report on-screen, it should look something like Figure 20-8.

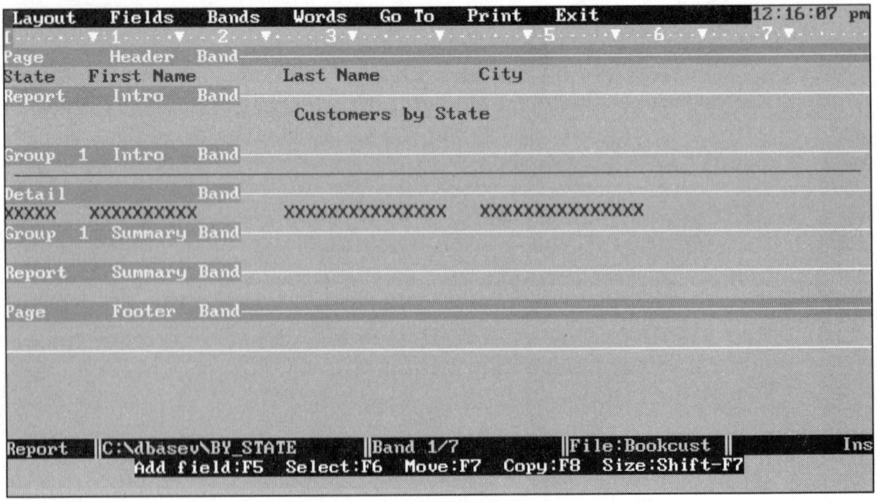

Figure 20-8: The grouped report with a record count for each group.

If the report looks okay, switch back to the Report Design screen. Open the **L**ayout menu and select **S**ave this report. If you want to keep the preceding version of the report, you can enter a different name.

Basing a Report on a Query

So far, all the reports you've created have used information from a table. But you can also base a report on a query. If you think about it, it's not too surprising, because the result of a query is a group of records and fields, very much like a table.

By using a query instead of a table, you can restrict the information that appears in a report. Suppose you want a report that includes only information about customers who live in California. The easiest way to produce such a report is to create a query that asks, "Which customers live in California?" The answer to the query contains the records you want for the report. When you base the report on the query, dBASE automatically prints information about California customers only.

Basing a report on a query is only slightly different from basing it on a table. Follow these steps:

1. **In the Control Center, highlight the query you want to use and press Enter.**

   A dialog box appears, asking what you want to do with the query.

2. **Select Use view.**

   dBASE opens the query you selected.

3. **In the Report panel, highlight `<create>` and press Enter.**

   The Report Design screen appears, just as it does when you base a report on a table.

After this point, everything else works the same as it does when you use a table.

In the exercise in the next section, you use the query-report combination for another very special purpose: to create a report that draws information from more than one table.

Creating a Multitable Report

The multitable report you're about to create isn't fancy. But you can use the process you learn in this example to construct more interesting reports.

To create the sample multitable report, use the Custsale query from Chapter 19. Because this query already includes the fields from the book's example Bookcust and Sales tables, all the data that the query draws from both tables can be printed in the report.

> **NOTE:** You're not limited to only two tables in a report or query. You can include as many as you need.

To create a multitable report, follow these steps:

1. **In the Control Center, select the multitable query the report should use.**

   In the dialog box, select Use view. This command opens the query so that the report can use it. If you're working with the book's example database, use the Custsale query from Chapter 19.

2. **In the Reports panel, select** <create>.

   The Report Design screen appears.

3. **Place the fields you want in the Detail band.**

4. **Position the cursor in the Detail band.**

5. **Open the Fields menu and select Add field.**

6. **Select the field you want and press Ctrl-End.**

   For the example report, use the LNAME, TITLE, and PRICE fields.

7. **In the Page Header band, add columns labels for the fields.**

   For the example report, use **Last Name**, **Title**, and **Price**.

8. **If needed, tell dBASE not to repeat fields on successive lines.**

   In the example report, you don't want dBASE to print the same customer's name on several lines for each book purchased. So position the cursor on the field that shouldn't repeat (LNAME), open the Fields menu, and select **Modify Field**. In the submenu, change Suppress repeated values to Yes, and then press Ctrl-End to save the change.

9. **Open the Print menu and select View report on screen to see the report.**

   Your report should look something like Figure 20-9, except much bigger.

10. **Press Esc to exit from print preview.**

11. Name and save the report.

For the example, use the name *Custsale*.

Figure 20-9: Preview of a multitable report.

State	First Name	Last Name	City
		Customers by State	
CA	James	West	Martinsville
	Teri	Lane	Santa Barbara
	Susan	Brown	Los Angeles
	Harris	Harrison	Goleta
	Tracy	Dancer	Zuma Beach
	Diane	Walker	San Francisco
	Number in this state:		6
ID	Arnold	Harris	Boise
	Number in this state:		1
IN	Shirley	Edison	Bloomington
	Don	Wilds	Bloomington
	Jack	Stein	Bloomington
	Irwin	Jones	Bloomington
	Number in this state:		4
LA	Thomas	Baker	Shreveport
	Number in this state:		1

Cancel viewing: ESC, Continue viewing: SPACEBAR

> **NOTE:** You can use other tricks to improve the report. In the sample report, for example, you can insert a summary field under the Price column to show the total amount spent by each customer. Use your imagination!

As usual, you can print the report by opening the **P**rint menu and selecting **B**egin printing.

In the next chapter, you learn how to use dBASE to create those annoying form letters that are always jamming your mailbox. But this time, you can send them to *other* people (plan on sending at least a thousand to Ed McMahon).

Chapter 21
Insanely Great Field Tricks in Forms and Reports

● ●

In This Chapter
- ▶ Using templates and picture functions
- ▶ Formatting field data
- ▶ Error-checking data entry
- ▶ Showing memo text in a form or report

● ●

*I*n previous chapters, you learn quite a few tricks for creating on-screen forms and printed reports. This chapter expands what you've learned by providing, in one place, a comprehensive explanation of *all* the important tricks you can use for things like

- ✔ Formatting data in a field of an on-screen form or printed report
- ✔ Preventing the user from putting something in a field unless it's in a list of specific values or in a range of values
- ✔ Making dBASE automatically fill in selected fields with default values that it uses unless you specify something else
- ✔ Making dBASE carry values from one record to the next
- ✔ Displaying memo field text in a window on a form or report

You perform these tricks in pretty much the same way whether you're creating a form or report. The big difference is not in how you *do* the tricks, but in their result. When used in a form, they control how data goes into your database; when used in a report, they control how data comes out.

To understand the ideas and techniques in this chapter, you need to

- ✔ Know basic database concepts, such as *table* and *field* (see Chapters 1 and 2).
- ✔ Create an on-screen form (see Chapter 9) and a report layout (see Chapter 16).

Using the Modify Field Submenu

Most of the tricks in this chapter apply to both on-screen forms and printed reports. You begin at the Modify field submenu, shown in Figure 21-1.

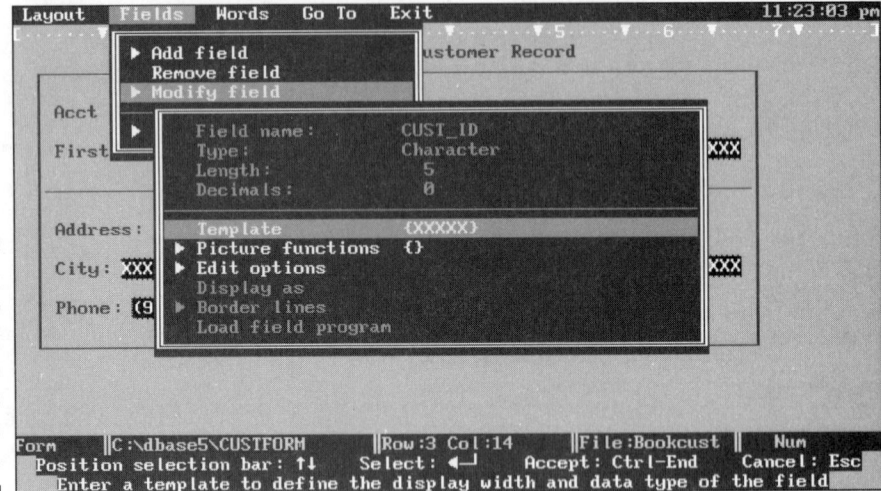

Figure 21-1: The Modify field submenu in the Forms Design screen.

You can get to the Modify field submenu in two ways. After opening a form or report layout on-screen and then moving the cursor onto the form or report field you want to change, you can either

- Open the **F**ields menu and select **M**odify field, or
- Press F5 (the hot key for modifying or inserting fields).

The submenu itself is almost the same in both the Forms Design screen and the Report Design screen. The most important change is that a menu line saying **S**uppress repeated values in the Report Design screen replaces the menu line saying **E**dit options in the Forms Design screen.

> **TIP:** In addition to modifying fields, you can use the F5 key to insert a field on a form or report. The only difference is that instead of positioning the cursor on a field blank before pressing F5, you position it on a blank part of the layout.

In the top part of the Modify field submenu, dBASE shows you basic information about the field, such as its name, type, width, length, and number of decimal places. The real action begins in the bottom part, where you can

Chapter 21: Insanely Great Field Tricks in Forms and Reports 251

✔ Enter a template to restrict or format the characters or digits that a user can put in the field.

✔ Display a menu of picture functions that do template tasks for you.

✔ Display a menu of editing options that let you prevent users from entering anything outside a particular range of values (for example, 1 to 10), tell dBASE to carry a value forward from one record to the next, set default values, or show help messages.

Templates and editing options are pretty much the same in all types of fields (character, numeric, date, and so on). They are covered in the next two sections. After that, we cover picture functions and other tricks for each main field type.

Tricks with Templates

To enter a template in a field, you move the cursor to the field blank and press F5 to open the Modify field submenu. From there, highlight the Template menu choice and press Enter. You can now delete the original field template (usually a bunch of Xs) and type a new one. dBASE displays a help window telling you how to do it, as shown in Figure 21-2.

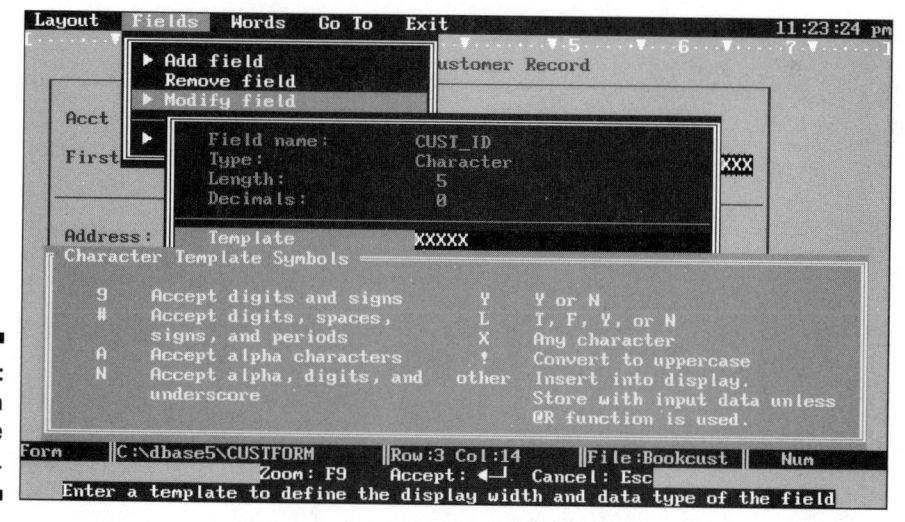

Figure 21-2: Entering a template into a field.

A template not only lets you format a field, but it also lets you restrict certain field positions to certain characters. That idea's pretty abstract, so here are a few examples with a character field five spaces wide to help you understand how these restrictions work:

Table 21-1 Examples of Templates and Their Meanings

Template	Meaning
99999	Only digits (0 to 9) can be entered in the field. (If the field is numeric, plus and minus signs are also allowed.)
A999#	Only a letter (A to Z, or a to z) in position 1; only digits in positions 2 to 4; and only a digit, space, period, plus sign, or minus sign in position 5.
!AAAA	Any character allowed in the first position (a letter in that position is converted to uppercase); only letters allowed in positions 2 to 5.
!!!!!	Any characters in any position, but letters are converted to uppercase.
(999)	Inserts parentheses at positions 1 and 5; allows only digits in positions 2 to 4.
@!	Allows any characters, but converts letters to uppercase. The at sign (@) tells dBASE to apply the exclamation mark to the entire field, regardless of the field's size. (This is a template you can enter that uses a picture function.) In a name field, for example, it would convert jones to JONES.

Many things you can do with templates can also be done, sometimes more easily, with picture functions. When you enter a template, however, you can use these symbols:

Table 21-2 Template Symbols and Their Effects

Symbol	What It Does
9	In a character field, restricts the field position to a digit (0 to 9). In a numeric field, restricts the field position to a digit, plus sign, or minus sign.
#	Restricts the field position to a digit, space, period, plus sign, or minus sign.
A	Restricts the field position to a letter — no punctuation marks, spaces, or digits.
N	Restricts the field position to a letter, digit, or underscore (_).
Y	Restricts the field position to Y, y, N, or n and converts lowercase y or n to uppercase.
L	Restricts the field position to a T, F, Y, or N.
X	Allows any character in the field position — no restrictions.
!	Allows any character in the field position and converts letters to uppercase.
Literal	A fancy word for any other character you put in a field template, such as parentheses.

To save a template or any change you make to the field definition, press Ctrl-End.

Using Edit Options

Editing options are used in forms for data entry and are pretty much the same for all types of fields. They let you set predetermined values for a field, prevent the user from entering data into the field, and so on. To get to the Edit options menu shown in Figure 21-3, you start at the Modify field submenu. Highlight Edit options and press Enter. Here's what you can do with the different choices:

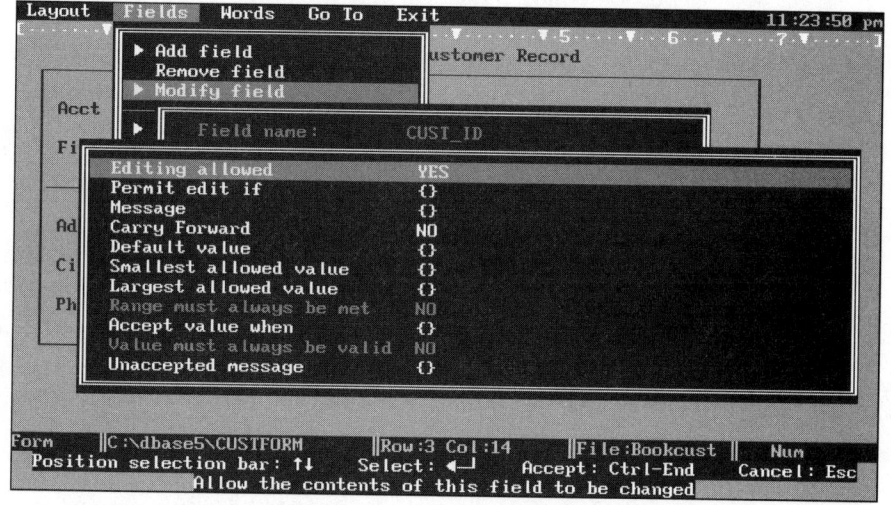

Figure 21-3: The Edit options menu.

- ✓ **Editing allowed** tells dBASE whether the user should be allowed to enter or change data in a field. Normally, this option is set to Yes, meaning that the user *can* enter new data or change what's already there. You use this option in two main situations. First, you can create a form intended only for use in displaying data. In that case, you want to keep users from changing the data while it's displayed. Second, you can set a default value for a field or create a calculated field: in that case, you may or may not want to let the user change the value.

- ✓ **Permit edit if** tells dBASE that changing a field's data is allowed only if something else is true, such as that another field contains a certain value. You probably won't use this option often.

- ✓ **Message** lets you create a customized help message that appears on-screen whenever a user moves the cursor into the field. The message can contain up to 80 characters (one line of text).

- **Carry Forward** tells dBASE to use the same data in this field as appeared in the preceding record. It's useful for tables in which certain fields repeat the same information over and over. For example, if you enter customer records in groups by city, there's no point in typing the same city name over and over. Once you've entered the city, you want it to stay the same until you get to the next city group, at which point you type a new city in the first record of the group, which is then carried forward. In a way, this option turns whatever you enter in the field into a sort of temporary default value.

- **Default value** lets you set a value that the field automatically has unless the user changes it. If most of your customers are in the same city, then you can enter the city's name as the default value in a City field. A user has to put something in the field only when a customer comes from a different city. This option not only saves time and effort, but it also reduces the chance of typing errors.

- **Smallest allowed value** lets you tell dBASE not to accept any values lower than the one you select. For instance, a bookstore may not sell books priced lower than $9.95. If a clerk attempts to enter a price of $7.00, you know in advance that such a value is a mistake. Therefore, you can use this option to tell dBASE to reject any values under $9.95.

- **Largest allowed value** lets you tell dBASE not to accept any values higher than the one you select. It works the same as **S**mallest allowed value.

- **Range must always be met** lets you turn off range checking (smallest to largest value) by setting this option to No.

- **Accept value when** is like **P**ermit edit if. The difference is that this option applies to entering new data, while **P**ermit edit if applies to changing data that you have already entered.

- If you set **Value must always be valid** to No, dBASE doesn't check to make sure that a value is valid.

- **Unaccepted message** lets you create a customized help message that appears on-screen whenever a user tries to enter a field value that's forbidden by the **A**ccept value when option. The message can contain up to 80 characters (one line of text).

To save edit options or other changes you make to the field definition, press Ctrl-End.

Tricks with Character Fields

Most specific tricks for different kinds of fields use the **Picture functions** submenu, shown in Figure 21-4. You open this submenu by selecting **P**icture functions from the **M**odify field submenu. Picture functions are often shortcuts

Chapter 21: Insanely Great Field Tricks in Forms and Reports 255

that let you do the same things you can do by creating a field template — but more easily and efficiently. The choices are as follows:

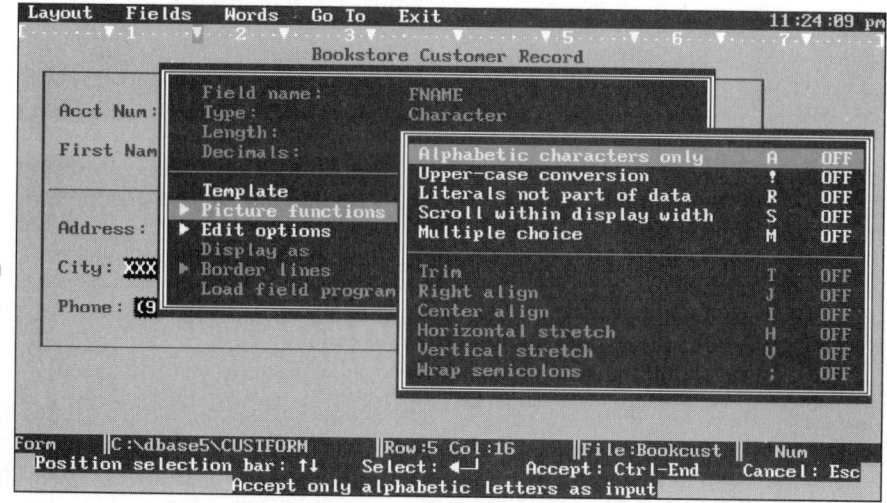

Figure 21-4: The Picture functions submenu for character-type fields.

- When you turn on **Alphabetic characters only** (by pressing Enter), dBASE allows only letters (uppercase or lowercase) in the field.

- **Upper-case conversion** tells dBASE to convert any letters in the field to uppercase. The section about templates explains how to use this picture function (@!) in a template.

- When you create a form template that contains formatting characters, such as parentheses, these characters (called *literals*) are actually inserted into the field data in the table, such as in the example table's PHONE field. **Literals not part of data** uses literals only to format the data when it's displayed in the form — they aren't actually part of the data in the table. The advantage of making literals part of the data is that no matter how the data is displayed (form, report, or Browse screen), the formatting characters are included. The disadvantage is that the field must be bigger to include the formatting characters, which is a concern if your database is large and you're trying to save space on your hard disk.

- You may have a field width of 80 but only have room on your form for a field blank that's 50 characters wide. In that case, some of the data may not be visible in the field blank on the form. With the **Scroll within display width** option on, a user can press the arrow keys to scroll right and left within the field blank to see all the data.

This option works only if Editing allowed is turned on in the Edit options submenu.

Part IV: Really Advanced Stuff to Impress Your Friends

✓ **Multiple choice** lets you set up a choice list from which a form's user can select values to enter into the field. It's useful when there are a limited number of possible values for a field and you want to make sure that no one enters another value. For example, a bookstore may service customers in only three states: Maryland, Pennsylvania, and New York. After highlighting **M**ultiple choice and pressing Enter to set up a choice list, you type each choice with the choices separated by commas. For the bookstore example, type **MD,PA,NY** and then press Enter to tell dBASE that you're finished entering items in the list.

To save the picture functions or other changes you make to the field definition, press Ctrl-End.

Tricks with Number Fields

As shown in Figure 21-5, the **P**icture functions submenu offers different choices for numeric fields than it does for character fields, simply because you need to do different things with numeric fields. When turned on, the choices perform as follows:

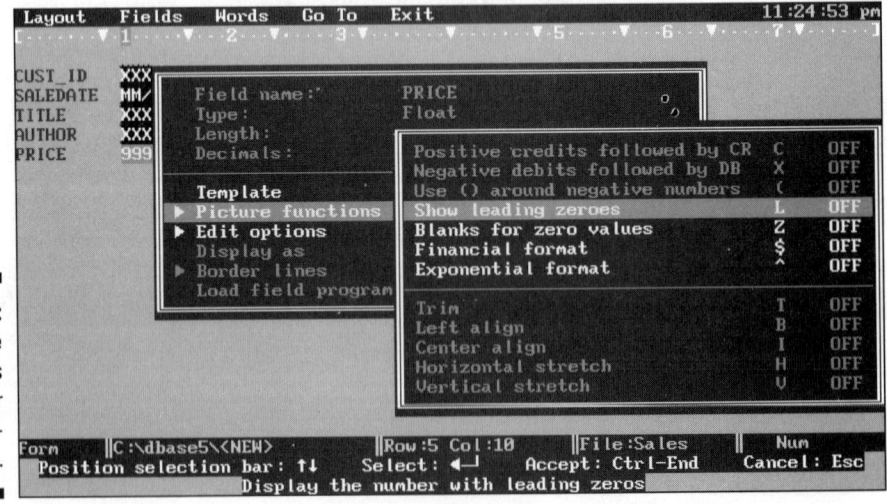

Figure 21-5:
The Picture functions submenu for numeric-type fields.

✓ **Positive credits followed by CR** makes the letters CR (for *credit*) display after positive numbers in the field. You can use this option only if you've set **E**diting allowed to **N**o in the **E**dit options submenu.

Chapter 21: Insanely Great Field Tricks in Forms and Reports

- **Negative credits followed by DB** makes the letters DB (for *debit*) display after negative numbers in the field. You can use it only if you've set Editing allowed to No in the Edit options submenu.

- **Use () around negative numbers** makes parentheses display around positive numbers in the field. You can use it only if you've set Editing allowed to No in the Edit options submenu.

- **Show leading zeroes** makes leading zeroes display to the number's left so that the number fills up the field — for example, 00012.

- **Blanks for zero values** turns off leading zeroes.

- **Financial format** displays a number in dollar format, with a $ sign in front of it.

- **Exponential format** displays a number in exponential format as a power of 10. For example, it displays the number 125 as .125000E+2, which is how a PC says "0.125 times 10 to the power of 2."

- **Trim** hides all blank spaces to the left and right of a field value. You can use it only if you've set Editing allowed to No in the Edit options submenu.

- **Left align** makes data align with the left end of the field blank. With character fields, this is the normal way to display data. Unless you turn this option on, numeric fields are aligned with the right end of the field blank. You can use it only if you've set Editing allowed to No in the Edit options submenu.

- **Center align** centers the data in the middle of the field blank. You can use it only if you've set Editing allowed to No in the Edit options submenu.

- **Horizontal stretch** makes the field blank in a report expand horizontally to show all the data.

- **Vertical stretch** makes the field blank in a report expand vertically to show all the data.

To save picture functions or other changes you make to the field definition, simply press Ctrl-End.

Displaying Memo Fields in a Form Window

Normally, as shown in Figure 21-6, you can't read a memo field right on a form. The form contains only a field marker. To read the memo, you position the cursor on the field marker and press Ctrl-Home to open the memo editor. Then, in the editor, you can see the text that is in the memo.

Part IV: Really Advanced Stuff to Impress Your Friends

Figure 21-6:
Normally, you can't read memo fields right on a form.

The main problem with this approach is that it wastes time and effort. You have to open the memo editor, read the text, and then close the memo editor. Okay, it's not as much work as balancing the federal budget, but it's still extra work that you're better off without.

The **Mo**dify field submenu, shown in Figure 21-7, gives you a way to display the memo text in a window on your form. That way, you don't have to open the memo editor; the text is already visible. Follow these steps:

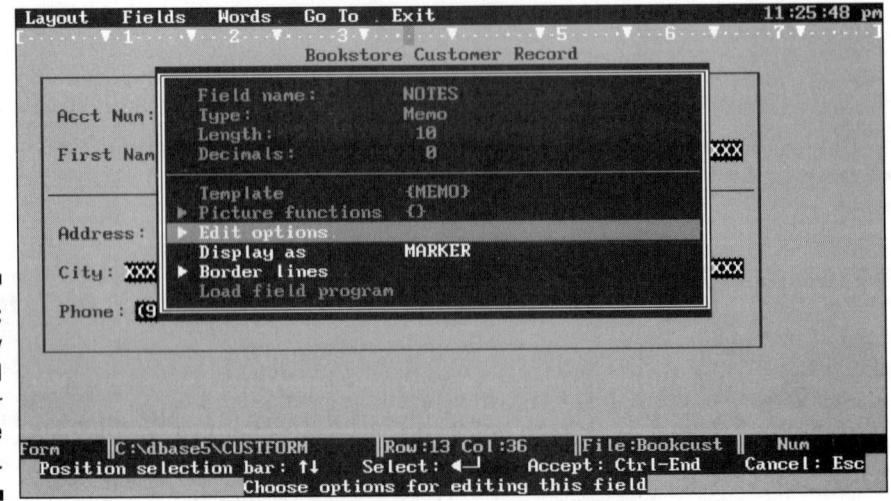

Figure 21-7:
The Modify field submenu for memo-type fields.

Chapter 21: Insanely Great Field Tricks in Forms and Reports   259

1. **Open the Forms Design screen with the form you want to modify.**

   In the Control Center, highlight the form you want to modify and press Enter. In the dialog box, select **M**odify layout.

2. **Position the cursor on the marker for the memo field and press F5.**

   The **M**odify field submenu appears. The **D**isplay as menu choice should say `Marker`.

3. **Highlight Display as and press Enter.**

   The word `Marker` changes to `Window`.

4. **Press Ctrl-End to save the change in the field.**

   The field now appears as a slightly oversized window on the form, as shown in Figure 21-8. Notice that the window is highlighted — it's already selected so that you can resize or move it.

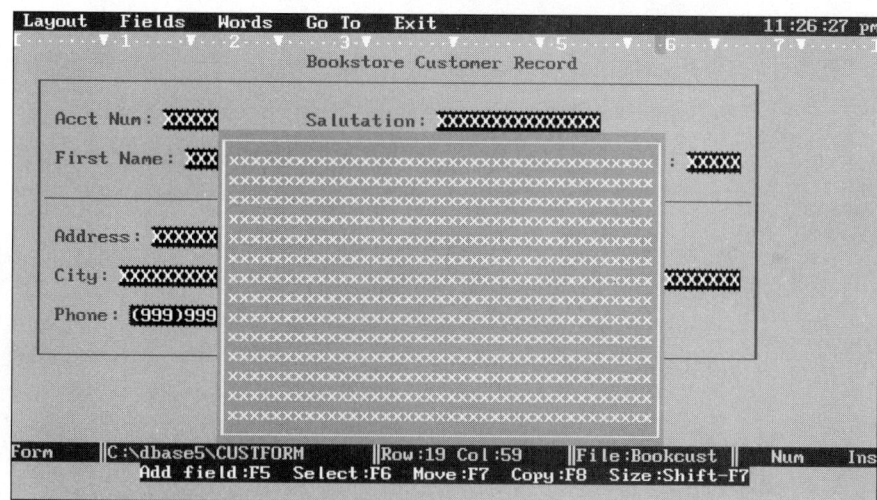

Figure 21-8: The memo window appears, but it's waaaaaay too big.

5. **Press Shift-F7.**

6. **Press the up- and left-arrow keys to shrink the window.**

   Make it a size that displays the memo text but also fits easily on the form.

7. **Press Enter.**

   This action tells dBASE that you're finished shrinking the window.

8. **Press F7 again.**

9. **Press the arrow keys to move the window into position, as shown in Figure 21-9.**

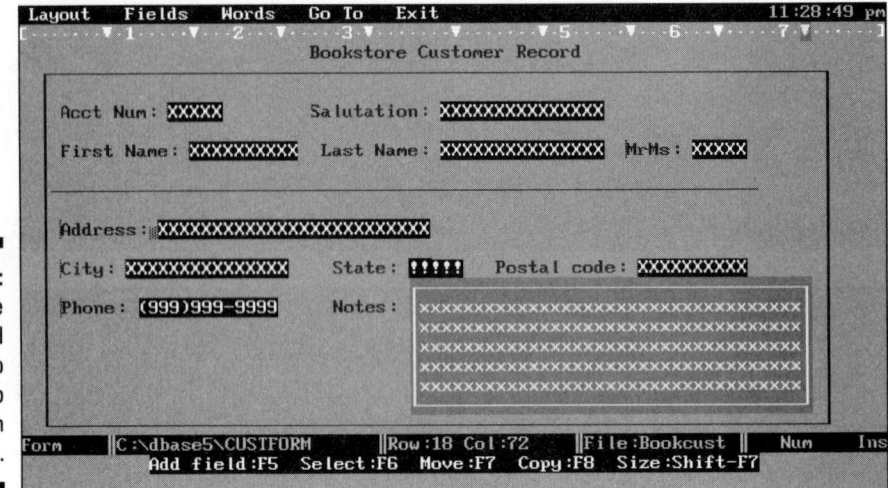

Part IV: Really Advanced Stuff to Impress Your Friends

Figure 21-9: Move the resized memo window into position on the form.

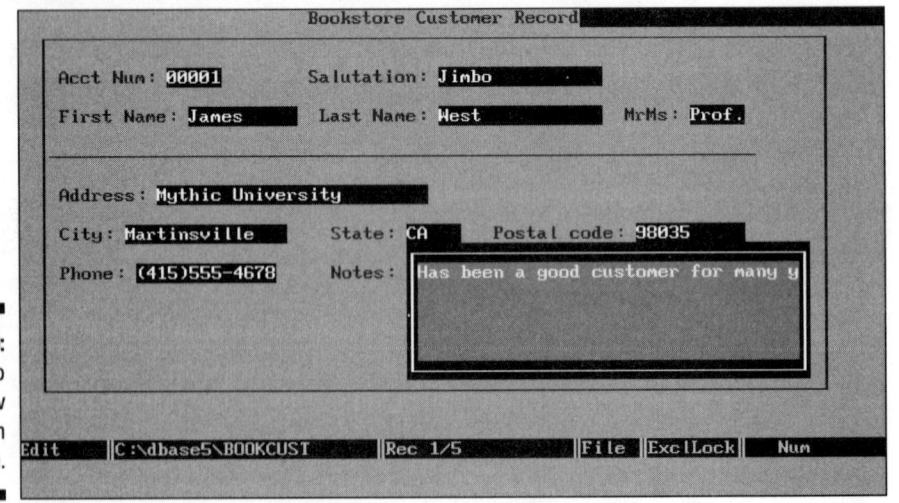

Figure 21-10: The memo text now appears on the form.

10. **Press Enter to confirm the move.**
11. **Open the Exit menu and select Save changes and exit.**

    You can now use the form to display memo text on-screen, as shown in Figure 21-10.

> **NOTE:** From the Modify field submenu, you can also select Border lines. This option tells dBASE to surround the memo window with a single line, double line, or line made of a character you choose.

The 5th Wave   By Rich Tennant

"WE HARDLY GET ANY COMPLAINTS FROM USERS ANYMORE. THINK IT'S BECAUSE WE HIRED A TROGLODYTE TO RUN THE DEPARTMENT?"

Chapter 22
dBASE Utilities and Power Tricks

In This Chapter
- Changing the default directory
- Creating macros
- Customizing dBASE's settings

This is the chapter where you will truly become a dBASE power user in the modern sense of the word. All that will remain is for you to get a cellular phone (if you don't already have one), a nice condo downtown, and a really cheesy smile. In this chapter, you'll learn how to change the default directory, create macros, and customize dBASE's appearance to meet your dreams of what an attractive database manager looks like. You'll also learn why each of those things is important, and how you can use them with your database.

Before embarking on this chapter, you should have

- An idea of what databases are and how they work (see Chapters 1 and 2)
- A data file (see Chapter 5)
- A firm grasp of the true nature of material wealth, and its place in the cosmos (you don't want to let power dBASEing go to your head)

Changing the Default Directory

If you're like most people, then you probably think that this section is about getting a new French telephone book. But alas, that is not the case. Changing the default directory is what you do when you want dBASE to save/load everything that you do to a different directory on your hard disk. This can be a useful feature for the person with multiple databases. For even though catalogs (covered in Chapter 3) help you to remember which dBASE tools go with which database, they can only help you when you are actually using dBASE. From the

Part IV: Really Advanced Stuff to Impress Your Friends

cold and lonely world of the DOS prompt, they can't do much, because they don't actually separate different databases on your hard disk. If you're the kind of person who needs to back up your databases often, then changing the default directory will be invaluable to you. It will allow you to keep various tools associated with the database that they belong with, by putting each database into its own directory. That way, when it's time to back up, there's no worrying about which tool goes with which database. A simple COPY *.* command will take care of everything.

To change the default directory in dBASE, just follow these quick and easy steps:

1. **Select DOS utilities from the Tools menu in the Control Center.**

   The DOS utilities screen appears, as shown in Figure 22-1.

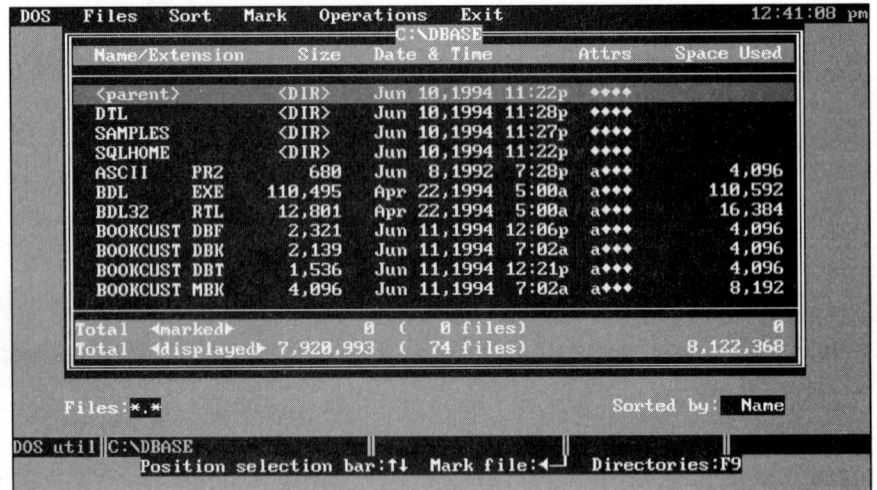

Figure 22-1: The DOS utilities screen, unmasked.

2. **Open the DOS menu and select Set default drive:directory.**

   A dialog box appears on the left side of the screen, asking you to enter the drive and directory that you want to set as the default.

3. **Enter the default drive and directory.**

   One note: The directory must already exist! You can enter the default directory just as you'd type any directory in MS-DOS — for example, C:\DBASE\STORE.

The directory that you enter becomes the default directory from now until you change it again or turn off dBASE. Everything that you do, see, hear, smell, save, and load will be from this directory.

Chapter 22: dBASE Utilities and Power Tricks *265*

> **WARNING!** Once you set the default directory, dBASE will use that directory unless you go through the same steps to switch to *another* directory as the default. What that means is that if you've already set up a database and then change the default directory, you'll need to copy all your database files to the new directory.

Creating Macros

A macro is something that you create to make your computer life faster and easier. Macros work by taking a long, complicated series of keystrokes (which you enter to perform some task) and combining them so that the same task can be done with just one keystroke. Pretty good idea, huh?

To create a macro from the Control Center, follow these steps:

1. Open the Tools menu and select Macros.

The Macros submenu appears in the top center of the screen (see Figure 22-2). If this will be the first macro that you create in dBASE, then most of the options in the submenu will be dimmed, meaning that you can't select them currently.

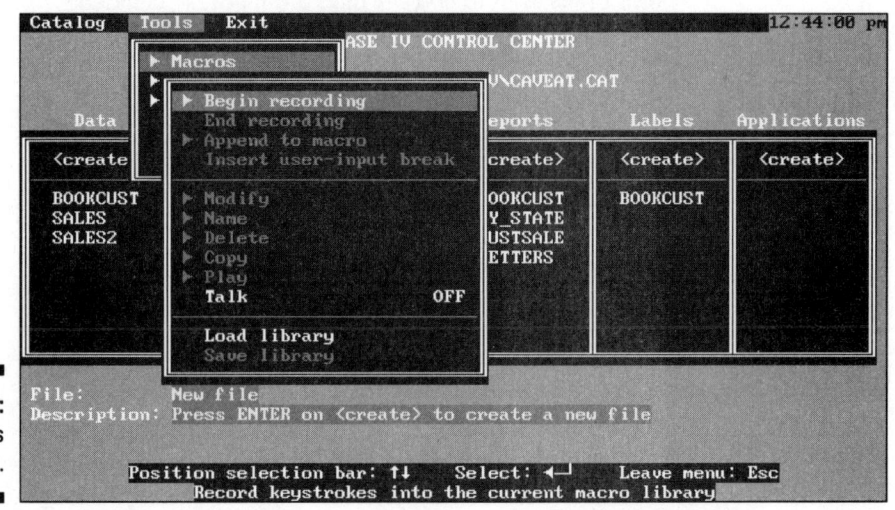

Figure 22-2: The Macros submenu.

2. Select the Begin recording option.

A macro selection table appears, prompting you to enter the keystroke that will run this macro.

3. **Enter the single keystroke that will run this macro.**

   The keystroke that you enter can be one of the function keys (for example, F7 or F8) or a letter of the alphabet.

4. **Enter the keystrokes that will be run by executing this macro.**

   Every keystroke that you press (including Enter and the arrow keys) will now be saved into the macro. All *entering keystrokes* means is that you should do whatever you want the macro to do. The macro recorder is whirring away in the background (well, it doesn't *actually* make a whirring sound), so every move you make gets recorded in the macro for later playback.

   > **TIP:** When recording a macro, you should avoid using the arrow keys or the Enter key outside of menus. Unless the cursor is at the exact same initial spot that it was in when you recorded the macro, the keystrokes will get out of line with the screen items that they're on. You can easily end up executing menu options that you don't want. Of course, if your macro opens a menu first, then you know exactly where the cursor is, so you can use the arrow and Enter keys with reckless abandon.

5. **Press Shift-F10 to stop recording keystrokes into the macro.**

   In the dialog box that appears, select End recording. This causes all recording of the macro to be stopped, and will save the macro. The Shift-F10 keystrokes used to end the macro will not be included.

Changing Macros

You can update the keystrokes contained in a macro by following these steps from the Control Center:

1. **Open the Tools menu and select Macros.**

   The Macros submenu appears in the top center of the screen.

2. **Select Modify from the Macros submenu.**

   A table of available macros appears.

3. **Select the macro you want to modify.**

   Type the keystroke that executes the macro. The macro that you select is displayed in the Macro Editor screen as in Figure 22-3.

Figure 22-3: A typical macro being inspected in the Macro Editor screen.

```
                                                        12:45:35 pm
  [....▼1.....▼.2....▼....3.▼....4▼....▼5....▼.6...▼..7.▼..
  {Alt-c}{Enter}
  {downarrow}{downarrow}
```

4. **Edit the macro.**

   You can delete a keystroke from the macro by using the Backspace or Delete keys (as you would in a word processor). You can add a keystroke by putting brackets { } around the command for the keystroke you want to add. If you don't know the command, you can add it by using the Append to macro option in the Macros submenu.

5. **Press Ctrl-End to save the modified macro.**

   When you're done editing the macro, press Ctrl-End to save it.

Customizing dBASE's Settings

Are you unhappy with that Nauseous Blue used by dBASE as a background color? Do you dislike it when dBASE beeps tauntingly at you? If you answered "Yes" to either of these questions, you may want to consider using dBASE's Settings menu. The makers of dBASE (in a stroke of genius) realized that everyone is different. For this reason, they included a wide range of features that each individual can change to his or her liking. You can change such varied settings as programming options and screen colors. Open the Tools menu in the Control Center and select the Settings option to see a menu of settings. Then select the Options heading to see a list of the options that you can change (see Figure 22-4). Here's what each one does:

- **Bell:** Turns the warning bell off and on. With the bell OFF, dBASE won't beep in the places that it normally does (like when a field is full and you get moved to the next one).
- **Carry:** With this ON, dBASE takes the data from the preceding record and puts it into a new record that you may be adding to your database.
- **Century:** When ON, this option causes the date to be displayed with the year showing all four digits (05/31/1994 as opposed to 05/31/94 when it's set to OFF).
- **Confirm:** Requires that you press Enter before it allows data to be put into a field or variable.
- **Date Order:** Cycles you through three options when you press Enter: MDY, DMY, and YMD. The option that you select is the order that dates will be displayed in (for example, MDY would cause the Month, Day, then Year to be displayed).
- **Date Separator:** Pressing Enter cycles through three different characters that you can use to separate the various parts of the date. The choices are /, -, and . (period).
- **Decimal Place:** Specifies the number of digits after the decimal point to use in calculations and unformatted displays. You can enter a number between 0 and 18.
- **Deleted:** Having this option ON while moving through a display of your data causes dBASE to skip over the records that are marked for deletion.
- **Exact:** When it's ON, it requires strings to match in length as well as in capitalization to be considered equal.
- **Exclusive:** When ON, prevents the use of shared files in a multiple-computer network.
- **Instruct:** When ON, displays information boxes.
- **Margin:** Lets you enter a number of spaces to skip for the left margin of printed reports.
- **Memo Width:** Lets you change the default width of the screen that's used to display memos.
- **Mouse:** When ON, it lets you use a mouse.
- **Safety:** When ON, asks for confirmation when you're about to overwrite a file.
- **Talk:** Displays the results of operations that you perform on your data.
- **Trap:** Turn it ON to enable the debugger option. This is useful if you're going to be creating dBASE programs.

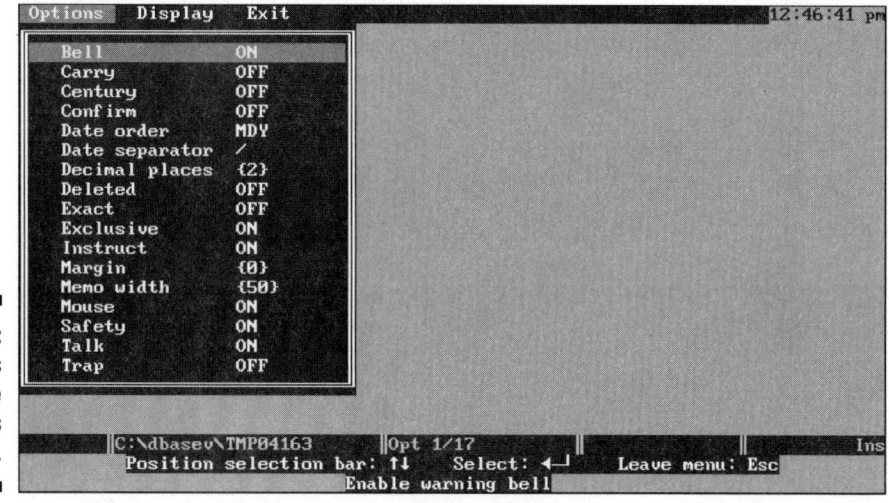

Figure 22-4: The Options menu in the Settings screen.

You can also tell dBASE to change the look and color of almost any part of your screen by using the Display menu in the Settings screen. The first option is the Display Mode. Use this to change the number of rows that can be displayed on the screen at one time. If you want to see large chunks of your data at once, for example, select the Display Mode option. The screen will change to display more lines (and therefore more data) at one time. You can cycle through the available screen modes by highlighting the option and pressing Enter. The three modes available (depending on your monitor) are VGA25, VGA43, and VGA50, where the two numbers at the end indicate the number of rows on the screen. VGA25 is the default.

You can change the colors of your screen by using the options in the rest of the Display menu. Just highlight the option that corresponds with the part of the screen you want to change and press Enter. You can then use the up- and down-arrow keys to select a foreground and background color. Press Ctrl-End when you're done.

That's all there is to customizing dBASE to your whims and desires. So return to the Control Center by opening the Exit menu and selecting Exit to Control Center. Then kiss your computer lovingly and turn it off. You deserve a break. Especially if you actually kissed your computer.

Chapter 23
Exchanging Data with Other Programs

In This Chapter
▶ Importing from a plethora of other programs
▶ Exporting to a plethora of other programs

*I*t's obvious that you're very smart. Since you're reading this book, it's likely that you have dBASE IV or 5. Since you're reading this chapter, someone you work with probably has something other than dBASE IV or 5.

This chapter tells you everything you need to know about moving data between dBASE and some of the other popular programs on the market today. It also gives you some general guidelines for transferring data to and from some of the not-so-popular programs. After you read this chapter, you should be able to share data with just about any other program.

Before you can exchange data with other programs, you must have

✔ A dBASE table (see Chapter 4) with data (see Chapter 5)
✔ Another program besides dBASE so that you have something with which to exchange data
✔ A good idea of which direction the data should go (that is, from dBASE to the other program or from the other program to dBASE)

Filename Extensions

In your quest for files that are compatible with dBASE, it helps to know what compatible files look like. Table 23-1 lists filename extensions for the data files of programs that dBASE can share data with.

Table 23-1 Extensions of dBASE Compatible Data Files

Program	Extension
ASCII files	TXT
dBASE II	DB2
Framework II	FW2
Framework III	FW3
Framework IV	FW4
Lotus 1-2-3 (version 1.x)	WKS
Lotus 1-2-3 (version 2.x)	WK1
PFS:FILE	none
RapidFile	RPD
SYLK-Multiplan	none
VisiCalc	DIF

Importing Data from Other Programs

dBASE imports almost to a trade deficit. It handles a variety of known formats as well as several generic ones — all at the flick of a button. To import a data file from another program, follow these steps:

1. **From the Control Center, open the Tools menu and select Import.**

   A submenu appears with a list of the data types that dBASE can recognize.

2. **Select the kind of file that you want to import.**

   If the kind of file that you want to import is listed in the submenu, then simply select it. dBASE opens a small dialog box that shows the files within the current directory that match the kind you specified. Don't be surprised if there is no match at first. That's probably because you're still in the dBASE default directory. To switch to another directory, select the <parent> option from the dialog box. Then look through the other directories on your hard disk to find the file(s) that you need to import.

   If you want to import a file that was created in a program not listed in the Import submenu, you have to design a table with the same structure as the file you want to import. Then put the records into it by using the Copy Records From Non-dBASE File option in the Append menu in the Table Design screen.

NOTE

For most of the programs listed in the Import submenu, simply select the program that you want to import from and then import the files you want. You don't have to change the data. dBASE II files are the exception. For dBASE II files, you must change from the extension .DBF to .DB2 before you import them. Any other dBASE files (from dBASE III.x, or dBASE IV.x) you can use right inside of dBASE 5 without importing or doing anything different.

Exporting Data to Other Programs

It's no surprise that exporting from dBASE is practically the opposite of importing. When you export, dBASE creates a brand new file (based on the one that you choose to export). To export a file to another program, simply follow these steps:

1. **From the Control Center, open the Tools menu and select Export.**

   A submenu appears, listing the available file types to export to, such as Lotus 1-2-3, Framework, RapidFile, and so on. Remember one thing: Although there's no option to export records to Paradox format (or that of some other database managers), virtually *all* database managers can *import* tables from dBASE. So if you're sending data to another database manager, you probably don't *need* to export the dBASE data: just make a copy of the table file, start the other database program, and use that program's features to import the table.

2. **Select the program to which you want to export.**

   If the program that you want to export to isn't listed in the submenu, and it's not a database program that can import dBASE files, try using one of the bottom three choices on the list. They tell dBASE that you want to export the file to ASCII format (American Standard Code for Information Interchange). The three ASCII formats listed (in order) are the most popular: text fields of a fixed length, text fields separated by blanks, or text fields separated by a character. The documentation that comes with the software program that you're exporting to has information about which ASCII format the program supports.

NOTE

When exporting to dBASE II, first export the file as you normally would and then rename the file. The new dBASE II file that dBASE creates will have the extension .DB2. Next, copy the .DB2 file to a different directory and change its .DB2 extension to .DBF (which dBASE II can recognize). If you don't copy it to a different directory, you may accidentally erase (overwrite) your original file in dBASE 5.

That's all there is to importing and exporting data. So why don't you shut down and take a break. Go for a drive. Watch an exercise video. Try to do both. At the same time. Just be careful.

Part V
The Part of Tens

The 5th Wave   By Rich Tennant

"It's really made the job a lot less complicated. Oh jeez— now what?"

In this part ...

This part talks about things you probably would rather not think about. What if you get in trouble on your PC while using dBASE? What are the secrets of dBASE that those M.I.T. computer wizards are hiding from you? And what will you do if a computer wizard corners you at a party and starts to spout a lot of database jargon?

In this part, you'll learn how to handle *all* those situations. Except how to get invited to a party in the first place. You already know that. (Don't you?)

Chapter 24
Ten Awful Database Terms (and Suggested Penalties for Using Them)

In This Chapter
▶ Application
▶ Field
▶ Easy
▶ Fourth-generation language (4GL)
▶ Key
▶ Normalize
▶ Post
▶ Powerful
▶ Relational
▶ SQL

Get ready for ten of the dumbest database terms in the world, and that means the *entire universe*, not just the planet Earth, although Earth people do seem to be awfully good at coming up with awful words to confuse everyone and especially Earth people are good at writing long run-on sentences that seem to keep going forever like did you ever try to read Hegel in the original German or make your way through a *New Yorker* magazine article about just about anything geez what a bore and when you think about how much money those people make it's really incredible, well, it's time for me to take a breath now so I have to stop.

What are you reading this part for? Get on with the chapter!

Application

The only defensible meaning of *application* is *program,* so the term is redundant because there's already a word for program, which is — guess what?! — *program.* Sometimes *application* is used to describe a program that's written in a database language, such as dBASE, and that works only inside a database program, in which case the program is called a *database application.* But that's just more clutter in the language.

Penalty: Application of three coats of wax to the offender's tongue, using the celebrated "wax on, wax off" method.

Field

By now, you know what *field* means in a database. But *field* must be one of the most obscure words ever to be swiped by computer science from agriculture. The official story is that the term originates with old-style punched computer cards. In reality, database fields are named after Syd Field, a legendary screenwriting instructor in Los Angeles, who is rumored to have started his career as a computer repairman for IBM. Not.

Penalty: Rewrite the screenplay for the movie *Field of Dreams,* making the characters say the word *database* at least once every five minutes.

Easy

The term means nothing. Every database program ever created is supposed to be *easy.* And if you got 800 (a perfect score) on your math section of the SAT, databases probably *are* easy.

Penalty: Keep retaking the math SAT test every day until a perfect score of 800 is achieved.

Fourth-Generation Language (4GL)

A *4GL* is a computer programming language that is both *easy* (see preceding definition) and *powerful* (defined later in this chapter). Because *easy* and *powerful* don't mean anything, *fourth-generation language* doesn't, either.

dBASE's own programming language, a little of which you used in this book, is a fourth-generation language, or maybe it's not — who knows?

Penalty: Learn m*achine language* for the PC — a first-generation language that is neither *easy* nor *powerful*.

Key

Key means either the main field by which a table is sorted or the thing you're looking for when you search a database. More often, it means what you're looking for when you can't get into your house.

Penalty: Watch all of the next "Green Acres" marathon on *Nick at Nite*. Even if it lasts a week.

Normalize

Normalize means getting rid of redundant data, though what getting rid of redundant data has to do with a word like *normalize* is a complete mystery. The idea is that you shouldn't store the same data in several different places because it wastes disk space and increases the chance of error. Each piece of data should be in a database only once. This is a very simple idea. People who use the word *normalize* just want to be sure you know they graduated from Stanford or M.I.T.

Penalty: Attend a monster truck show and make friends with three people who are definitely *not* "normal."

Post

When you have one table to hold data about sales transactions and two other tables that hold inventory and customer balance data, you update the latter two tables by *posting* the data from the transaction table. This term seems to be derived from accounting, which explains a lot.

Penalty: Think of at least one anagram of the word *post* that begins with the letters *s* and *t*. Then do it.

Powerful

The term means nothing. Every database program ever created is supposed to be *powerful*. People who call a program powerful mean that the program does what it's supposed to do. Arnold Schwarzenegger is *powerful,* but database programs either work or they don't. In that sense, dBASE really *is* powerful.

Penalty: Go to a discount store and buy a really *powerful* cologne. Then, wear it to the office all week.

Relational

Relational has three meanings. First, it can mean that a database "conforms to the relational model," one of those heavy-duty computer science things that is long on theory but doesn't make much difference in practice. Second, it can mean that a database has linked tables, in which case the word is being used incorrectly because nonrelational databases can have linked tables, too. Third, it can mean "Good! Buy this!" — its most common meaning.

Penalty: Attend this year's family reunion and get reacquainted with all those "relations" that you've tried so hard to forget.

SQL

SQL stands for Structured Query Language, a database language that's used to find and manipulate data. More often, SQL simply means good. People look for database managers that support SQL even though they have no idea what SQL is or what they'd do with it if they knew.

Penalty: Learn what SQL is and figure out what you'd do with it if you knew.

Chapter 25
Ten dBASE Problems and How to Survive Them

In This Chapter
- When you get a disk error
- When you can't start the Control Center
- When your disk drive "isn't ready"
- When files don't open
- When dBASE runs soooooo slow
- When queries crash and burn
- When your disk is "too full" to save a memo
- When you've lost indexes and memo fields
- When you can't delete a blank report line
- When you don't know where to get help with dBASE

Problems are a part of life. For the most part, the only people who have no problems are dead or hopelessly insane or have read too many books on positive thinking.

This chapter shows you how to cope with some most common dBASE problems. But the most important resource for solving dBASE problems isn't in this book: it's just behind your forehead. If you use your brain and don't get too anxious, you can solve a lot of dBASE problems on your own.

Problem #1: Getting a Disk Error

Sometimes, when you're trying to save a file to your PC's hard disk (usually the C drive), you get an *alarming* message from dBASE: "A serious disk error has occurred when attempting to write to drive C: Abort, Retry?" And then, when you select Retry, nothing happens, the message is still there, and you end up restarting your computer.

Don't panic. It may be something very simple — not serious at all. (On the other hand, it may be something *absolutely awful* that will totally ruin your life, but why jump to that conclusion?)

The most likely cause of this error message (other than *really* serious disk errors, which we cover in a moment) is that you may be running two *disk cache* programs at the same time. A disk cache program speeds up your hard disk by keeping recently used stuff in the PC's electronic memory, where it's available much faster than if it has to be read from the disk again.

Running one cache program is good, but *two* at the same time are likely to conflict with each other. You may not know that dBASE comes with *its own* disk cache program. This program is designed to work only with dBASE and only when dBASE is running. If the dBASE installation program sets up this cache and you also run a general-purpose cache like Microsoft's SmartDrive, you can have this mysterious disk error problem.

To find out if the dBASE cache program is installed, search your PC's hard disk for the file dbase1.exe (it might be in any of several directories). This file will exist only if dBASE is doing its own disk caching. If the file is present, then you know that dBASE disk caching is the likely cause of the problem. At the `C:\>` (assuming that your hard disk is the C drive), follow these steps:

1. **Switch to the root directory.**

    Type **cd** and press Enter.

2. **Search for the dbase1.exe file.**

    Type **dir/s dbase1.exe** and press Enter. If the file is on your hard disk, this will find it.

3. **If dbase1.exe is on your hard disk, tell dBASE to stop using the cache program.**

    Type **cd\dbase** and press Enter. This switches you to the dBASE directory. Then, type **cachedb.off** and press Enter. You should see the message `dBASE caching is OFF`. This change is permanent, so you only need to do it once.

4. **If dbase1.exe *isn't* on your hard disk, then look elsewhere for the problem.**

Chapter 25: Ten dBASE Problems and How to Survive Them **283**

The other likely explanation is that you *really do* have a disk error. But you still don't need to panic: a lot of disk errors are easy to fix. If you have a disk diagnostics program such as the Central Point's *diskfix* (included with the PC Tools software package) or Norton Disk Doctor (included with Symantec's Norton Utilities package), then run it. These programs can not only detect disk errors but also can repair many of them — often, they can even save data that may be in danger.

If you don't have one of these programs, then follow these steps:

1. **Switch to the root directory.**

    Type **cd** and press Enter.

2. **Use the MS-DOS chkdsk command to check the disk for errors.**

    Type **chkdsk /f** and press Enter. MS-DOS scans your hard disk, looking for errors. The slash-f tells MS-DOS to fix any errors that it can. When the scan is finished, you see a report on any errors that were found and/or fixed.

3. **Restart dBASE and try again.**

    If the problem is fixed, you're in good shape. If not, then you may need to take your PC back to the store to have it checked by a technician.

Problem #2: The Control Center Won't Start

Sometimes the dBASE Control Center won't start even though everything else seems to be working all right. If this happens and you get the error message *Not a dBASE database,* then your catalog file has probably been damaged.

Remember that when the Control Center starts up, it automatically reopens the same catalog it used the last time it ran. If anything has happened to damage the catalog file, then the Control Center can't start up because it can't load the catalog.

The solution is to create a new catalog, add the files you need, then rename it. Follow these steps:

1. **Create and open a new catalog.**

    In the Command window (which should be on your screen, since you can't start the Control Center), type **set catalog to frank** and press Enter.

    It's important to name the catalog Frank, after Borland's spiritual leader, Frank Borland. (Legends of Frank Borland and his burro, Lotus, are part of the folklore of the American Southwest. At least in Silicon Valley.)

2. **Start the Control Center.**

   It should work this time because it's using a brand-new catalog that (we hope!) has nothing wrong with it.

3. **Add all the tables and other database files that were in the old catalog.**

   To do this, just open the Catalog menu and select Add file to catalog.

4. **Rename the new catalog to wipe out the old, damaged catalog.**

   Open the Exit menu and select Exit to Command window. Then, in the Command window, type **copy file frank.cat to blahblah.cat** where *blahblah* is the name of your old catalog.

5. **Restart the Control Center with the new catalog.**

   In the Command window, type **set catalog to blahblah** and press Enter. Then, press F2 to restart the Control Center. The next time the Control Center starts, it will load your new, renamed catalog.

Problem #3: A Drive Not Ready

If you get the error message "Drive not ready A:" when you open a catalog, then you've probably added a file to the catalog from your PC's floppy drive. Remember that when you open a catalog, the catalog must be able to find all the files you've told it to keep track of. If one of the files is on a floppy disk, then the disk must be in your disk drive so that the catalog can find it.

The short-term solution is to find the floppy disk and put it in the drive. The better, long-term solution is to copy the file to your hard disk, delete the floppy file from your catalog, and add the file from the hard disk. That way, you won't have the problem in the future.

Problem #4: Files Don't Open

When you open a table in the Control Center, all the other files associated with it (reports, forms, queries, and so forth) are supposed to open, too. If the files are open, you see them above the horizontal lines in their panels. But sometimes, the files don't open as they should.

When the files don't open, the links between the table and its associated files have been broken somehow. One thing that can break the links is deleting a file from the catalog and then adding it back.

To restore the links, modify each file that should go with the table. In the appropriate design screen, open the **L**ayout menu and select **U**se different database file or view. Then, select the table with which the file should be linked. When you save the file, *don't* simply use **S**ave changes and exit. Instead, open the **L**ayout menu and select **S**ave this form (and so on) — the Exit menu option won't do the job in this case.

Problem #5: dBASE Runs Really Slow Under Windows

The modern versions of dBASE need quite a lot of PC memory. If you're a little bit short on memory, then dBASE can run pretty slowly — *especially* if you're running it under Microsoft Windows.

The easy, expensive answer is to buy more PC memory. But there are other things you can do.

First, you can go into your dBASE disk directory and run a program called PMINFO. PMINFO evaluates your PC's available memory, speed, and a few other things, and optimizes dBASE to work on your machine. To run PMINFO, follow these steps:

1. **Switch to your main dBASE disk directory.**

    At the C:\>, type **cd\dbase** and press Enter.

2. **Run the PMINFO program.**

    At the C:\>, type **pminfo** and press Enter. The program analyzes your PC and displays a report on the screen. PMINFO also sets up dBASE to work as well as it can on your PC.

Second, if you have at least an 80386-based PC and some available disk space, you can increase the amount of *virtual memory* used by Windows — a tricky operation. You can find out more about it in IDG's *Windows For Dummies*.

Problem #6: Queries Quickly Quietly Quit

Your query doesn't run right! Not only does it fail to give you the information you need, but it flashes an annoying error message on the screen, telling you that there's a syntax error.

The most common cause of a syntax error is that you've tried to use a query condition but didn't type the *entire* condition that dBASE needs for the query. For instance, you may be looking for a sales record in which the price of a book is greater than $5.00 and less than $15.00. In the Condition box, you might type **price > 5.00 .AND. < 15.00**.

Now, that's perfectly plain to *you:* but you're a human and thereby (whether you believe it or not) much smarter than dBASE or your PC. When you enter a condition for a dBASE query, you need to spell everything out in great detail. The correct way to enter the query condition is to type **price > 5.00 .AND. price < 15.00** in the Condition box. Other query conditions work the same way: you must be careful to include *all* the details that dBASE needs to process the query. (By the way, dBASE doesn't care if you capitalize the AND: it's capitalized here just to make things easier to read.)

Problem #7: Is Your Disk "Too Full" for a Memo?

If you try to save a memo but get the error message `Disk full, delete old files Y/N`, then your table's memo file as almost certainly damaged.

Remember that when a table has a memo field, the memo data isn't stored in the table itself. The data is stored in another file with the same name as the table, but ending with an extension .DBT. If this file is damaged, you can have a number of problems with the table's memo data. The "disk full" problem is the most common. Other indications that a memo file is damaged are

- ✔ You get the error message "End of file encountered," when you *know* that you aren't at the end of the file.
- ✔ You open a memo and see "happy faces" or other garbage characters in the text.
- ✔ Your PC locks up when you try to view or edit a memo but your hard disk is going crazy, whirring like it's looking for something.

If you think that you have a damaged memo file, get out of dBASE: if you have to, reboot your PC by pressing Ctrl-Alt-Delete or the Reset button (some PCs don't have them). As a last resort, if you can't exit or reboot your PC, turn your PC off. Wait at least 30 seconds, then turn it back on.

As soon as you're out of the dBASE trouble and back in control of your PC, run the MS-DOS *chkdsk* program or another disk diagnostic program to fix any errors in the logical structure of your disk. (See IDG's *DOS For Dummies* if you need complete details about the *chkdsk* program.)

The easiest way to get your memo data back is to restore an older version of the memo file from a backup copy — one that, you hope, was made before the memo file was damaged.

If you can't restore an older version of the file, download the DBT CHECK program, either from the Borland computer bulletin board (BBS) or from the Borland dBASE Forum on CompuServe. The number of the Borland BBS is (408)439-9096 and the program file is called DBTCK153.EXE. If you download the program from CompuServe, the program has a different name: DBTCHK.EXE. Whatever the name, the program is designed to repair your damaged memo file — if it can *be* repaired at all.

If you need instructions on how to get DBTCHECK153.EXE from the Borland BBS, fax a request for Technical Information Report TI1099 to Borland's Fax Automated System (TECHFAX) at (800)822-4269.

Problem #8: You Lost Memo Fields and Indexes

You restore your database from a backup copy, but your memo fields and indexes are gone!

Remember that memo data and indexes are kept in files *separate* from the main table, whose filename ends in .DBF. If you only make a backup copy of your table, then you lose the memo data and indexes that are associated with it. The safest thing to do is to keep all your data files (tables, reports, indexes, memo files, and so forth.) in a separate disk directory. Then, when you make a backup copy, just back up everything in the directory.

As for your missing memo fields and indexes, you can't do much unless you have another backup copy that contains the necessary files. The files have the same name as the table (.DBF) file, but end in the letters .MDX (for the index file) and .DBT (for the memo file).

Problem #9: You Can't Delete a Blank Report Line

The dBASE Report Design screen won't let you delete the bottom line in a report band. If you need to delete the line, follow these steps:

1. Move the cursor to the line above the one you want to delete.

2. **Select the line.**

    Press F6 to start selecting the line, then press End. Finally, press Enter to tell dBASE that you finished selecting stuff.

3. **Press the down-arrow key and move the cursor to the start of the next line.**

4. **Press F7, then press Enter.**

    The selected line moves down.

5. **Press the up-arrow key to move the cursor up one line.**

6. **Press Ctrl-Y to delete the line.**

Problem #10: You Don't Know Where to Get dBASE Help

If you don't know where to get help with dBASE, you're in luck: there are *hundreds* of places to get help. The problem is simply deciding which one to use. Here are just a few of them:

- **Help with installation:** Call Borland's dBASE Installation Hotline at (408)431-9060. It's open from 6 a.m. to 5 p.m. Pacific Time.

- **General help from a machine:** Call Borland's 800-Automated Support line. This lets you select and listen to recorded messages with help for common dBASE problems. The number is (800)524-8420, and it's open 24 hours a day, seven days a week.

- **General help on CompuServe:** If you subscribe to the CompuServe Information Service, you can get into the dBASE Forum by entering **go dbase**. In the forum, you can get answers to all your questions and read the answers to *other* people's questions as well. There are also dozens of help files and hundreds of tips on how to use dBASE.

- **Help in your town:** Your local PC user group almost certainly has a large number of dBASE users who get together at least once a month to exchange ideas. In addition, many user groups have help lines staffed by group members who volunteer their expertise in specific areas. For dBASE help, your local PC user group is an excellent resource.

- **General help from an actual person:** If you're a registered user (as indeed, you should be!), you can call Borland's help line. You may have to wait a few minutes because there are millions of dBASE users but you eventually get to talk to an actual, live person for help with your problem. This is often *not* the best way to get help: the Automated Support Line is fastest, with CompuServe being next best.

Chapter 26
Ten Fun Facts About dBASE

- dBASE originated in the 1960s with *Retriev,* a database manager developed at the Jet Propulsion Laboratories (JPL) in Palo Alto, California.

- In the 1970s, Wayne Ratliff at JPL built on the ideas in Retriev to create *Vulcan,* which brought things one step closer to dBASE.

- *dBASE* spelled backwards is *ESABd,* which means absolutely nothing.

- In 1979, the rights to Vulcan were bought by Ashton-Tate, a small software company in Southern California. Ashton-Tate renamed the program *dBASE II*.

- In 1981, Microrim, Inc., released *MicroRIM,* the first major competitor to dBASE. The *RIM* stood for *Relational Information Management,* and the product was eventually renamed *R:BASE*.

- In 1983, *Data Based Advisor, featuring dBASE II,* became the first database magazine for PCs.

- In 1984, Ashton-Tate competitor Micro Data Base Systems renamed its flagship database package several times, from *KnowledgeMan* to *Knowledge Manager* to *The Knowledge Manager,* then finally back to *KnowledgeMan.* And everyone got really, *really* confused.

- In the late 1980s, a controversy raged over "who owned the dBASE language." Eventually, an industry committee was formed to standardize the dBASE language. The standardized language was called Xbase.

- In 1991, Ashton-Tate and dBASE were acquired by Borland International, which had also acquired the *Paradox* database manager by purchasing Ansa Software.

- In 1994, Borland updated the venerable dBASE program with dBASE 5 for DOS and created the very first version of dBASE for Windows.

Part VI
Appendixes

In this part ...

You can't do much with a database until you've put some data in it. In this part, Appendix A gives you sample data for the Bookcust and Sales tables that are used in this book's example database.

Likewise, you can't do much with dBASE until you've got it installed on your PC. Appendix B shows you how to set up the program on your PC's hard disk

And in case there's a bit of a programmer in you, Appendix C gives you a quick look at dBASE5's Developer's Desktop.

Appendix A
Database Data for This Book

*T*o work through the example database in this book, you have to enter some data into the dBASE tables. You could hire a high school kid to do the data entry, of course. But what if the student is distracted by something really great on MTV? *Where would you be then?* Out of data and out of luck, thank you. So you should probably enter the data yourself.

On the bright side, you can enter as many or few of these data records as you like. But if something really great does come on MTV, restrain yourself and keep at it.

The "Customer Records" Table

00001
Prof. James West
Jimbo
Mythic University
Martinsville, CA 98035
(415) 555-46780

0002
Ms. Harriett Stowe
Ms. Stowe
14 Parakeet Lane
New York, NY 10087
(212) 555-23450

0003
Mr. Jules Twombly
Jules
The ABC Hotel
Las Vegas, NV 34567
(201) 555-62130

0004
Mr. Arnold Harris
Arnie

101 Fifth Avenue
Boise, ID 23413
(321) 555-98760

0005
Ms. Teri Lane
Ms. Lane
5678 15th St., #5-A
Santa Barbara, CA 93101
(805) 555-12340

0006
Ms. Susan Brown
Ms. Brown
5541 LaBrea
Los Angeles, CA 90069
(310) 555-86170

0007
Dr. Thomas Baker
Tom
342 Gallifrey St.
Shreveport, LA 14325
(205) 555-76810

0008
Ms. Janet White
Janet
745 Microsoft Way
Redmond, WA 98052
(206) 555-31110

0009
Mr. Harris Harrison
Mr. Harrison
21 El Embarcadero
Goleta, CA 93105
(805) 555-90260

0010
Ms. Tracy Dancer
Tracy
11 Waterside Place
Zuma Beach, CA 90078
(213) 555-77410

0011
Ms. Diane Walker

Ms. Walker
551 Second St.
San Francisco, CA 94107
(415) 555-10790

0012
Ms. Shirley Edison
Ms. Edison
Bloomington University
Bloomington, IN 47401
(812) 555-58730

0013
Mr. Don Wilds
Don
114 E. 6th St.
Bloomington, IN 47408
(812) 555-97700

0014
Mr. Jack Stein
Jack
113 E. 6th St.
Bloomington, IN 47408
(812) 555-12990

0015
Prof. Irwin Jones
Prof. Jones
Dept. of Prognostication
Bloomington University
Bloomington, IN 40401
(812) 555-1191

The "Sales" Table

Although there are 15 customers in the Customer Records table, the Sales Table only lists account numbers 1 to 5 in case you didn't enter all 15 customer records. The fields are listed in order: Cust ID, Sale Date, Title, Author, and Price.

00004
8/21/94
How to Write a Computer Book
Obscurantis, Jargun
2.95

00001
8/25/94
In Praise of Idleness
Russell, Bertrand
12.95

00002
8/26/94
Getting Your Husband Off His Lazy Butt
Russell, Mrs. Bertrand
12.95

00005
8/27/94
How I Turned $25 Cash into a Successful Business
Fleiss, Heidi
24.95

00005
8/23/94
dBASE For DOS for Dummies
Palmer, Scott
19.95

00005
8/26/94
Fershlugginers I Have Known
Smith, Joe
11.66

00001
8/27/94
Atlas Shrugged
Rand, Ayn
12.95

00002
8/28/94
Love in the Time of Cholera
Garcia-Marquez, Gabriel
12.00

00004
8/30/94
Deep Thoughts
Clinton & Quayle
1.95

00003
8/31/94
"Supertrain" Forever!
Silverman, Fred
1.95

Appendix B
Installing dBASE

Installing dBASE really *is* easy. But before you install dBASE on your PC — in fact, before you even *buy* dBASE — it's essential that you make sure that your PC is capable of running it.

What You Need to Install and Run dBASE

Like most modern programs, dBASE requires a lot of PC horsepower and disk space to work properly. You don't need to understand what all these things are, but you should make sure that your PC has *at least*

- **An 80386 processor**

    An 80486 or Pentium (80586) processor is better. Processor speeds are rated in "Megahertz" (MHz), so a 33-MHz 80386 processor is faster than a 20-MHz 80386 processor. However, higher-numbered processors are faster, so a 33-MHz 80486 processor is faster than a 33-MHz 80386 processor.

- **A hard disk with at least 6MB of free disk space — that's for a *minimum* installation, with just the essential stuff**

    More free space is better. For full installation of dBASE, you need 14.5MB of free disk space (16.5MB if you're installing from Microsoft Windows). Afterward, the program requires "only" 9MB of disk space, but you need the full 14.5MB or 16.5MB of free space for the installation itself.

- **At least 4MB of RAM**

    Six megabytes of RAM (electronic memory) is better, 8MB is terrific, and more than that is *spectacular*. The more RAM you have, the faster dBASE is likely to run.

- **A monochrome, CGA, EGA, or VGA monitor**

- **DOS version 3.3 or later, and Windows 3.1 or later**

Installing dBASE on Your PC

To install dBASE on your PC, follow these steps:

1. **Put the first dBASE disk into the appropriate floppy disk drive.**

    Usually, this drive is drive A, but it can also be drive B.

2. **At the DOS prompt, switch to the floppy disk drive that has the disk in it.**

    To switch to the floppy disk drive, type the drive name with a colon (such as **a:**), and press Enter.

3. **At the DOS prompt, type install and press Enter.**

4. **Follow the instructions that appear on your screen.**

    That's it!

Appendix C
Stepping Up to the Developer's Desktop

In This Appendix
- What is the Developer's Desktop?
- Good-bye, dot prompt; hello, Command window
- A glimpse of creating your own database programs with the dBASE compiler and linker
- A look at creating event-driven forms
- A taste of messing around with the Object Inspector
- Organizing your applications with the dBASE Project Manager

For the most part, this book has explained the easy, user-oriented features of dBASE. With the exception of a few tweaks here and there, these features are pretty much the same in dBASE 5 as they were in dBASE IV.

But there's another side to dBASE 5 — an incredibly powerful side that lets you create your own database programs, including all the most advanced tricks of the computer expert's trade. This side is called the *Developer's Desktop,* and even though you don't have to use it to benefit from dBASE, it can (if you're adventurous) help you do incredible things with your database.

In this appendix, you get a quick overview of what you can do if you decide to become a real dBASE expert and get into using the Developer's Desktop (to understand everything in this appendix, you probably *need* to be a dBASE expert).

What's on the Developer's Desktop

As the name implies, the Developer's Desktop is, well, for developers. If all you want to do is set up a table or create simple forms and reports, you don't need it. But if you want to create database applications for other people to use — even applications you can sell — the Developer's Desktop has all the tools you need to accomplish this goal.

Introducing the Command window

The Command window replaces the venerable dBASE dot prompt, which inspires fear among normal database users and adoration among dBASE experts. The Command window is more flexible than the dot prompt. The Command window automatically keeps a history of your previously typed commands so that you can repeat them without having to retype them. You can also cut and paste text from one command line to another, which can be useful if you're doing several complex commands.

If you're in the dBASE Control Center, you can get to the Command window by opening the **Exit** menu and selecting **Exit to Command window**. In the Command window, you can enter dBASE commands or start the dBASE program editor to write your own programs in the dBASE programming language.

The dBASE compiler and linker

Suppose that you create a database that includes tables, report layouts, on-screen forms, and standard queries. It could be a big database, such as a list of bad movies, or a little database, such as a customer list for a mom-and-pop store that sells ice cream.

Consider something interesting: now that you've gone to the trouble of designing the database, other people with similar needs can save time by using the database setup you've created. All they need to do is plug their own data into your database.

The Developer's Desktop gives you a way to distribute your database setups to other users by compiling dBASE programs. The details aren't important to you at this stage, but when you create a form, report, or other database item, dBASE is usually writing code behind the scenes, such as the following code:

```
PROCEDURE Cust

* Link to external procedure file of "tool" procedures
SET PROCEDURE TO Library

* Set up database environment
DO Set_env

SET COLOR TO &c_standard.

* Declare variables used:
* Database memory variables
STORE "" TO cust_id, category, customer, address1, address2,
           city, state
STORE "" TO zip, phone, contact, phone_cont, phone_ext,
           date_last, terms
STORE "" TO comments

* Miscellaneous variables - used to pass parameters to
           Library
STORE "CUST" TO dbf, mlist           && Standard report & mail
           list available
STORE "N/A"  TO cust_rpt             && No custom reports
           available
* BLAH BLAH BLAH BLAH SODA WATER BUBBLES
```

If you decide to create a customized database program (a database application) to give to other users, you can write your own dBASE code, although the techniques for doing so are beyond the scope of this book. When you compile and link your code, it becomes a PC program, just like dBASE itself. You can then send copies of your own program to other dBASE users.

Creating event-driven forms

This book is designed to get you up and running with dBASE quickly. Because of this goal, the forms you've learned how to create are simple and easy. They do everything that most dBASE users ever need.

But dBASE also lets you create more powerful, intelligent forms — what computer geeks call *event-driven* forms. These are forms with special tools, such as list boxes and radio buttons, that know how to respond to mouse clicks and other things that the user does. They can include menus and on-screen help — just like dBASE itself!

The Object Inspector

You probably never thought about it (there's no reason why you would), but everything you put on a form in dBASE is an *object*. An object is just something that has its own properties and knows how to behave — like a basketball, which has the properties of roundness and brownness. As for its behavior, it bounces when you dribble and goes *whoosh* through the basket when you throw it just right.

In the same way, a field, button, or label on a form is also an object. The Object Inspector lets you view and change the properties of each object on your form. For example, you can change what happens when you click on a button or move the cursor into a field as well as how much space the object takes up on your form and what happens when the user activates a list box or menu choice.

Like the other features available from the Developer's Desktop, the Object Inspector is a fairly high-end computer expert kind of thing. But don't let that intimidate you: it's not hard to use once you sit down and get the knack.

The Project Manager

When you create a database, you end up with lots of different files working together: tables, forms, reports, queries, and so on. To keep track of them, you create a database catalog that keeps all the files together.

A database application works the same way. It has lots of files that work together. From the Developer's Desktop, you can create a project file that keeps track of all your dBASE program files in a database application. When you get ready to compile and link the application, the project manager automatically integrates everything from the different files in the project.

If you're a computer geek and have used the C programming language to write heavy-duty computer programs, then the idea of creating and compiling a project is very familiar. If not, then you probably have a social life, which is almost as much fun as programming in C.

Don't worry about it anyway: The dBASE Project Manager will always be there if you need it. If and when you start writing dBASE applications, using the Project Manager will be crystal clear.

Index

• A •

Add Field submenu, 153
Add Field to Form (F5) key, 101
Alt key, with menu selections, 18, 26
American Standard Code for Information Interchange (ASCII), 127
AND operator, 136–142
  combining conditions, 137–140
  range of values, 141–142
append command, 61
Append menu, 59
  Enter records from keyboard option, 59
ascending
  ASCII sort, 165
  dictionary sort, 165
  sort, 126, 163
ASCII codes, sorting by, 163
assist command, 20, 22
asterisk (*) wild card, 114
asterisk–space, with command line comments, 26
automatic error–checking, 154–155
Avery mailing label, 210

• B •

Backspace key, 60
bands
  Detail, 192
  Group Intro, 242
  Group Summary, 242
  Page Footer, 192
  Page Header, 192
  report, 191–192
  Report Intro, 192
  Report Summary, 192
book
  conventions, 2–4
  hands–on steps, 2
  icons, 4–5
  instruction, 2
  organization, 2–4
  overview, 1
Boolean operators, 136
Box submenu, 150
boxes, form, 150–151
Browse mode, 34
  accessing, 61
  entering data, 61–62
  entering memo in memo field, 91–92
Browse screen, 61
  column lock, 74–75
  column widths, 73

customizing, 72–75
field lock, 74–75
navigating, 76–78
skipping, 77

• C •

calculated field, 143–144, 153–154
  adding to form letter, 207–208
calculations, query, 143–144
Caps Lock key, 63–64
CAT filename extension, 40
Catalog menu, 38–39, 48–49, 99
  Add file to catalog option, 28, 48–49
  Edit description of catalog option, 28, 39
  Modify catalog name option, 28
  overview, 28
  Remove Highlighted file from catalog option, 49
  Use a different catalog option, 28, 39, 99
catalogs
  closing, 48
  creating, 32–33, 38–41
  deleting data, 49–50
  deleting files, 50
  entering data, 48–49
  hands on exercise, 40–41
  limitations, 32
  naming conventions, 32, 39–40
  opening, 48
  removing files, 49–50
  vs DOS utilities, 176
character fields, 47, 254–256

  numbered, 167–168
codes, ASCII, 163
colors, form, 151–152
Column Layout report, 190–191
column widths, 73
columns
  changing report names, 194–195
  changing report widths, 195–197
  deleting/undeleting report, 193–194
  locking, 74–75
command line
  asterisk–space with comments, 26
  comments, 26
Command window, 172, 300
  Developer's Desktop, 22
commands
  append, 61
  assist, 20, 22
  quit, 20
  reindex, 172
  Skip, 78
  UPPER( ), 173–174
  use, 60
  Window, 20, 22
  ZAP, 66
comments, command line, 26
compiler, 300–301
computerized databases, advantages of, 11–12
conditions, query syntax error, 286
CONFIG.DB file, 25
Control Center, 17, 23–26
  creating files, 24
  current catalog, 23–24
  current file, 24

Index

current time, 24
Data panel, 24
default startup, 25–26
Display data option, 60–62, 103
Forms panel, 99
Menu Bar, 23
menus, 23
Modify layout option, 103, 148
Modify structure/order option, 59, 83
opening, 19–20, 22
opening on startup, 25–26
panels, 23–24
Reports panel, 24
startup problems, 283–284
Status Bar, 23
Control Center (F2) key, 20, 22, 26
controlling index, 234
current catalog, Control Center, 23–24
current file, 24
current time, 24
customer records table data, 293–295

• D •

data entry, 13
Data panel, 24
data
  adding to table, 58–63
  catalog, 48–50
  editing, 64–66
  entering in Browse mode, 61–62
  error-checking, 154–155
  exchanging, 14–15
  extracting, 13
  form, 104–105
  hands on exercise, 66–69
  importing/exporting, 271–274
  organizing, 32
  replacing table, 144–145
  searches, 112–114
  table organization, 33–35
  types, 35
database
  catalogs, creating, 38–41
  data editing, 64–66
  data entry, 13, 57–70
  data exchange, 14–15
  data extraction, 13
  data organization, 32
  data types, 35
  default directory, 263–265
  Developer's Desktop, 299–302
  error-checking, 154–155
  fields, 34–35, 44–47, 82–88
  file, *see* tables
  form letters, 201–208
  form window, 257–260
  forms, 36, 97–110
  glossary of terms, 277–280
  hands on exercise data, 293–296
  importing/exporting data, 271–274
  index, 168–174
  index fields, 115
  indexing, 211–212
  macros, 265–267
  mailing labels, 209–220
  management system, 9–10

memo fields, 89–96
multiple tables, 223–230
multiple-condition query, 136–143
one-to many relation, 225–226
one-to-one relation, 225–226
organizing, 32–33
planning, 37–38
printing reports, 14
query, 35–36, 119–134
records, 34–35, 64–65
relational, 12
reports, 37, 187–200, 231–247
searches, 111–118
setting up, 31–42
simple sorts, 162–168
single table, 224
tables, 12, 33–35, 50–51, 81–88
templates, 251–253
date field, 47
dBASE
  accessing help, 288
  Command window, 17
  computerized database advantages, 11–12
  CONFIG.DB file, 25
  Control Center, 17, 19–20
  customizing settings, 267–269
  database management system, 9–10
  default filename extensions, 185
  Developer's Desktop, 17, 22, 299–302
  development history, 11, 289
  DOS utilities, 175–186
  dot prompt, 11
  form letters, 201–208
  hardware requirements, 297
  installing, 297–298
  mailing labels, 209–220
  memory requirements, 285
  Object Inspector, 302
  opening screens, 21–30
  organizing receipts, 10
  overview, 9–15
  Project Manager, 302
  quitting, 20
  relational database, 12
  reports, 187–200
  runs slowly under Windows, 285
  starting, 15–16
  troubleshooting, 281–288
  utilities, 263–270
  Windows program icon, 16
DBF filename extension, 40
default directory, changing, 263–265
definitions, field, 82–83
Delete key, 50, 60
descending
  ASCII sort, 165
  dictionary sort, 165
descending sort, 126, 163
Detail band, 192
Developer's Desktop, 17, 22, 299–302
  Command window, 22, 300
  compiler, 300–301
  event-driven forms, 301
  linker, 300–301
  Menu Bar, 17, 22
  Object Inspector, 302
  Project Manager, 302
  quitting dBASE, 20
  Status Bar, 17, 22

Index 307

Dimensions menu, Predefined Size option, 213
directory, 32
  default, 263–265
disk cache programs, problems with, 282
disk diagnostics programs, 283
disk drives, error messages, 284
disk files, 32
Display window, 152
DOS menu, 182–183
  Go to DOS option, 183
  Perform DOS command option, 182
  Set default directory option, 183
DOS utilities, 175–186
  accessing, 177
  deleting files, 178–180
  DOS menu, 182–183
  Exit menu, 185
  Files menu, 183
  Mark menu, 184
  marking files, 178
  moving/copying files, 181–182
  Operations menu, 184
  preprogrammed commands, 176
  renaming files, 182
  utilities screen, 177, 264
  shell, 176
  Sort menu, 183–184
  vs catalogs, 176
  wild cards, 182
DOS, starting dBASE, 15–16
dot prompt, 11

• E •

Edit Options menu, 154–155, 253–254
  Accept value when option, 254
  Carry forward option, 254
  Default value option, 254
  Editing allowed option, 254
  Largest allowed value option, 254
  Message option, 254
  Permit edit if option, 254
  Range must always be met option, 254
  Smallest allowed value option, 254
  Unaccepted message option, 254
  Value must always be valid option, 254
End key, (Right End of Line), 101
equal (=) key, setting tab stops, 207
Esc key
  closing menus with, 18
  deselecting form text/field, 101
event–driven forms, 301
Exit menu, 17, 20, 29
  DOS utilities, 185
  Exit to the Command window option, 29
  Quit to DOS option, 20, 29
  Save changes and exit option, 52
  Transfer to query design option, 125
Exit to Command window, 17
Export submenu, 273
expression, field, 153

• F •

field types, memo, 89–96
Fields menu, 74–75, 103
  Add field option, 153
  Create Calculated Field option, 144
  Freeze field option, 75
  Lock fields on left option, 74
  Modify field option, 103
  Sort on this field option, 127
fields, 34–35
  adding to table, 83–84
  adding/deleting mailing label, 217–218
  calculated, 143–144, 153–154, 207–208
  character, 47, 254–256
  date, 47
  definition, 82–83
  deleting, 84
  deleting/undeleting report, 193–194
  edit options, 253–254
  entering data, 59–61
  entering templates, 251–253
  expression, 153
  float, 47
  form, 148–149
  form formats, 103–104
  formulas, 153
  freezing, 75
  index, 115
  index tag, 170
  indexing, 51
  locking, 74–75
  logical, 47
  master tag, 170
  memo, 47, 89–96, 287
  moving form, 102
  moving mailing label, 218
  multiple index, 172–174
  multiple sort, 165–167
  naming conventions, 46
  new, 83–84
  number conventions, 60
  number fields, 256–257
  numbered character, 167–168
  numeric, 47
  query, 123
  renaming, 149
  reordering query answer, 128
  searches, 112–114
  shared, 226–227
  size limitations, 47
  sort, 162
  structure, 44–46
  summary, 243–245
  template, 154–157
  types of, 46–47
  unfreezing, 75
  unlocking, 75
File menu, 18
filename extensions, 32
  CAT, 40
  DBF, 40
  default, 185
  MDX, 170
  QBE, 126
  supported, 272
files
  CONFIG.DB, 25
  creating, 24
  current, 24

database, 13
deleting with DOS utilities, 178–180
disk, 32
marking in DOS utilities, 178
master index, 170
moving/copying with DOS utilities, 181–182
opening, 24
printing to, 198
removing vs deleting, 49
selecting for index, 171
unable to open, 284
writing to, 198
Files menu, DOS utilities, 183
  Change drive/directory option, 183
  Display only option, 183
float field, 47
form letter reports, 232
form letters, 14
  adding calculated field, 207–208
  creating, 203–208
  glorified report, 203
  Mailmerge layout, 203–208
  setting margins, 206–207
  tab stops, 206–207
  type styles, 208
Form mode, data entry, 59–61
form window, displaying memo fields, 257–260
formal report, 188
forms, 97–110
  adding text, 101
  calculated fields, 153–154
  changing colors, 151–152
  changing/adding/text, 149
  creating, 98–101
  customizing, 147–158
  data entry, 36
  deleting fields, 101
  deleting lines, 101
  deselecting text/field, 101
  drawing boxes/lines, 150–151
  entering/changing data, 104–105
  event-driven, 301
  field formats, 103–104
  hands on exercise, 105–110
  inserting lines, 101
  moving fields/text, 101–102, 148–149
  moving to
    left end of line, 101
    next text/field, 101
    preceding text/field, 101
    right end of line, 101
  navigating, 101–103
  on-screen, 97–110
  Quick Layout, 99–100
  selecting text/field, 101
  shortcuts, 101
  uses for, 98
  viewing/moving table data, 102–103
Forms Design screen, 99–100, 103
formulas, field, 153
functions, *see* commands

• G •

glossary, 277–280
Go To menu, 77–78, 113
  Backward search option, 113
  Forward search option, 113

Match Capitalization option,
    113–114
  Record Number option, 78
  Skip option, 77
grouped reports, 232
  adding sections, 238–240
  calculations, 243–245
  creating, 234–243
  group field indexing, 234–236
  inserting summary field, 243–245
  previewing, 239
  resizing bands, 243
  saving, 243
  section breaks, 240–242
  setup, 236–238

table query, 140
tables, 52–55
hard disk, error messages, 282–283,
    286
hardware requirements, 297
help
  accessing, 19, 29–30
  program support, 288
Help (F1) key, 19, 30
Help menu, 19
Help window, 30
  Choosing Contents option, 30
  printing contents, 30
Home key, (Left End of Line), 101
hot keys, 17

• H •

hands on exercise
  adding/deleting fields, 85–87
  catalogs, 40–41
  creating/changing forms, 105–108
  customer records table data,
    293–295
  database data, 293–296
  entering memos, 93–94
  finding a customer record, 115–117
  formatting and filling PHONE field,
    109–110
  multiple table database, 227–230
  partial word search, 117
  records editing, 69–70
  sales table, 295–296
  sales table setup, 131–133
  table data entry, 66–69

• I •

icons
  book, 4–5
  dBASE program, 16
Import submenu, 272–273
index, 168–174
  controlling, 234
  database, 211–212
  fields, 115
  grouped field report, 234–236
  master tag, 170
  multiple fields, 172–174
  preparation, 170
  record order, 171–172
  selecting fields, 171
  tag, 170
  uses, 168–169
  vs sort, 168–169

Insert key, 101
Insert mode, 64, 101
installation program, 297–298

• K •

key combinations
  Alt+C (Catalog), 38
  Alt+P (Print), 198
  Alt-H (Help), 19
  Ctrl+End (Save), 36, 52
  Ctrl-A (Preceding), 101
  Ctrl-F (Next), 101
  Ctrl-PgDn (Last Record), 62, 77
  Ctrl-U (Delete), 65, 84
  Ctrl-Y (Delete), 101
  F6-Enter (Select form text/field), 101
  Shift+F2 (Query), 121
keyboard
  Browse screen navigation keys, 76
  changing column width, 73–74
  opening a table, 58
  opening menus with, 26
  selecting menu items, 26
  table navigation keys, 62
  vs mouse, 16
keys
  = (equal), 207
  Alt, 18
  Backspace, 60
  Caps Lock, 63–64
  Delete, 50, 60
  Esc, 18, 101
  F1 (Help), 19, 30
  F2 (Control Center), 20, 22, 26
  F2 (Toggle modes), 59
  F3 (view skeleton), 128
  F5 (Add Field to Form), 101
  F5 (Modify field), 250
  F6 (Select), 102, 123
  F7 (Move), 102, 148
  F10 (Go To), 113
  Home, 101
  Insert, 101
  Num Lock, 63–64
  right arrow, 18
  shortcut, 27
  Tab, 61

• L •

Label Design screen, 212
labels, mailing, 14, 209–220
Layout menu, 99–100, 189, 241
  Box option, 150
  Edit description of query option, 125
  Line option, 151
  Quick Layout option, 99–100
  Save this label design option, 216
  Save this report option, 191, 197
  Use different database file or view, 285
  Write view as a database file option, 126
layouts
  Mailmerge, 203–208
  Quick Layout, 99–100
  report, 232–234
Line submenu, 151, 241

lines
  deleting form, 101
  form, 150–151
  inserting form, 101
  report, 287–288
linker, 300–301
linking, multiple tables, 225, 228–230
links, restoring, 284–285
logical
  fields, 47
  operators, 136–143

• M •

macros, 265–267
Macros submenu, 265–267
  changing, 266–267
  creating, 265–266
mailing label reports, 232
mailing labels, 14, 209–220
  adding/deleting fields, 217–218
  adding/removing text, 218
  Avery, 210
  creating, 212–215
  custom sizing, 215–216
  dimensioning, 213
  label design, 210
  Measured, 210
  moving fields, 218
  printing, 217
  redesigning, 217–219
  Rolodex, 210
  saving designs, 216
  switching size, 218–219
  text styles, 216

Mailmerge layout, 203–208
  accessing, 204
  form letters, 203–208
margins, form letters, 206–207
Mark menu, DOS utilities, 184
  Mark all option, 184
  Reverse marks option, 184
  Unmark all option, 184
marked files, deleting in DOS utilities, 179–180
master index file, 170
MDX filename extension, 170
Measured mailing label, 210
Memo Editor
  entering memo, 92
  viewing/editing memo, 92
memo fields, 47, 89–96
  entering memo, 91–92
  pointer, 91
  viewing/editing memo, 92
memo files
  displaying in form window, 257–260
  restoring, 287
  viewing/editing, 92
memos, entering, 91–92
Menu Bar
  bold letters in, 18
  Control Center, 23
  Developer's Desktop, 17, 22
menus
  Add Field, 153
  Append, 59
  Box, 150
  Catalog, 28, 38–39, 48–49, 99
  closing, 18
  Dimensions, 213

Index **313**

DOS utilities
  DOS, 182–183
  Exit, 185
  Files, 183
  Mark, 184
  Operations, 184
  Sort, 183–184
Edit Options, 154–155, 253–254
Exit, 17, 20, 29, 52, 125
Export, 273
Fields, 74–75, 103, 127, 144, 153
File, 18
Go To, 77–78, 113
Help, 19
Import, 272–273
Layout, 99–100, 125–126, 150, 189, 197, 241, 285
Line, 151, 241
Macros, 265–267
Modify field, 103–104, 156, 240, 250–251, 258
navigating, 26–29
opening, 17–18
opening with keyboard, 26
opening with mouse, 26
Operations, 179–181
Organize, 65, 163–164, 171, 173
Picture functions, 154, 254–255
Print, 189, 198
selecting items, 27
Settings, 267–269
Sorting, 127
submenus, 27
Tools, 29, 177
viewing with right-arrow key, 18
Words, 152, 204, 207, 216

messages
  Disk full, delete old files Y/N, 286
  Drive not ready, 284
  hard disk error, 282–283
modes
  Browse, 34, 61–62, 91
  Form, 59–61
  Insert, 64, 101
  overstrike, 64
  toggling, 59, 101
Modify field (F5) key, 250
Modify field submenu, 103–104, 240, 250–251, 258
  Suppress repeated values option, 240
  Template option, 104, 156
mouse
  changing column width, 73
  Control Center, opening, 20, 22
  menus, opening, 17–18, 26
  selecting menu items, 26
  starting dBASE, 16
  table, opening, 58
  vs keyboard, 16
Move (F7) key, 102, 148
multiple index fields, 172–174
multitable report, 246–247

• N •

Num Lock key, 63–64
number fields, 256–257
numbered character fields, sorting, 167–168

numbers, conventions, 60
numeric fields, 47

• O •

Object Inspector, 302
on–screen help, accessing, 30
one–to–many table relation, 225–226
one–to–one table relation, 225–226
Operations menu
  Copy option, 181, 184
  Delete option, 179–180
  Displayed Files option, 180
  DOS utilities, 184
    Delete option, 184
    Edit option, 184
    Rename option, 184
    View option, 184
  Move option, 181, 184
operators
  AND, 136–142
  logical operators, 136–143
  OR, 142–143
  query, 129–130
  relational, 129
Options menu
  Bell option, 268
  Carry option, 268
  Century option, 268
  Confirm option, 268
  Date Order option, 268
  Date Separator option, 268
  Decimal Place option, 268
  Deleted option, 268

Exact option, 268
Exclusive option, 268
Instruct option, 268
Margin option, 268
Memo Width option, 268
Mouse option, 268
Safety option, 268
Talk option, 268
Trap option, 268
OR operator, 142–143
Organize menu, 65
  Create New Index option, 173
  Erase marked records option, 65
  Order Records by Index option, 171
  Sort Database on Field List option, 163–164
overstrike mode, 64

• P •

Page Footer band, 192
Page Header band, 192
panels
  Control Center, 24
  Data, 24
  Reports, 24
parent table, 225
Picture functions menu
  Alphabetic character only option, 255
  Blanks for zero values option, 257
  Center align option, 257
  Exponential format option, 257
  Financial format option, 257

Horizontal stretch option, 257
Left align option, 257
Literals not part of data option, 255
Multiple choice option, 256
Negative credits followed by DB option, 257
Positive credits followed by CR option, 256
Scroll within display width option, 255
Show leading zeroes option, 257
Trim option, 257
Upper-case conversion option, 255
Use ( ) around negative numbers option, 257
Vertical stretch option, 257
Picture functions submenu, 154, 254–255
place holders, 193
pointers, memo field, 91
Predefined Size window, 213
Print menu, 198
  Begin printing option, 198
  Destination option, 198
  Print Report option, 198
  View report on screen option, 189
printing
  Help window contents, 30
  mailing labels, 217
  reports, 14, 198
program
  accessing help, 288
  customizing settings, 267–269
  development history, 289
  disk cache, 282
  disk diagnostics, 283

hardware requirements, 297
importing/exporting data, 271–274
installing, 297–298
quitting, 20
starting, 15–16
supported filename extensions, 271–274
troubleshooting, 281–288
Project Manager, 302

• Q •

QBE filename extension, 126
query, 35–36, 119–134
  adding search values, 138–139
  AND operator, 126–142
  basing report on, 245
  calculations in, 143–144
  creating, 36, 123–129
  fails to run, 285–286
  instructions, 124
  keys, 120–122
  linking tables, 225, 228–230
  logical operators, 136–143
  multiple-condition, 136–143
  naming conventions, 125
  no-conditions, 125
  operators, 129–130
  OR operator, 142–143
  reordering answer fields, 128
  rerunning, 129
  running, 120, 124–125
  saving answer as table, 125–126
  selecting fields, 123

sorting answer records, 126–128
sorting options, 139
syntax error, 286
wild cards, 130
Query Design screen, 121–122
 navigating, 122
 Replace values in option, 145
 replacing table data, 144–145
 Save this query option, 125
Query Design window, 229
Question mark (?) wild card, 114
Quick Layout, 188–191
 Column Layout option, 189
quit command, 20

• R •

range of values, AND operator, 141–142
range-checking, *see* error-checking
receipts, organizing, 10
records, 34–35
 deleting, 64–65
 deleting with ZAP command, 66
 displaying in indexed order, 171–172
 hands on exercise, 69–70
 sorting, 163–165
 sorting query answer, 126–128
 undeleting, 65
 viewing, 62
reindex command, 172
relational
 database, 12
 operators, 129

Report Design screen, 189, 233, 237, 242
 Detail band, 242
 Group Intro band, 242
 Group Summary band, 242
 Page Footer band, 242
 Page Header band, 242
 Report Intro band, 242
 Report Summary band, 242
Report Intro band, 192
report line, deleting blank, 287–288
Report Summary band, 192
Reports panel, 24
reports, 37, 187–200
 bands, 191–192
 basing on query, 245
 changing column widths, 195–197
 Column Layout, 190–191
 column names, 194–195
 creating, 188–191, 233–234
 deleting/undeleting columns, 193–194
 deleting/undeleting fields, 193–194
 editing, 193–197
 form letter, 232
 grouped, 232
 layouts, 232–234
 mailing label, 232
 multitable, 246–247
 place holders, 193
 printing, 14, 198
 Quick Layout tool, 188–191
 row-and-column, 232
 saving, 197
 sophisticated, 231–247

types of, 188
right–arrow key, viewing menus with, 18
Rolodex mailing label, 210
row–and–column reports, 232

• S •

sales table, 295–296
screens
  Browse, 61, 72–75
  Developer's Desktop, 22
  DOS utilities, 177, 264
  Forms Design, 99–100, 103
  Label Design, 212
  opening, 21–30
  Query Design, 121–122
  Report Design, 189, 233, 237, 242
  Settings, 269
  Table Design, 50–52, 90–91
searches
  see also query
  database, 111–118
  field, 112–114
  query, 35–36, 119–134
  string, 112–114
  wild cards, 114
section breaks, grouped reports, 240–242
sections, grouped reports, 238–240
Select (F6) key, 102
Settings menu, 267–269
Settings screen, 269
shell, DOS, 176

shortcut keys, *see* key combinations, 27
simple sorts, 162–168
Skip command, 78
Sort dialog box, 164
  Field order column, 144
Sort menu, DOS utilities, 183–184
sort
  ascending/descending, 126, 163
  changing order, 173
  multiple field, 165–167
  numbered character fields, 167–168
  options, 139
  query answer records, 126–128
  simple, 162–168
  supported fields, 162
  types of, 165
  vs index, 168–169
Sorting submenu, Ascending ASCII option, 127
special–purpose report, 188
Status Bar, 63–64
  Caps Lock key status, 63
  Control Center, 23
  current record number, 63
  Developer's Desktop, 17, 22
  network information, 63
  Num Lock key status, 63
  on–screen data source, 63
  table name/directory path, 63
string search, 112–114
submenus, 27
  Add field, 153
  Box, 150
  Export, 273

Import, 272–273
Line, 151, 241
Macro, 265–267
Modify field, 103–104, 240, 250–251, 258
Picture Function, 154, 254–255
Sorting, 127
summary field, grouped report, 243–245
symbols, template, 156, 252
syntax error, query, 286

• T •

Tab key, navigating tables, 61
tab stops, form letter, 206–207
Table Design screen, 50–52
  Field Type column, 90–91
tables, 33–35
  adding data to, 58–63
  adding fields, 83–84
  Browse mode, 34
  cataloging, 47–50
  child, 225
  creating, 50–52
  customer records, 293–295
  data editing, 64–66
  data replacement, 144–145
  database, 12–13
  deleting fields, 84
  field definition, 82–83
  field index, 51
  form, 102–103
  hands on exercise, 52–55, 131–133
  linking with query, 225, 228–230
  multiple, 224–230
  multiple database hands on exercise, 227–230
  naming conventions, 51, 164
  navigating, 62–63
  one-to-many relation, 225–226
  one-to-one relation, 225–226
  parent, 225
  query answer, 125–126
  redesigning, 81–88
  sales, 295–296
  saving design, 51–52
  selecting, 83
  shared fields, 226–227
  single table database, 224
  types of changes, 82
tags
  index, 170
  master, 170
templates, 251–253
  fields, 154–157
  symbols, 156, 252
terms, 277–280
text
  form, 148–149
  mailing label, 218
time, current, 24
toggle modes (F2) key, 59
toggling between modes, 59
Tools menu, 29
  DOS utilities option, 29, 177
  Export option, 29
  Import option, 29
  Macros option, 29

Protect data option, 29
Settings option, 29
troubleshooting guide, 281–288
type styles, form letter, 208

• U •

UPPER( ) command, 173–174
use command, 60
utilities, DOS, 175–186

• V •

view skeleton (F3) key, 128

• W •

wild cards
  * (asterisk), 114
  moving/copying files with DOS utilities, 182
  query, 130
  ? (question mark), 114
  search string, 114
Window command, 20, 22
Windows
  dBASE program icon, 16
  dBASE runs slowly, 285
  memory requirements, 285
  starting dBASE, 15–16
windows
  Command, 22, 172, 300
  dBASE command, 17
  Display, 152
  Exit to Command, 17
  form, 257–260
  Help, 30
  Predefined Size, 213
  Query Design, 229
Words menu, 152
  Display option, 152
  Enable automatic Indent option, 204
  Modify ruler option, 207
  Style option, 216

• Z •

ZAP command, 66

Notes

Notes

Notes

Notes

Notes

Notes

Notes

Notes

Notes

Notes

IDG BOOKS' ... FOR DUMMIES™ SERIES

Find out why over 6 million computer users love IDG'S ...FOR DUMMIES BOOKS!

"I laughed and learned..."
Arlene J. Peterson, Rapid City, South Dakota

DOS FOR DUMMIES,™ 2nd EDITION
by Dan Gookin

This fun and easy DOS primer has taught millions of readers how to learn DOS! A #1 bestseller for over 56 weeks!

ISBN: 1-878058-75-4
$16.95 USA/$21.95 Canada
£14.99 UK and Eire

INTERNATIONAL BESTSELLER!

WINDOWS FOR DUMMIES™
by Andy Rathbone

Learn the Windows interface with this bestselling reference.

ISBN: 1-878058-61-4
$16.95 USA/$21.95 Canada
£14.99 UK and Eire

#1 BESTSELLER!

THE INTERNET FOR DUMMIES™
by John Levine

Surf the Internet with this simple reference to command, service and linking basics. For DOS, Windows, UNIX, and Mac users.

ISBN: 1-56884-024-1
$19.95 USA/$26.95 Canada
£17.99 UK and Eire

NATIONAL BESTSELLER!

PCs FOR DUMMIES,™ 2nd EDITION
by Dan Gookin & Andy Rathbone

This #1 bestselling reference is the perfect companion for the computer phobic.

ISBN: 1-56884-078-0
$16.95 USA/$21.95 Canada
£14.99 UK and Eire

NATIONAL BESTSELLER!

MACs FOR DUMMIES,™ 2nd Edition
by David Pogue

The #1 Mac book, totally revised and updated. Get the most from your Mac!

ISBN: 1-56884-051-9
$19.95 USA/$26.95 Canada
£17.99 UK and Eire

#1 MAC BOOK

WORDPERFECT FOR DUMMIES™
by Dan Gookin

Bestseller Dan Gookin teaches all the basics in this fun reference that covers WordPerfect 4.2 - 5.1.

ISBN: 1-878058-52-5
$16.95 USA/$21.95 Canada/£14.99 UK and Eire

NATIONAL BESTSELLER!

UPGRADING AND FIXING PCs FOR DUMMIES™
by Andy Rathbone

Here's the complete, easy-to-follow reference for upgrading and repairing PCs yourself.

ISBN: 1-56884-002-0
$19.95 USA/$26.95 Canada

NATIONAL BESTSELLER!

WORD FOR WINDOWS FOR DUMMIES™
by Dan Gookin

Learn Word for Windows basics the fun and easy way. Covers Version 2.

ISBN: 1-878058-86-X
$16.95 USA/$21.95 Canada
£14.99 UK and Eire

NATIONAL BESTSELLER!

WORDPERFECT 6 FOR DUMMIES™
by Dan Gookin

WordPerfect 6 commands and functions, presented in the friendly ...For Dummies style.

ISBN: 1-878058-77-0
$16.95 USA/$21.95 Canada
£14.99 UK and Eire

NATIONAL BESTSELLER!

1-2-3 FOR DUMMIES™
by Greg Harvey

Spreadsheet guru Greg Harvey's fast and friendly reference covers 1-2-3 Releases 2 - 2.4.

ISBN: 1-878058-60-6
$16.95 USA/$21.95 Canada
£14.99 UK and Eire

NATIONAL BESTSELLER!

EXCEL FOR DUMMIES,™ 2nd EDITION
by Greg Harvey

Updated, expanded—The easy-to-use reference to Excel 5 features and commands.

ISBN: 1-56884-050-0
$16.95 USA/$21.95 Canada
£14.99 UK and Eire

NATIONAL BESTSELLER!

UNIX FOR DUMMIES™
by John R. Levine & Margaret Levine Young

This enjoyable reference gets novice UNIX users up and running—fast.

ISBN: 1-878058-58-4
$19.95 USA/$26.95 Canada/ £17.99 UK and Eire

NATIONAL BESTSELLER!

For more information or to order by mail, call 1-800-762-2974. Call for a free catalog! For volume discounts and special orders, please call Tony Real, Special Sales, at 415-312-0644. For International sales and distribution information, please call our authorized distributors:

CANADA   Macmillan Canada   UNITED KINGDOM   Transworld   AUSTRALIA   Woodslane Pty Ltd.
         416-293-8141   44-81-231-6661   61-2-979-5944

IDG BOOKS' ... FOR DUMMIES™ SERIES

"*DOS For Dummies* is the ideal book for anyone who's just bought a PC and is too shy to ask friends stupid questions."

MTV, Computer Book of the Year,
United Kingdom

"This book allows me to get the answers to questions I am too embarrassed to ask."

Amanda Kelly, Doylestown, PA on Gookin and Rathbone's PCs For Dummies

"If it wasn't for this book, I would have turned in my computer for a stereo."

Experanza Andrade, Enfield, CT

CORELDRAW! FOR DUMMIES™
by Deke McClelland

This bestselling author leads designers through the drawing features of Versions 3 & 4.

ISBN: 1-56884-042-X
$19.95 USA/$26.95 Canada/17.99 UK & Eire

QUICKEN FOR WINDOWS FOR DUMMIES™
by Steve Nelson

Manage finances like a pro with Steve Nelson's friendly help. Covers Version 3.

ISBN: 1-56884-005-5
$16.95 USA/$21.95 Canada
£14.99 UK & Eire

NATIONAL BESTSELLER!

QUATTRO PRO FOR DOS FOR DUMMIES™
by John Walkenbach

This friendly guide makes Quattro Pro fun and easy and covers the basics of Version 5.

ISBN: 1-56884-023-3
$16.95 USA/$21.95 Canada/14.99 UK & Eire

MODEMS FOR DUMMIES™
by Tina Rathbone

Learn how to communicate with and get the most out of your modem — includes basics for DOS, Windows, and Mac users.

ISBN: 1-56884-001-2
$19.95 USA/$26.95 Canada
14.99 UK & Eire

1-2-3 FOR WINDOWS FOR DUMMIES™
by John Walkenbach

Learn the basics of 1-2-3 for Windows from this spreadsheet expert (covers release 4).

ISBN: 1-56884-052-7
$16.95 USA/$21.95 Canada/14.99 UK & Eire

NETWARE FOR DUMMIES™
by Ed Tittel & Denni Connor

Learn to install, use, and manage a NetWare network with this straightforward reference.

ISBN: 1-56884-003-9
$19.95 USA/$26.95 Canada/17.99 UK & Eire

OS/2 FOR DUMMIES™
by Andy Rathbone

This fun and easy OS/2 survival guide is perfect for beginning and intermediate users.

ISBN: 1-878058-76-2
$19.95 USA/$26.95 Canada/17.99 UK & Eire

QUICKEN FOR DOS FOR DUMMIES™
by Steve Nelson

Manage your own finances with this enjoyable reference that covers Version 7.

ISBN: 1-56884-006-3
$16.95 USA/$21.95 Canada/14.99 UK & Eire

WORD 6 FOR DOS FOR DUMMIES™
by Beth Slick

This friendly reference teaches novice Word users all the basics of Word 6 for DOS

ISBN: 1-56884-000-4
$16.95 USA/$21.95 Canada/14.99 UK & Eire

AMI PRO FOR DUMMIES™
by Jim Meade

Learn Ami Pro Version 3 with this friendly reference to the popular Lotus word processor.

ISBN: 1-56884-049-7
$19.95 USA/$26.95 Canada/17.99 UK & Eire

WORDPERFECT FOR WINDOWS FOR DUMMIES™
by Margaret Levine Young

Here's a fun and friendly reference that teaches novice users features and commands of WordPerfect For Windows Version 6.

ISBN: 1-56884-032-2
$16.95 USA/$21.95 Canada/14.99 UK & Eire

For more information or to order by mail, call 1-800-762-2974. Call for a free catalog! For volume discounts and special orders, please call Tony Real, Special Sales, at 415-312-0644. For International sales and distribution information, please call our authorized distributors:

CANADA Macmillan Canada
416-293-8141

UNITED KINGDOM Transworld
44-81-231-6661

AUSTRALIA Woodslane Pty Ltd.
61-2-979-5944

IDG BOOKS' ...FOR DUMMIES QUICK REFERENCE SERIES

IDG's bestselling ...For Dummies Quick Reference Series provides a quick and simple way to remember software commands and functions, written in our down-to-earth, plain English style that guides beginners and experts alike through important commands and hidden troublespots.

Fun, Fast & Cheap!

"Thanks for coming up with the simplest idea ever, a reference that you really can use and understand."
Allison J. O'Neill, Edison, NJ

WORDPERFECT FOR DOS FOR DUMMIES™ QUICK REFERENCE
by Greg Harvey

With this guide you'll never have to worry about deciphering cryptic WordPerfect commands again!

ISBN: 1-56884-009-8
$8.95 USA/$11.95 Canada
£7.99 UK & Eire

WORD FOR WINDOWS FOR DUMMIES™ QUICK REFERENCE
by George Lynch

End your stress over style sheets, mail merge, and other pesky Word features with this quick reference. Covers Word 2.

ISBN: 1-56884-029-2
$8.95 USA/$11.95 Canada

ILLUSTRATED COMPUTER DICTIONARY FOR DUMMIES™
by Dan Gookin, Wally Wang, & Chris Van Buren

This plain English guide to computer jargon helps with even the most techie terms.

ISBN: 1-56884-004-7
$12.95 USA/$16.95 Canada
£11.99 UK & Eire

1-2-3 FOR DUMMIES™ QUICK REFERENCE
by John Walkenbach

Keep this quick and easy reference by your desk and you'll never have to worry about forgetting tricky 1-2-3 commands again!

ISBN: 1-56884-027-6
$8.95 USA/$11.95 Canada
£7.99 UK & Eire

WINDOWS FOR DUMMIES™ QUICK REFERENCE
by Greg Harvey

The quick and friendly way to remember Windows tasks & features.

ISBN: 1-56884-008-X
$8.95 USA/$11.95 Canada
£7.99 UK & Eire

EXCEL FOR DUMMIES™ QUICK REFERENCE
by John Walkenbach

A fast, fun and cheap way to remember bothersome Excel commands.

ISBN: 1-56884-028-4
$8.95 USA/$11.95 Canada
£7.99 UK & Eire

DOS FOR DUMMIES™ QUICK REFERENCE
by Greg Harvey

A fast, fun, and cheap way to remember DOS commands.

ISBN: 1-56884-007-1
$8.95 USA/$11.95 Canada
£7.99 UK & Eire

WORDPERFECT FOR WINDOWS FOR DUMMIES™ QUICK REFERENCE
by Greg Harvey

The quick and friendly "look-it-up" guide to the leading Windows word processor.

ISBN: 1-56884-039-X
$8.95 USA/$11.95 Canada/£7.99 UK & Eire

For more information or to order by mail, call 1-800-762-2974. Call for a free catalog! For volume discounts and special orders, please call Tony Real, Special Sales, at 415-312-0644. For International sales and distribution information, please call our authorized distributors:

| CANADA | Macmillan Canada | UNITED KINGDOM | Transworld | AUSTRALIA | Woodslane Pty Ltd. |
| 416-293-8141 | | 44-81-231-6661 | | 61-2-979-5944 | |

IDG BOOKS' PC WORLD SERIES

"I rely on your publication extensively to help me over stumbling blocks that are created by my lack of experience."

Fred Carney, Louisville, KY on
PC World DOS 6 Handbook

PC WORLD MICROSOFT ACCESS BIBLE
by Cary N. Prague & Michael R. Irwin

Easy-to-understand reference that covers the ins and outs of Access features and provides hundreds of tips, secrets and shortcuts for fast database development. Complete with disk of Access templates. Covers versions 1.0 & 1.1

ISBN: 1-878058-81-9
$39.95 USA/$52.95 Canada
£35.95 incl. VAT UK & Eire

PC WORLD WORD FOR WINDOWS 6 HANDBOOK
by Brent Heslop & David Angell

Details all the features of Word for Windows 6, from formatting to desktop publishing and graphics. A 3-in-1 value (tutorial, reference, and software) for users of all levels.

ISBN: 1-56884-054-3
$34.95 USA/$44.95 Canada
£29.95 incl. VAT UK & Eire

PC WORLD DOS 6 COMMAND REFERENCE AND PROBLEM SOLVER
by John Socha & Devra Hall

The only book that combines a DOS 6 Command Reference with a comprehensive Problem Solving Guide. Shows when, why and how to use the key features of DOS 6/6.2.

ISBN: 1-56884-055-1
$24.95 USA/$32.95 Canada
£22.95 UK & Eire

QUARKXPRESS FOR WINDOWS DESIGNER HANDBOOK
by Barbara Assadi & Galen Gruman

ISBN: 1-878058-45-2
$29.95 USA/$39.95 Canada/£26.95 UK & Eire

PC WORLD WORDPERFECT 6 HANDBOOK
by Greg Harvey, author of IDG's bestselling 1-2-3 For Dummies

Here's the ultimate WordPerfect 6 tutorial and reference. Complete with handy templates, macros, and tools.

ISBN: 1-878058-80-0
$34.95 USA/$44.95 Canada
£29.95 incl. VAT UK & Eire

PC WORLD EXCEL 5 FOR WINDOWS HANDBOOK, 2nd EDITION
by John Walkenbach & Dave Maguiness

Covers all the latest Excel features, plus contains disk with examples of the spreadsheets referenced in the book, custom ToolBars, hot macros, and demos.

ISBN: 1-56884-056-X
$34.95 USA/$44.95 Canada /£29.95 incl. VAT UK & Eire

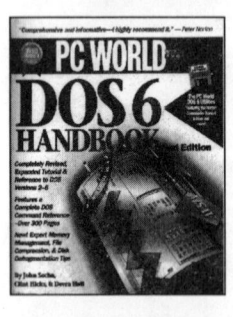

PC WORLD DOS 6 HANDBOOK, 2nd EDITION
by John Socha, Clint Hicks & Devra Hall

Includes the exciting new features of DOS 6, a 300+ page DOS command reference, plus a bonus disk of the Norton Commander Special Edition, and over a dozen DOS utilities.

ISBN: 1-878058-79-7
$34.95 USA/$44.95 Canada/£29.95 incl. VAT UK & Eire

OFFICIAL XTREE COMPANION, 3RD EDITION
by Beth Slick

ISBN: 1-878058-57-6
$19.95 USA/$26.95 Canada/£17.99 UK & Eire

For more information or to order by mail, call 1-800-762-2974. Call for a free catalog! For volume discounts and special orders, please call Tony Real, Special Sales, at 415-312-0644. For International sales and distribution information, please call our authorized distributors:

CANADA   Macmillan Canada   UNITED KINGDOM   Transworld   AUSTRALIA   Woodslane Pty Ltd.
416-293-8141   44-81-231-6661   61-2-979-5944

IDG BOOKS' INFOWORLD SECRETS™ SERIES

...SECRETS

"Livingston is a Windows consultant, and it is hard to imagine any tricks or tips he has ommitted from these 990 pages. True to the name, there are lots of undocumented hints that can make life easier for the intermediate and advanced user."
Peter H. Lewis, New York Times *on Brian Livingston's* Windows 3.1 SECRETS

"Brian Livingston has worked his magic once again. *More Windows 3.1 SECRETS* is well worth any serious Windows user's time and money."
Stewart Alsop, Editor in Chief, InfoWorld

"...Probably the most valuable book on computers I've ever seen, and I work in a library."
Jacques Bourgeios, Longueuil, Quebec, on Brian Livingston's Windows 3.1 SECRETS

"David Vaskevitch knows where client/server is going and he tells it all."
Dr. Robert Metcalfe, Publisher/CEO, InfoWorld *on David Vaskevitch's* Client/Server Strategies

Over 750,000 SECRETS Books In Prints

WORDPERFECT 6 SECRETS™
by Roger C. Parker and David A. Holzgang

Bestselling desktop publishing wizard Roger C. Parker shows how to create great-looking documents with WordPerfect 6. Includes 2 disks with Bitstream fonts, clip art, and custom macros.

ISBN: 1-56884-040-3; $39.95 USA/
$52.95 Canada/£ 35.99 incl. VAT UK & Eire

DOS 6 SECRETS™
by Robert D. Ainsbury

Unleash the power of DOS 6 with secret work-arounds and hands-on solutions. Features "Bob's Better Than DOS" shareware Collection with over 25 programs.

ISBN: 1-878058-70-3; $39.95 USA/
$52.95 Canada/£ 35.99 incl. VAT UK & Eire

MORE WINDOWS 3.1 SECRETS™
by Brian Livingston   **BESTSELLER!**

IDG's Windows guru, Brian Livingston, reveals a host of valuable, previously undocumented, and hard-to-find Windows features in this sequel to the #1 bestseller.

ISBN: 1-56884-019-5
$39.95 USA/$52.95 Canada
£ 35.99 incl. VAT UK & Eire

PC SECRETS™
by Caroline M. Halliday   **BESTSELLER!**

IDG's technical support expert shows you how to optimize your PC's performance. Includes two disks full of valuable utilities.

ISBN: 1-878058-49-5; $39.95 USA/
$52.95 Canada/£ 35.99 incl. VAT UK & Eire

WINDOWS 3.1 SECRETS™
by Brian Livingston   **BESTSELLER!**

The #1 bestselling Windows book/disk by the renowned *InfoWorld* and *Windows Magazine* columnist. Over 250,000 in print! A must-have!

ISBN: 1-878058-43-6
$39.95 USA/$52.95 Canada
£35.99 incl. VAT UK & Eire

HARD DISK SECRETS™
by John M. Goodman, Ph.D.

Prevent hard disk problems altogether with the insider's guide. Covers DOS 6 and SpinRite 3.1. Includes a disk of hard disk tune-up software.

ISBN: 1-878058-64-9; $39.95 USA/
$52.95 Canada/£ 37.99 incl. VAT UK & Eire

NETWORK SECURITY SECRETS™
by David Stang & Sylvia Moon

Top computer security experts show today's network administrators how to protect their valuable data from theft and destruction by hackers, viruses, corporate spies, and more!

ISBN: 1-56884-021-7;
$49.95 USA/$64.95 Canada
£ 44.99 incl. VAT UK & Eire

WINDOWS GIZMOS™
by Brian Livingston and Margie Livingston   **BESTSELLER!**

The best Windows utilities, applications, and games— over 30 programs on 4 disks!

ISBN: 1-878058-66-5
$39.95 USA/$52.95 Canada
£35.99 incl. VAT UK & Eire

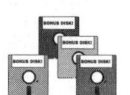

CLIENT/SERVER STRATEGIES: A SURVIVAL GUIDE FOR CORPORATE REENGINEERS
by David Vaskevitch

An essential read for anyone trying to understand the data highways that will drive successful businesses through the '90s and beyond.

ISBN: 1-56884-064-0; $29.95 USA/$39.95 Canada
£ 26.99 incl. VAT UK & Eire

For more information or to order by mail, call 1-800-762-2974. Call for a free catalog! For volume discounts and special orders, please call Tony Real, Special Sales, at 415-312-0644. For International sales and distribution information, please call our authorized distributors:

CANADA Macmillan Canada   **UNITED KINGDOM** Transworld   **AUSTRALIA** Woodslane Pty Ltd.
416-293-8141   44-81-231-6661   61-2-979-5944

IDG BOOKS

Order Form

Order Center: (800) 762-2974 (8 a.m.-5 p.m., PST, weekdays) or (415) 312-0650

For Fastest Service: Photocopy This Order Form and FAX it to: (415) 358-1260

Quantity	ISBN	Title	Price	Total

Shipping & Handling Charges

Subtotal	U.S.	Canada & International	International Air Mail
Up to $20.00	Add $3.00	Add $4.00	Add $10.00
$20.01-40.00	$4.00	$5.00	$20.00
$40.01-60.00	$5.00	$6.00	$25.00
$60.01-80.00	$6.00	$8.00	$35.00
Over $80.00	$7.00	$10.00	$50.00

In U.S. and Canada, shipping is UPS ground or equivalent.
For Rush shipping call (800) 762-2974.

Subtotal _____
CA residents add applicable sales tax _____
IN and MA residents add 5% sales tax _____
IL residents add 6.25% sales tax _____
RI residents add 7% sales tax _____
Shipping _____
Total _____

Ship to:
Name _____
Company _____
Address _____
City/State/Zip _____
Daytime Phone _____

Payment: ❑ Check to IDG Books (US Funds Only) ❑ Visa ❑ Mastercard ❑ American Express

Card# _____ Exp. _____ Signature _____

Please send this order form to: IDG Books, 155 Bovet Road, Suite 310, San Mateo, CA 94402.
Allow up to 3 weeks for delivery. Thank you!

IDG BOOKS WORLDWIDE REGISTRATION CARD

RETURN THIS REGISTRATION CARD FOR FREE CATALOG

Title of this book: **dBASE V For DOS For Dummies**

My overall rating of this book: ❏ Very good [1] ❏ Good [2] ❏ Satisfactory [3] ❏ Fair [4] ❏ Poor [5]

How I first heard about this book:

❏ Found in bookstore; name: [6] _____ ❏ Book review: [7] _____
❏ Advertisement: [8] _____ ❏ Catalog: [9] _____
❏ Word of mouth; heard about book from friend, co-worker, etc.: [10] _____ ❏ Other: [11] _____

What I liked most about this book:
_____
_____

What I would change, add, delete, etc., in future editions of this book:
_____
_____

Other comments: _____

Number of computer books I purchase in a year: ❏ 1 [12] ❏ 2-5 [13] ❏ 6-10 [14] ❏ More than 10 [15]

I would characterize my computer skills as: ❏ Beginner [16] ❏ Intermediate [17] ❏ Advanced [18] ❏ Professional [19]

I use ❏ DOS [20] ❏ Windows [21] ❏ OS/2 [22] ❏ Unix [23] ❏ Macintosh [24] ❏ Other: [25] _____
(please specify)

I would be interested in new books on the following subjects:
(please check all that apply, and use the spaces provided to identify specific software)

❏ Word processing: [26] _____ ❏ Spreadsheets: [27] _____
❏ Data bases: [28] _____ ❏ Desktop publishing: [29] _____
❏ File Utilities: [30] _____ ❏ Money management: [31] _____
❏ Networking: [32] _____ ❏ Programming languages: [33] _____
❏ Other: [34] _____

I use a PC at (please check all that apply): ❏ home [35] ❏ work [36] ❏ school [37] ❏ other: [38] _____
The disks I prefer to use are ❏ 5.25 [39] ❏ 3.5 [40] ❏ other: [41] _____
I have a CD ROM: ❏ yes [42] ❏ no [43]
I plan to buy or upgrade computer hardware this year: ❏ yes [44] ❏ no [45]
I plan to buy or upgrade computer software this year: ❏ yes [46] ❏ no [47]

Name: _____ **Business title:** [48] _____ **Type of Business:** [49] _____
Address (❏ home [50] ❏ work [51]/Company name: _____)
Street/Suite# _____
City [52]/**State** [53]/**Zipcode** [54]: _____ **Country** [55] _____

❏ **I liked this book!** You may quote me by name in future
IDG Books Worldwide promotional materials.

My daytime phone number is _____

IDG BOOKS
THE WORLD OF COMPUTER KNOWLEDGE

☐ **YES!**
Please keep me informed about IDG's World of Computer Knowledge. Send me the latest IDG Books catalog.

BUSINESS REPLY MAIL
FIRST CLASS MAIL   PERMIT NO. 2605   SAN MATEO, CALIFORNIA

IDG Books Worldwide
155 Bovet Road
San Mateo, CA 94402-9833

NO POSTAGE
NECESSARY
IF MAILED
IN THE
UNITED STATES